THE JUNK FOOD ALTERNATIVE

LINDA BURUM

Illustrations By
Andra Rudolph

101 Productions
San Francisco

Second Printing, June 1981

Copyright © 1980 Linda Burum
Drawings copyright © 1980 Andra Rudolph

Published by 101 Productions
834 Mission Street
San Francisco, California 94103

Distributed to the book trade in the United States by
Charles Scribner's Sons, New York.

Library of Congress Cataloging in Publication Data

Burum, Linda.
    The junk food alternative.

    Bibliography: p.
    Includes index.
    1. Cookery.   2. Nutrition.   3. Snack foods.
I. Title.
TX652.B88   641.5'63   80-17799
ISBN   0-89286-163-0

Contents

Preface

This is a health-food cookbook that won't try to change your eating habits but will change your ideas about junk food. Without giving up fast foods, snacks, chips, dips and desserts, you can enjoy a wholesome, nutrient-rich diet. Eating all the nutrients your body needs doesn't have to involve three sit-down meals a day, complicated menu plans, dieting or feeling guilty about craving snacks and desserts. The recipes in this book are designed to help you break the unhealthful junk food syndrome painlessly.

You can still eat on the run, substituting a snack or even a dessert for a meal without denying your body the nourishment it needs. How? By packaging your own high-nutrient "take-out" foods.

The ingredients used in the recipes in this book have been carefully selected to combine complementary proteins and to provide complex carbohydrates, fiber and loads of vitamins and minerals so that foods normally low or entirely lacking in nutritive value become wholesome foods high in complete protein.

Complete protein is emphasized because that's what meal-skippers need for a sustained blood sugar level, and that's what junk foods don't provide. When protein is added to sweets, it helps to slow down the release of glucose into the bloodstream and prevents it from upsetting the body's metabolic balance. And the use of complementary proteins reduces the need for meat in the diet, too.

As a teacher of foods and nutrition in high school, I watched hundreds of students eat thousands of pounds of junk. This led me to do some experimenting. First I introduced some Adelle Davis recipes for cookies and brownies, since these are ever-popular foods in school. They were wolfed down with great delight. I decided the same principle of using complementary proteins could be applied to all sorts of treat foods. One experiment led to another. Students began to contribute their ideas, and soon we had developed an entire array of high-nutrient snack foods. Many of the recipes in this book have been sampled and tested by numerous high school students.

So here is a book for all the parents who want to feed their children healthy foods but have to compete with busy schedules, fast food chains and TV junk food ads; and the people who crave desserts but don't want to go off their diet by eating empty calories (they may now have cake instead of lunch); and all the kids at school who eat chocolate-covered doughnuts for "nutrition" because they don't eat breakfast at home; and for those who, like me, could live on bread and snacks and don't feel like cooking a meal after every working day. And for all of us who skip breakfast (a most necessary meal) because we don't have time to fix anything but are starving by 10:30 am.

The symbols on the recipe pages will show you how easy it is to prepare foods for meals and then package or freeze them so they will be available at a moment's notice (see inside of front or back cover for an explanation of the symbols).

Now you can eat on the run, confident that the food you're eating will help you to keep on running.

Introduction

As I have explained to my high school classes, the food industry does not care about your health. Its primary concern is profit. With the use of artificial colors and preservatives, food chemists have become veritable wizards at creating taste-addicting, eye-catching products with a very long shelf life. Protein and good nutrients, however, are avoided like the plague.

These tempting morsels are, unfortunately, always available. Wherever we turn there are candy machines, potato chip racks, catering trucks or deli and liquor stores, all beckoning with crackers, cheezies, chips, oversized or undersized cookies and sweet trips in every nutritionless form imaginable. They are packaged so they can be easily transported lest a craving hits when you are not near a junk food depot. To make matters worse, it is very difficult to find a similar array of items that offer our body nutritional rewards.

The appeal of these goodies is constantly advertised on television and on radio and in beautiful palate-provoking magazine photographs to remind you of your latest craving (or to create a new one for you). The image created is of foods that are desirable because they are so delicious. They are symbolic of good times, of socializing and of hospitality. We are trained to respond to these junk foods in a certain manner, and Madison Avenue is there to make sure we continue to do so. Unfortunately for most of us, we do!

To understand why junk food really is junk, compared to foods with high-nutrient value, it is necessary to know a few basic facts about how your body uses food. Too many poor food choices are made because of lack of information.

The nerves, the brain and every cell in your body need a constant supply of energy. This energy is supplied to them in the form of blood sugar, or glucose. When the blood's supply of sugar is low, there are two ways it can be raised. The body converts energy that has been stored in the body as either glycogen or fat into blood sugar, or it converts newly digested food into blood sugar.

When you supply your body with energy by eating refined carbohydrate food (especially at breakfast), your blood sugar rises quickly but then dissipates almost as quickly. This is because refined carbohydrates are rapidly digested, producing a temporary oversupply of sugar in the blood. This situation stimulates the pancreas and liver to withdraw the excess in order to keep the blood's sugar at a desirable level. The excess energy is then converted into starch in the liver and is stored in the cells as glycogen, then is eventually converted into fat.

After the withdrawal of excess energy, the blood sugar level drops and a person experiences hunger, fatigue and a craving for more energy food. If no food is eaten, the blood sugar will remain at an undesirably low level until glycogen stored in the body is reconverted to blood sugar. Because he experiences hunger, however, a person will often eat before the glycogen is reconverted into glucose. Excess unused or unconverted glucose is then converted into body fat. If more refined carbohydrates are eaten the whole process is renewed, and more and more fat is stored in the body.

High and low swings in the blood sugar level are extremely detrimental to the liver, the pancreas and the entire body. Over a period of years, eating this way is devastating to the human organism, resulting in rapid aging, bodily deterioration and susceptibility to sickness and disease. Replacing granulated sugar with honey, brown sugar or Turbinado sugar (see page 186) is not the answer to this problem. It is true that these sweeteners and molasses, unlike granulated sugar, contain small amounts of trace minerals. But all of these sweeteners, like granulated sugar, are refined carbohydrates. They are all composed of the same basic simple sugar molecules, fructose and glucose, and are used exactly the same way by the body. Unless they are eaten in combination with other nutrients, they are too rapidly digested and converted into blood sugar.

This is why naturally occurring sugars, such as those in vegetables and whole grains, are "better for you"—they are complex carbohydrates containing vitamins and other nutrients bound up in cellulose fiber that takes longer to digest and enter the bloodstream. The sugar in fruit, though rapidly digested, is also combined with valuable fiber, vitamins and minerals.

The important thing is not what kind of sweetener is used, but what kind of nutrients are combined with it. When sweeteners are mixed in the right proportions with complex carbohydrates, proteins and fats, this food is digested more slowly, and the glucose level in the bloodstream remains at a high, even level for a longer period of time.

On the following page is a comparison of a typical junk food with a high-nutrient dessert, listing the main ingredients in each food and explaining how each ingredient functions in the body.

As you can see, the doughnut provides a fast energy "hit" that zooms the blood sugar level up and then lets it drop with a crash, shattering your body's delicate mechanisms. The applesauce cake, however, gives a slow, steady release of energy because it is made from ingredients that are concentrated sources of complete protein and complex carbohydrates. The doughnut contains quick energy while the applesauce cake contains fiber and B vitamins, which build health in many ways. The doughnut contains quick energy while the applesauce cake supplies valuable minerals such as calcium (which builds bones) and iron (which builds blood cells). The doughnut supplies quick energy while the applesauce cake provides a supply of body-building and body-replenishing protein. And the applesauce cake also provides energy—but the long-lasting kind!

If that's not impressive, maybe you should be

A TYPICAL DOUGHNUT

White Flour
Supplies mostly energy and a few vitamins

White Sugar
Supplies quick energy; raises the blood sugar level quickly for a short time

Oil (for frying)
Provides a little longer-lasting energy

Salt and Flavorings
None

HIGH-PROTEIN APPLESAUCE CAKE

Whole-Wheat Flour
Provides fiber, complete protein (when mixed with soy flour or dry milk) and slowly digested complex carbohydrates, vitamins and minerals

Wheat Germ
A concentrated source of B vitamins, iron and protein for a sustained blood sugar level and the building and repair of worn body cells

Dry Milk
Provides protein for a sustained energy level in the bloodstream. Combines with the incomplete protein in the wheat products to form complete protein. Provides additional vitamins and minerals.

Soy Flour
Provides protein for sustained energy level and replacement of worn body cells. Provides some energy.

Applesauce
Provides quick energy, fiber and vitamins

Sugar (or Honey)
Provides quick energy but is more slowly released into the bloodstream when eaten in combination with protein foods such as dry milk or soy flour and complex carbohydrates as contained in whole-wheat flour

Unsaturated Oil
Provides slowly released energy and some important essential fatty acids

Salt and Flavorings
None

reminded of the importance of complete protein. Keep in mind that virtually every part of you is made from protein: your hair, nails, blood, muscles and all of your various tissues. The cells that build the different parts of you don't stick around your whole lifetime (with a few exceptions). They are constantly being destroyed or dying of old age, and your body must manufacture new ones. For example, a blood cell lives only about eighty days. You can readily see that your hair grows and falls out. This process is constantly occurring with most of the cells in your body. Cells are dying and being manufactured every second of your life! The raw material needed for the constant rebuilding of cells and body tissue is complete protein. You need a continuous supply of it in your bloodstream to replace your dying cells on cue. Without the required amount, the aging process is speeded up.

In addition to keeping your energy level high and replacing worn tissue, protein has some other important roles to play in your body's life processes. You know you need vitamins and iron. But did you know that all body energy is produced with the help of enzymes? Enzymes are organic substances made up largely of protein. Vitamins fail to do their job and are useless to the body if certain necessary enzymes are not also present in the blood to collaborate with them. Though a person might get plenty of iron, anemia can result if there is not enough protein in the blood to build red corpuscles that carry oxygen to all the cells in the body.

In addition to these enzymes you need the protein albumin in your blood to attract the waste products of metabolism (energy burning) and old broken-down body tissue into the bloodstream. The blood then carts this debris off to the kidneys and the lungs to be disposed of. Without sufficient protein levels in the blood, this waste collection system becomes inefficient. Wastes then remain in the body tissues causing fatigue (mental and physical), stress, susceptibility to disease and sickness and, in extreme cases, varying degrees of edema or retention of body fluids. These are but a few of the many ways protein contributes to bodily functioning.

The body is a fabulous machine and, if given the right materials, it can be kept in tune. Without the right materials, it will just barely putter along (breaking down more often than not) in a weakened and debilitated condition, getting old before its time. And don't forget—with your body, there are no trade-ins. The key to feeling energetic and to maintaining your body's nutritional equilibrium is to eat a balance of protein, carbohydrates and fats together at comfortably spaced intervals throughout the day. The following section will show you how to make your own high-nutrient alternatives to junk food.

The Healthy Kitchen

TURNING JUNK FOODS INTO HIGH-NUTRIENT FOODS

The main problem with treat foods, snack foods and fast-food meals is their inability to contribute a *balance* of food elements necessary for good nutrition. If you are going to substitute snacks or fast foods for balanced meals (and who doesn't these days), they should be as complete as possible.

Complete food begins with the use of whole-food ingredients rather than ingredients that have had much of their goodness refined out of them. The glossary of ingredients beginning on page 184 will give you important information on whole-food ingredients and how to use and store them. Using wholesome, unrefined ingredients is only part of the answer. Many of the foods in this book contain complete protein, because that's what is usually missing in the sweets and snacks that often replace nutritious food. The sweets

and snacks in this book can help to supplement a low-protein diet, and some of them (see the "Have Some Dessert for Breakfast" and the "Make a Meal of Appetizers" sections) are high enough in protein that they can be eaten as light meals. The emphasis in this book is on complementary proteins that, used together, create a protein that is as complete as meat but is lower in cost, calories and animal fats.

Protein is not just a simple substance but a combination of specific chemicals known as amino acids. Scientists have discovered about twenty-two amino acids. There are many different kinds of proteins made up of various combinations of amino acids, just as musical notes are rearranged to form different melodies, or letters of the alphabet are combined and recombined to form different words. Each of the hundreds of proteins your body needs to function is made up of different combinations of amino acids. For example, hair protein contains different amino acids (or amino acids combined in a different way) than muscle protein or fingernail protein.

There are eight amino acids that the body needs but cannot manufacture: tryptophane, lysine, methionine, phenylalanine, threonine, valine, leucine and isoleucine. These are called the *essential* amino acids, because they must be consumed simultaneously and in the right proportions if the body is to use them for growth and tissue replacement. Foods containing all eight of these essential amino acids are called complete protein foods.

Many foods contain protein but not all of the eight essential amino acids required for the body's needs. These are called *incomplete protein* foods and their amino acids are converted into glucose and used as energy. In order to take advantage of the amino acids in incomplete protein foods, they may be combined, or complemented, with another food containing the missing amino acids. By combining these complementary protein foods, many foods not usually considered protein can supply the body with the same complete protein as meat or dairy products.

In order to simplify the combining of complementary proteins, I like to divide non-meat protein foods into three groups. All of the foods in each group are missing or are low in the same amino acids and are complemented by the other groups that can supply those needed amino acids. By combining foods from group A with foods from group B or C you will maximize the protein in all of these foods.

Group A	Group B	Group C
Wheat products	Milk	Soy beans
Other grains and their products: corn, oats, rice, etc.	Cheeses	Soy flour
	Eggs	Dry beans
	Wheat germ	Dry peas
Nuts		
Seeds		

As an example of the benefits of combining complementary proteins, only 2 tablespoons of non-fat dry milk added to 1 cup of grain flour increases the protein quality by about 45 percent. Most of the recipes in this book combine two or more incomplete protein foods in order to take advantage of all the different protein sources.

Many food labels show the amount of protein in a certain portion of food. What they rarely tell you is whether or not that protein is actually complete. Foods advertised as "high in protein" are not always high in *complete* protein. If you want to be sure you'll be getting complete protein in a product, you need to become familiar with the combinations of ingredients that produce it. Remember, you must eat all eight of the amino acids *together* to have them function as protein in your body.

Because protein is used for growth and tissue replacement, it is especially important for children and teenagers. Ideally, one third of the body's protein should be consumed at breakfast, making that meal most important for the day's activities. Yet children and teenagers are notorious breakfast-skippers, and often ruin their appetite for regular meals with junk food snacks. Many adults, on the other hand, get too much protein in the form of meat, high in both calories and animal fat.

How can you be sure you are getting enough protein without eating a lot of meat? If you are in good nutritional shape and don't need to build up your body's supply of protein, the Food and Nutrition Board of the National Research Council recommends the following daily totals of grams of complete protein.

Children					
Under 12 years		**Over 12 years**		**Adults**	
1-3	40 g	Girls		Men	65 g
4-6	50 g	13-15	80 g	Women	58 g
7-9	60 g	16-20	75 g	Pregnancy	85 g
10-12	70 g	Boys		Lactation	100 g
		13-15	85 g		
		16-20	100 g		

This is an estimate of how much protein the average person needs and many people feel it is high. These figures allow for individual differences and a margin of safety. There is evidence that about 40 grams of complete protein for women and 50 grams of complete protein for men would be more than adequate. To help you figure out your protein intake, complete-protein counts are provided for each recipe in this book. *Note:* Optional ingredients and suggested alternative ingredients are not included in the protein counts.

This book will show you many good ways to get complete protein into snack foods and sweets by including dry milk, cheese, soy products, whole-wheat flour and wheat germ. You can eat cheesecake or coffeecake for breakfast and still get the nutrients you need. If you're watching your calories, you can eat carrot cake or sesame cheese snacks at noon and forget about lunch without ruining your health. You can package lunchbox treats that will build health in your children. Many of the treats in this book are portable. They can be frozen in individual servings and be ready when cravings hit, or when you need a quick meal, helping you to avoid that Danish at work. They help the kids survive the afternoon hungries without cheating them of their needed nutrients.

BASIC INGREDIENTS

With just a few special ingredients on hand you'll be ready to start making everything you cook count nutritionally. Here is a list of the ingredients you will find most often in the following recipes. For additional information on buying and storing healthy ingredients, please refer to the ingredient list beginning on page 184.

Cottage cheese, dry and creamed
Honey
Neufchatel cheese
Non-instant nonfat dry milk
"Old-fashioned" peanut butter
Ricotta cheese
Rolled oats
Safflower margarine
Safflower or corn oil
Soy flour
Turbinado and brown sugar
Unbleached all-purpose flour
Unhulled sesame seeds
Unsalted soy nuts
Unsalted sunflower seeds
Walnuts
Wheat germ
Whole-wheat flour

CHEESE

The unique secret ingredient in many of the dishes in this book is cheese. It adds protein as well as complementing the incomplete protein in wheat, nuts and seeds. Cheese also contains moisture or oil that is released during the cooking process, adding more moisture to the final product. The following chart shows how cheeses vary in protein and calorie content.

PROTEIN AND CALORIE COUNTS
PER 4-OUNCE PORTION OF CHEESE

Cheese	Grams Protein	Calories
Bakers' (hoop) cheese	18	90
Cheddar cheese	28.4	451
Cottage cheese	15	120
Cream cheese	9.1	424
Dry cottage cheese	18	80
Farmers' cheese	17.2	160-200
Low-fat cottage cheese	14-15	90
Neufchatel	12.8	280
Parmesan	41	446
Pot cheese	14	120
Ricotta cheese	12	180
Swiss cheese	31.1	419

Note: Four ounces of ricotta, cottage, bakers' (hoop), pot, cream or Neufchatel cheese equals about 1/2 cup. Four ounces of farmers', Swiss, Cheddar or Parmesan cheese, grated, equals about 1 cup.

● For best results, be sure to use the type of cheese specified in each recipe. Though Neufchatel and cottage cheese are often used in this book because they are low in fat and high in protein, cream cheese and ricotta cheese are used in certain recipes where a creamier texture is desirable.

● Dry cottage cheese is often found in bags in the dairy section of your market. If you are unable to find it, rinse off ordinary creamed cottage cheese in a strainer and squeeze it dry in a piece of cheesecloth. Measure *after* squeezing cheese dry. Bakers' (hoop) cheese is uncreamed and has no lumps. It may be used in place of sieved or pureed dry cottage cheese. Squeeze it dry if it seems very moist.

● Many of the recipes in this book call for sieved or pureed cottage cheese (use low-fat for fewest calories). To prepare sieved or pureed cottage cheese, press it through a sieve or puree in a blender or food processor until smooth. You'll have to stop the blender several times to push the cheese into the blades. Always measure the cheese *before* sieving or pureeing.

SWEETENERS

Any of the recipes in this book containing sugar or honey can have the amount of sweetening altered according to taste. You may want to experiment with using slightly less honey or sugar than is called for, or using the smaller amount when alternative amounts are given. I like the flavor of brown and Turbinado sugar in baking (see ingredient list, page 184), and they are a mite healthier since they have a few vitamins and minerals. Turbinado is more unrefined than granulated sugar and can be substituted for granulated in most recipes, but it is usually more expensive. If you substitute brown sugar for granulated in a recipe, however, you will often find a big difference in the texture of baked goods, especially cookies. Here are some substitutes for granulated sugar you might find useful:

● For 1 cup Turbinado or granulated sugar substitute 2/3 cup packed brown sugar plus 1/3 cup granulated sugar, or 3/4 cup granulated sugar plus 1/4 cup molasses (reduce liquid in recipe by 2 teaspoons).

● Exchanging sugar for honey does not always work, especially in cookies, but 7/8 cup honey may sometimes be used in place of 1 cup Turbinado or granulated sugar (reduce liquid in recipe by 3 tablespoons and add a pinch of baking soda to neutralize the acid in the honey).

SALT

I have used salt in these recipes because most taste buds have come to expect it. I have found if things don't taste "right" they don't get eaten even if they are healthy. But you can train taste buds, so cut down on or omit salt little by little and soon you won't miss it.

FLOUR

You can fortify all-purpose flour and get excellent results in traditional recipes if you use the following substitutes:

● For 1 cup all-purpose flour substitute 1/2 cup unbleached all-purpose flour mixed with 1/3 cup whole-wheat flour, 2 tablespoons wheat germ and 2 tablespoons non-instant nonfat milk.

● Or, for 1 cup all-purpose flour substitute 1/2 cup unbleached all-purpose flour mixed with 1/3 cup whole-wheat flour, 3 tablespoons soy flour and 1 tablespoon wheat germ.

● You may also fortify whole-wheat flour simply by stirring in 3 tablespoons non-instant nonfat dry milk.

When you use these substitutes you will be complementing all of the amino acids in the wheat flour as well as adding fiber and B vitamins.

EQUIVALENTS AND SUBSTITUTES

● You can improve the protein value of baked goods by replacing nuts with a mixture of half soy nuts and half nuts or 1 cup nuts with 1/3 cup each sunflower seeds, soy nuts and nuts.

● You may substitute instant nonfat dry milk for non-instant in all recipes except those for frostings and candies; add 1 extra tablespoon instant dry milk for each 1/4 cup dry milk called for (for example, 1-1/4 cups instant dry milk replaces 1 cup non-instant).

● You can retain the flavor butter gives to baked goods even if you substitute safflower margarine for up to two-thirds of the butter.

● Always use unsaturated vegetable oils, either safflower oil, which is preferred, or corn oil; soy bean oil is also a good choice.

● Carob chips may be substituted for chocolate or carob powder for cocoa (you may want to reduce your sweetener by one fifth as carob is slightly sweeter than cocoa).

● One ounce of baking chocolate may be replaced with 3 tablespoons carob powder, 1 tablespoon margarine and 1 tablespoon water (reduce your sweetener by one fifth, if you wish).

● Four ounces of cheese is equal to 1 cup shredded cheese.

● One clove of garlic is equal to 1/8 teaspoon garlic powder.

● Garlic salt may be made by crushing a clove of garlic into 1 tablespoon salt; remove the clove before use.

COOKING TIPS

After all my experiments I gathered together all of the techniques I found or devised to save time and to make cooking easier and more fun.

● Try to use your equipment more than once. For example, mix your dry ingredients in a bowl or in the baking pan, then place them on a paper towel or waxed paper while you deal with the moist ingredients.

● Keep your measuring spoons handy in a glass of hot water. Just wipe them dry to reuse them over and over.

● Get a tiny pan for melting small quantities of butter or margarine, or softening gelatin.

● Oil measuring cups before measuring honey or peanut butter—it will slide right out.

● Chop dates, dried apricots and other dried fruit with floured scissors, or chop dried fruit in a food processor by first flouring the fruit and the blade of the processor.

● When using freshly grated orange or lemon peel (there's nothing like it for flavoring) grate the whole peel (only the orange or yellow part, not the white) and freeze the rest in aluminum foil for future use.

● Freeze leftover egg whites in little waxed paper cups covered with aluminum foil. They may be used just like fresh egg whites when they are thawed.

● When adding non-instant nonfat dry milk to a liquid, place the liquid in a bowl and sprinkle dry milk over gradually while beating with a whisk; blend thoroughly. Or place liquid in a blender, cover and turn on blender, then uncover and sprinkle in dry milk; turn off motor as soon as milk has blended so mixture does not foam.

● Flour in any amount larger than 1/4 cup should be stirred vigorously with a fork or wire whisk before measuring. (Or fluff in a food processor.) This is an important step, as there can be a considerable difference in volume between unsifted and sifted or stirred flour, and even presifted flour will pack down in its container.

● When using glass baking dishes for cakes, pies and bar cookies, reduce oven heat by 25 degrees.

● Foods will have the most freshness and the best flavor if you use freshly squeezed lemon and lime juice and freshly grated lemon and orange rind. Freshly grated Parmesan cheese and fresh parsley are always preferable to packaged grated cheese and dried parsley.

STORAGE TIPS

- For portable meals, use individual foil pie tins or individual muffin tins for casseroles, pies, quiches, etc. Use plastic-coated paper cups for puddings. Cottage cheese cartons also make good portable containers.
- Most foods that have been wrapped in aluminum foil and frozen can be reheated without thawing by placing them in a 350°F oven until heated through.
- Cakes and other baked foods may be wrapped in aluminum foil and kept frozen for about two months.Cakes with frosting, sticky candies and unbaked loaves of bread should be frozen solid, then wrapped in aluminum foil; be sure to unwrap before thawing.
- Divide cookie dough into small portions, wrap in aluminum foil and freeze; thaw and bake one portion when you want only a few cookies at a time.
- Nut mixtures and savory snacks may be stored in covered glass jars, plastic containers or tins in the refrigerator for a few weeks. Or they may be frozen for two months. To restore their crispness place them in a preheated 350°F oven for 5 to 6 minutes, then remove and cool thoroughly.
- Remember to refrigerate baked goods and candies made with dry milk.

BIBLIOGRAPHY

Aurand, L.W., and A.E. Woods. *Food Chemistry.* Westport, Conn.: Avi Publishing, 1979.

Bogert, Jean L. *Nutrition and Physical Fitness,* 9th ed. Philadelphia: W.B. Saunders Co., 1966.

Labuza, Theodore. *Food and Your Well-being.* St. Paul, Minn.: West Publishing Co., 1977.

Lappe, Francis M. *Diet for a Small Planet,* revised ed., New York: Ballantine Books, 1975.

Pearson,David. *The Chemical Analysis of Foods,* 6th ed. New York: Chemical Publishing Co., 1971.

Williams, Sue Rodwell. *Essentials of Nutrition and Diet Therapy,* 2nd. ed. St. Louis, Mo.: C.V. Mosby Co., 1978.

Other books of interest:

McNutt, Kristen W., and David R. *Nutrition and Food Choices.* Chicago: Science Research Associates, 1978

Whalen, E., and F. Stare. *Panic in the Pantry.* New York: Atheneum, 1976.

Have Some Dessert
For Breakfast

It may seem like sacrilege to suggest dessert for breakfast, yet coffee and "a little something" is a favorite combination for people who can't face eggs and bacon at 8 am. Youngsters who snub eggs and toast can be found nibbling on junk food soon after breakfast time, and breakfast skippers often find their hunger pangs arrive midmorning when there is nothing nutritious in sight.

The problem with ordinary coffeecakes and pastries is their refined carbohydrate energy. This type of energy food is quickly absorbed into the bloodstream, soon leaving you hungry and craving more sugar.

In this chapter you'll find recipes for desserts that are extra high in complete protein and filled with other wholesome nutrients. These treats will give Danish- and cake-lovers the long-lasting kind of energy they need to get them through the morning. Most of them are more nutritious than a typical cold cereal, milk and juice breakfast. As you look over the ingredients you will see that they are just the sort of thing recommended for a wholesome and nourishing breakfast:cheeses, whole grains, wheat germ, eggs and milk.

These are complementary-protein-rich treats that weight-conscious people can enjoy without feeling deprived or guilty. They'll be less tempted to "cheat" by eating no-nutrient foods between meals.

Many of these dishes can be made way ahead so they'll be ready for breakfast without a fuss. Some may be frozen, and there are portable foods that can be tucked into handbags or lunch-boxes to help avoid the midmorning urge for something less nutritious. And you don't have to limit these desserts to breakfast: They can round out any meal low in protein while allowing you to indulge your taste buds.

QUICK FRUIT BREAD, COFFEECAKES, MUFFINS AND DOUGHNUTS

Delicious fruit bread, coffeecakes and muffins can be made ahead in a flash if you use the High-Protein Baking Mix, following. And all of these recipes, including the Real Food Doughnuts, freeze well. Just pop a serving into the oven while you're getting dressed. Complete-protein counts range from 8 to 9.9 grams for the large-sized servings.

Note: Freeze individual servings wrapped in foil. Reheat in a preheated 350°F oven for 15 minutes or until heated through.

High-Protein Baking Mix

Make things easy on yourself and mix up a big batch of this nutritious baking mix. When you want to bake in a hurry, you won't have to get out a lot of ingredients.

5 cups stirred whole-wheat flour
6-1/4 cups stirred unbleached all-purpose flour
2-1/2 cups wheat germ
1-1/4 cups stirred soy flour
5 teaspoons salt
5 teaspoons baking soda
1/4 cup plus 1 tablespoon baking powder
2 tablespoons grated orange rind mixed with
    1 tablespoon grated lemon rind (optional)

Mix all ingredients together well in a large mixing bowl. Store in an airtight container in the refrigerator.
Makes 15-1/2 cups
19 grams protein per cup

Orange-Nut Coffeecake or Muffins

This is the parent recipe for all the following quick coffeecakes.

3 cups plus 2 tablespoons High-Protein Baking Mix, preceding, or 1-1/4 cups stirred unbleached all-purpose flour, 1 cup stirred whole-wheat flour, 1/2 cup wheat germ, 1/4 cup soy flour, 3 teaspoons baking powder, 1 teaspoon salt and 1 teaspoon baking soda
1/4 pound butter or safflower margarine, at room temperature
1 cup packed brown sugar
2 eggs
1/2 cup thawed frozen orange juice concentrate
2 tablespoons grated orange rind
1 teaspoon grated lemon rind
1 teaspoon vanilla extract
1-1/2 cups small-curd cottage cheese
1-1/4 cups chopped walnuts, or a mixture of chopped walnuts and unsalted sunflower seeds
Streusel Topping, following

Use High-Protein Baking Mix or combine dry ingredients well. With an electric mixer or a food processor, cream butter and sugar together until very fluffy. Add eggs and beat until creamy. Add orange juice, grated rinds, vanilla and cottage cheese and blend well. Add nuts to dry ingredi-

ents and combine with wet ingredients until just moistened. Spread into 2 greased 8 × 8-inch cake pans or fill 24 greased muffin cups two-thirds full. Sprinkle with Streusel Topping. Bake in a preheated 350°F oven 30 to 40 minutes for cakes and 25 minutes for muffins or until a toothpick inserted in center of a cake or muffin comes out clean. Cool in pans on racks.
Makes 16 servings or 24 muffins
9.8 grams protein per serving
6.5 grams protein per muffin

STREUSEL TOPPING Combine 3 tablespoons soft butter or safflower margarine, 1/3 cup wheat germ, 2 tablespoons whole-wheat flour and 1/3 cup packed brown sugar; mix well with a fork. Add 1/2 cup chopped nuts or unsalted sunflower seeds, if desired.

Blueberry Buckle or Muffins

3 cups plus 2 tablespoons High-Protein Baking Mix, page 20, or 1-1/4 cups stirred unbleached all-purpose flour, 1 cup stirred whole-wheat flour, 1/4 cup soy flour, 1/2 cup wheat germ, 3 teaspoons baking powder, 1 teaspoon baking soda and 1 teaspoon salt
1/4 pound butter or safflower margarine, at room temperature

3/4 to 1 cup packed brown sugar
2 eggs
1 tablespoon grated orange rind
1 teaspoon grated lemon rind
1 teaspoon vanilla extract
2 tablespoons milk
1-1/2 cups small-curd cottage cheese
2 cups fresh, frozen or well-drained canned blueberries
Streusel Topping, preceding

Use High-Protein Baking Mix or combine dry ingredients well. With an electric mixer or a food processor, cream butter and sugar together until very fluffy, using the smaller amount of sugar if using canned berries. Add eggs and beat until creamy. Add rinds, vanilla, milk and cottage cheese and mix well. Combine dry ingredients with wet ingredients until just moistened. Gently fold in blueberries. Spread into 2 greased 8 × 8-inch cake pans or fill 24 greased muffin cups two-thirds full. Sprinkle with Streusel Topping and bake in a preheated 350° F oven 30 to 40 minutes for cakes or 25 minutes for muffins, or until a toothpick inserted in center of a cake or muffin comes out clean. Cool in pans on racks.
Makes 16 servings or 24 muffins
8 grams protein per serving,
5.5 grams protein per muffin

Cottage Cheese Fruit Bread or Muffins

This is the parent recipe for the following quick coffeecakes.

3 cups plus 2 tablespoons High-Protein Baking Mix, page 20, or 1-1/4 cups stirred unbleached all-purpose flour, 1 cup stirred whole-wheat flour, 1/4 cup soy flour, 1/2 cup wheat germ, 3 teaspoons baking powder, 1 teaspoon baking soda and 1 teaspoon salt
1/4 pound butter or safflower margarine, at room temperature
1 cup packed brown sugar
2 eggs
1/4 cup milk
1 teaspoon vanilla extract
1 tablespoon grated orange rind
1 teaspoon grated lemon rind
1-1/2 cups small-curd cottage cheese
1/2 cup chopped walnuts
1/3 cup unsalted sunflower seeds
1 cup chopped dates
1/2 cup snipped dried apricots or mixed chopped dried fruit

Use High-Protein Baking Mix or combine dry ingredients well. With an electric mixer or a food processor, cream butter and sugar together until very fluffy. Add eggs and beat until creamy. Add milk, vanilla, rinds and cottage cheese and blend well. Add nuts and fruit to dry ingredients and mix well to coat with flour. Combine this mixture with wet ingredients until just moistened. Spread into 2 greased 5 × 7-inch loaf pans or fill 24 greased muffin cups two-thirds full. Bake in a preheated 350°F oven 40 to 45 minutes for loaves and 25 minutes for muffins or until a toothpick inserted in center of a loaf or muffin comes out clean. Cool in pans on racks for 10 minutes, then remove from pans and cool thoroughly on racks.

Makes 16 servings or 24 muffins
8.5 grams protein per serving,
5.7 grams protein per muffin

RAISIN SPICE NUT BREAD OR MUFFINS Follow directions for Cottage Cheese Fruit Bread or Muffins. Mix 2 teaspoons ground cinnamon, 1/2 teaspoon ground allspice and 1/2 teaspoon ground nutmeg into dry ingredients. Add 1-1/2 cups raisins to flour—omit dates and other fruit. Use 1-1/3 cups chopped walnuts or mixed chopped nuts and unsalted sunflower seeds.

Carob or Chocolate Chip Coffeecake

Carob (or chocolate) plus good nutrition. Great for breakfast or after-school snacks.

3 cups plus 2 tablespoons High-Protein Baking Mix, page 20, or 1-1/4 cups stirred unbleached all-purpose flour, 1 cup stirred whole-wheat flour, 1/4 cup soy flour, 1/2 cup wheat germ, 1 teaspoon salt, 3 teaspoons baking powder and 1 teaspoon baking soda
1/4 pound butter or safflower margarine, at room temperature
1 cup packed brown sugar
2 eggs
1/3 cup milk
1 teaspooon vanilla extract
1-1/2 cups small-curd cottage cheese
Carob or Chocolate Streusel Topping, following
1 teaspoon ground cinnamon
1 cup chopped walnuts, or 1 cup mixed chopped walnuts and unsalted sunflower seeds

Use High-Protein Baking Mix or combine dry ingredients well. With an electric mixer or a food processor, cream butter and sugar together until very fluffy. Add eggs and beat until creamy. Add milk, vanilla and cottage cheese and blend well. Add cinnamon and nuts to dry ingredients and combine this mixture with wet ingredients until just moistened. Spread one fourth of the batter into each of 2 greased 8 X 8-inch cake pans. Sprinkle each with one third of the Carob or Chocolate Streusel Topping. Divide remaining batter between the 2 pans and sprinkle with remaining topping. Bake in a preheated 350°F oven for 30 to 40 minutes or until a toothpick inserted in center of cake comes out clean. Cool in pans on racks.
Makes 16 to 18 servings
9.9/8.8 grams protein per serving

CAROB OR CHOCOLATE STREUSEL TOPPING
Combine 4 tablespoons soft butter or safflower margarine, 1/2 cup wheat germ, 2 tablespoons non-instant nonfat dry milk, 1/2 cup packed brown sugar and 2 teaspoons carob powder or cocoa. Add 1-1/2 cups carob or chocolate chips.

Pineapple Coffeecake or Muffins

1-1/3 cups crushed pineapple
3 cups plus 2 tablespoons High-Protein Baking
   Mix, page 20, or 1-1/4 cups stirred unbleached
   all-purpose flour, 1 cup stirred whole-wheat
   flour, 1/4 cup soy flour, 1/2 cup wheat germ,
   1 teaspoon salt, 3 teaspoons baking powder
   and 1 teaspoon baking soda
1/4 pound butter or safflower margarine, at
   room temperature
3/4 to 1 cup packed brown sugar
2 eggs
2 teaspoons grated lemon rind
1/2 teaspoon vanilla extract
1-1/2 cups small-curd cottage cheese
1/2 cup unprocessed wheat bran (optional)
Streusel Topping, page 21

Place pineapple in a sieve and allow to drain; reserve pineapple juice. Use baking mix or combine dry ingredients well. With an electric mixer or a food processor, cream butter or margarine and sugar together until very fluffy. Add eggs and beat until creamy. Add lemon rind, vanilla, 1/3 cup pineapple juice and cottage cheese and blend well. Mix in pineapple. Add bran to dry ingredients and add this mixture to wet ingredients just until moistened. Spread into 2 greased 8 × 8-inch cake pans or fill 24 greased muffin cups two-thirds full. Sprinkle with Streusel Topping. Bake in a preheated 350°F oven 30 to 40 minutes for cakes, 25 minutes for muffins, or until a toothpick inserted in center of cake or muffin comes out clean. Cool in pans on racks.
Makes 16 servings or 24 muffins
8 grams protein per serving,
5.5 grams protein per muffin

COCONUT-PINEAPPLE COFFEECAKE OR MUFFINS Add 1/2 cup unsweetened grated coconut to preceding recipe; omit bran.

Real Food Doughnuts

These doughnuts contain real food; even the glaze is good for you. They are nice served slightly warm.

1-3/4 cups stirred unbleached all-purpose flour
1-1/4 cups stirred whole-wheat flour
1/2 cup non-instant nonfat dry milk
1/4 cup wheat germ
4 teaspoons baking powder
1 teaspoon salt
1/2 teaspoon ground cinnamon
3 eggs
1 cup packed brown sugar
2 tablespoons butter or safflower margarine, at
    room temperature
3/4 cup milk
Safflower or corn oil
Milk and Honey Glaze, page 182, or Fabulous
    Apple Juice Glaze or Quick Milk Glaze, page
    183 (optional)

Combine flours, dry milk, wheat germ, baking powder, salt and cinnamon. With an electric mixer or food processor, beat eggs with brown sugar and butter until very light and fluffy. Add dry ingredients to egg mixture alternately with milk until combined and smooth; dough will be soft. Cover bowl with plastic wrap; refrigerate until well chilled, about 1 hour. Remove half the chilled dough to a well-floured pastry cloth or board (keep rest in refrigerator until ready to use). Turn over dough to coat with flour, then roll out 1/3 inch thick. Cut with a floured 3-inch doughnut cutter. With a wide spatula, transfer cut doughnuts to top edge of pastry cloth or board. Press dough trimmings together, reroll and cut; let rest, uncovered, 10 minutes. Meanwhile, in an electric skillet or heavy saucepan, slowly heat 1-1/2 to 2 inches oil to 375° F on a deep-frying thermometer. Gently drop doughnuts, 3 or 4 at a time, into hot oil. As they rise to the surface, turn over with a slotted utensil. Fry until golden-brown on both sides, about 3 minutes in all. With a slotted utensil, lift doughnuts from oil; hold over skillet a few seconds to drain slightly. Drain well on paper towels. Glaze with one of the suggested glazes, if you like.

Makes about 24 doughnuts
7.9 grams protein per doughnut

SWEET ROLLS AND YEAST COFFEECAKES

A sweet roll and coffee is standard breakfast fare for many people. Here are some high-protein versions that won't give you a low blood sugar attack. Some of the coffeecakes, for example, contain approximately 11.9 grams of complete protein for the larger servings, the same amount of nutrition as two eggs. An exception is the Cheese Kuchen, which is even higher in protein. All of these sweet rolls and coffeecakes freeze well, and you can make them in stages using Extra-High-Protein Refrigerator Sweet Dough.

Note: Freeze individual servings wrapped in foil. Reheat in a preheated 350°F oven for 15 minutes or until heated through.

Extra High-Protein Refrigerator Sweet Dough

1 cup small-curd cottage cheese
1-1/2 cups stirred unbleached all-purpose flour
1/4 cup soy flour
3/4 cup wheat germ
1/2 teaspoon salt
1/2 teaspoon baking soda
1 tablespoon (1 package) active dry yeast
1/4 cup warm water (80° to 90°F)

3 to 4 tablespoons butter or safflower margarine
2 eggs
2 egg yolks
1/3 to 1/2 cup honey or packed brown sugar
2 teaspoons grated orange rind
1 teaspoon grated lemon rind
1/2 teaspoon ground cardamom (optional)
1 to 1-1/2 cups or more stirred whole-wheat flour
Melted butter or safflower margarine

Place cottage cheese in a large bowl over hot water until heated to lukewarm (about 80°F). Combine flours, wheat germ, salt and soda; set aside. Sprinkle yeast over water and stir to dissolve. In a small saucepan, melt butter or margarine. Remove from heat and cool to lukewarm; stir into cottage cheese. Add yeast, eggs, egg yolks and honey or sugar. Stir in rinds and cardamom. With an electric mixer, beat in dry mixture a little at a time until combined. Beat this mixture for about 5 minutes with the mixer. Continue to mix, adding whole-wheat flour a little at a time until you can no longer use the mixer. Add remaining flour, mixing it in by hand. Turn out onto a lightly floured board and knead until smooth, about 5 minutes. Brush a large bowl with melted butter or margarine, add dough and brush top with melted butter or margarine. Cover dough and let rise in a warm place until doubled in bulk, about 2 hours. Punch dough down and knead it several times on a lightly floured board. Divide dough in half and freeze 1 half, if you like; use other half in any of the following recipes. Dough may be covered and refrigerated up to 3 days before shaping and baking.
Enough for 2 coffeecakes
62 grams protein per portion

ORANGE HIGH-PROTEIN REFRIGERATOR SWEET DOUGH Follow preceding recipe, adding 1/4 cup thawed frozen orange juice concentrate to cottage cheese before warming. Increase orange rind to 1 tablespoon and omit cardamom. (You may have to use slightly more whole-wheat flour because of the added liquid.)

Orange Swirl Rolls

My first-period class tested these and could not believe how much better they were than the cinnamon rolls sold in the cafeteria. They were especially impressed with the dry milk-orange juice glaze. You can't even tell what it is, they claimed!

1/2 recipe Orange High-Protein Refrigerator
  Sweet Dough, above
2 tablespoons butter or safflower margarine, at
  room temperature
High-Protein Streusel Filling, following, using
  3/4 cup packed brown sugar
Nutritious Orange Juice Glaze, following
Chopped nuts (optional)

Roll dough out to a 12 × 9-inch rectangle. Spread dough with butter or margarine to within 1/2 inch of edges. Sprinkle dough with streusel filling. Roll dough lengthwise like a jelly roll, being careful to include all of the streusel. Pinch edge of dough to seal roll. Cut roll into 12 slices and place them cut side down, slightly apart, in a greased 9 × 9-inch cake pan. Cover with a damp cloth and allow to rise in a warm place until doubled in bulk, 1 to 2 hours. Bake in a preheated 375°F oven for 30 to 35 minutes or until lightly browned. Cool in pan on a rack about 10 minutes and invert on a plate. When completely cooled, frost with orange juice glaze. Sprinkle with a few nuts, if desired.
Makes 12 rolls 9.7 grams protein per roll
9.7 grams protein per roll

HIGH-PROTEIN STREUSEL FILLING Combine 1/3 cup toasted wheat germ, 4 tablespoons soft butter or safflower margarine, 1/2 cup packed brown sugar and 1/2 teaspoon ground cinnamon; blend thoroughly. Press 1/2 cup dry cottage cheese through a sieve or puree in a blender, or use 1/2 cup crumbled bakers' (hoop) cheese. Mix cheese into wheat germ mixture along with 1 teaspoon vanilla extract and 1 tablespoon grated orange rind. Add 1/3 to 1/2 cup chopped nuts or unsalted sunflower seeds, if desired.

NUTRITIOUS ORANGE JUICE GLAZE Mix together 1 tablespoon thawed frozen orange juice concentrate, 2 tablespoons honey, 1/4 cup non-instant nonfat dry milk, and 1/2 teaspoon vanilla extract. Add a few drops of water to thin glaze if necessary.

Cinnamon Sticky Buns

A bit of advice from Tina who had never baked with yeast before trying out these sweet roll recipes: "Don't use all whole-wheat flour unless you want Cinnamon Sticky Bricks."

1/2 recipe Extra-High-Protein Refrigerator
   Sweet Dough, page 26
3 tablespoons butter or margarine, at room
   temperature
High-Protein Streusel Filling, page 27
1-1/2 teaspoons ground cinnamon
4 tablespoons butter or safflower margarine
1/2 cup packed brown sugar or honey
Chopped nuts or unsalted sunflower seeds
   (optional)

Roll dough out to a 12 × 9-inch rectangle. Spread dough with butter or margarine to within 1/2 inch of edges. Sprinkle dough with streusel filling and cinnamon. Roll dough lengthwise like a jelly roll, being careful to include all of the streusel. Pinch edge of roll to seal dough. Cut roll into 12 slices. Melt butter or margarine in a 9 × 9-inch cake pan. Sprinkle with the nuts or seeds, if desired. Place the slices, cut side down, slightly apart in pan. Cover with a damp cloth and allow to rise in a warm place until doubled, about 1 to 2 hours. Bake in a preheated 375°F oven 30 to 35 minutes or until buns are lightly browned. Cool for 5 minutes and invert buns on a plate.

Makes 12 buns
9.1 grams protein per bun

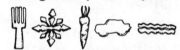

Danish Apple Coffeecake

For a nice portable breakfast, slice before freezing, then take a piece out of the freezer the night before. This looks very elegant—but it's easy to assemble.

4 tablespoons butter or safflower margarine
1/3 to 1/2 cup packed brown sugar or honey
2 medium apples, peeled and thinly sliced
1 teaspoon ground cinnamon
High-Protein Streusel Filling with walnuts,
   page 27
1/4 cup raisins or currants (optional)
1/2 recipe High-Protein Refrigerator
   Sweet Dough, page 26
1 tablespoon butter or safflower margarine,
   melted

Melt butter or margarine in a 9-inch round or 9-inch square cake pan. Over heat, thoroughly stir in sugar or honey and distribute evenly over bottom of pan. Remove from heat. Arrange sliced apples over sugar-butter mixture, overlapping apples so that none of pan is showing. Sprinkle with cinnamon, streusel and raisins or currants, if desired. Roll dough out to fit shape of pan and fit it into pan. Press dough lightly into apples. Brush dough lightly with melted butter. Cover pan with a damp cloth and place it in a warm place until the dough is doubled in bulk, about 1 hour. Bake in a preheated 375°F oven for about 30 minutes or until cake is lightly browned and shrinks slightly from edge of pan. Cool in pan on a rack for 5 minutes and invert on a plate, shaking pan to loosen cake.

Makes 8 to 10 servings
13.5/10.8 grams protein per serving

Date-Nut Coffeecake

A delicious strudel-like coffeecake.

1/2 recipe High-Protein Refrigerator
  Sweet Dough, page 26
3 tablespoons butter or safflower margarine, at
  room temperature
2/3 cup chopped dates
2/3 cup chopped nuts, or a mixture of chopped
  nuts and unsalted sunflower seeds
1/4 cup unsweetened shredded coconut
  (optional)

1/2 teaspoon ground cinnamon
2 egg whites, at room temperature
1/4 teaspoon salt
1/3 cup Turbinado or granulated sugar
1/4 cup non-instant non-fat dry milk

Roll dough out into a 12 × 10-inch rectangle. Spread dough with butter or margarine to within 1/2 inch of edges. Prepare filling by combining dates, half of the nuts, coconut and cinnamon. Beat egg whites until they form soft peaks. Beat in salt and sugar gradually, until stiff peaks form. Sprinkle in dry milk gradually, while beating. Reserve 1/3 cup of this mixture, folding date-nut mixture into remaining meringue.

Spread date-nut filling over buttered dough. Roll up lengthwise like a jelly roll. Pinch edges to seal ends of roll together. Place coffeecake on a greased baking sheet, seam side down, curving to form a narrow U-shape. Cover with a damp cloth and allow to rise in a warm place for 1 to 2 hours or until doubled in bulk. Bake in a preheated 350°F oven for 20 minutes. Spread reserved 1/3 cup meringue lightly over top of roll, sprinkle with remaining chopped nuts and bake 8 to 10 minutes longer.

Makes 10 servings
9.7 grams protein per serving

VARIATIONS Replace dates with raisins, snipped dried apricots, chopped dried apples or a mixture of chopped dried fruits.

Cheese Kuchen

For cheese Danish fans: A wonderful cheese coffeecake with lots of complete protein to get you through the morning. Make this with or without the topping.

1/2 recipe High-Protein Refrigerator
   Sweet Dough, page 26
1 tablespoon melted butter or safflower
   margarine

Filling
1-1/2 cups cottage, bakers' (hoop) or ricotta
   cheese
1 egg
1 egg yolk
2 tablespoons butter or safflower margarine,
   melted
1/3 to 1/2 cup honey
1/2 teaspon vanilla extract
1/2 teaspoon grated lemon rind

Topping
1/3 cup wheat germ
4 teaspoons butter or safflower margarine, at
   room temperature
2 tablespoons packed brown sugar

Pat dough evenly into a greased 9 × 9-inch baking pan, forming a rim around edge. Brush with melted butter or margarine. Blend filling ingredients together in a blender or food processor and pour filling all over dough, except for rim. Cover pan with a damp cloth and put in a warm place to rise, about 40 minutes to 1 hour, or until rim looks doubled in bulk. Mix together topping ingredients and sprinkle over dough. Bake in a preheated 375 °F oven for 25 to 35 minutes or until rim is browned and filling is set. Cool in pan on a rack for about 30 minutes.
Makes 8 to 12 servings
15.8/10.5 grams protein per serving

FRUIT AND CHEESE KUCHEN Prepare Cheese Kuchen and let rise. Just before baking, decorate top with your favorite fresh or thawed frozen fruit (well-drained sweet cherries, apricots, pineapple, plums or peaches). If you like, add a glaze after the cake has cooled thoroughly: In a saucepan blend 2/3 cup fruit juice (drained from fruit, above), 2 tablespoons honey, 2 tablespoons cornstarch and a few drops of almond extract. Cook over medium heat, stirring, until thickened and clear. Pour evenly over fruit on top of kuchen; do not freeze.

PUDDINGS AND CUSTARDS

Puddings have always been in the healthy dessert category. They are especially good for young finicky eaters who snub eggs and milk in other forms. More protein and nutrients have been squeezed into these recipes so that they meet nutritious food standards. Most of these puddings are quick and easy and are great for breakfast because you can make them ahead—and they're much better than unimaginative cold cereal. Make several at the beginning of the week, and breakfast will always be ready.

Early-Morning Pudding

This pudding tastes like dessert, but it's loaded with extra protein. Even those who complain that they just can't eat breakfast manage to enjoy this. The optional egg adds even more nourishment.

2 cups milk
Dash salt
5 tablespoons cornstarch
1/4 to 1/2 cup honey or Turbinado or granulated sugar
1 egg, beaten (optional)
1 cup cottage cheese
1-1/2 teaspoons vanilla extract

In a saucepan, mix 1/3 cup milk, salt and cornstarch, blending until smooth. Add honey or sugar to taste and blend well. Add remaining milk and cook over medium heat, stirring constantly until mixture is thick and loses its starchy taste, about 5 minutes. If adding an egg, add some hot pudding to egg, then add egg to pudding and cook about half a minute; remove from heat. Press cottage cheese through a sieve or puree in a blender or food processor; add to saucepan with vanilla and mix well. Pour into 5 custard cups and chill well.
Makes 5 servings
10 grams protein per serving

BANANA EARLY-MORNING PUDDING Prepare Early-Morning Pudding, increasing cornstarch to 6 tablespoons. Add a very ripe mashed banana to pudding after cooking.

COCONUT EARLY-MORNING PUDDING Add 1/4 to 1/3 cup unsweetened flaked or shredded coconut to Early-Morning Pudding after cooking.

Fruit Cheese Parfaits

I served this at a brunch because it looks so pretty and you can put it together in ten minutes. Who's to know it's so healthy? For smooth parfaits, sieve cottage cheese or puree in a blender or food processor.

1 tablespoon (1 envelope) unflavored gelatin
2 tablespoons lemon juice
2 tablespoons cold water
2 cups small-curd cottage cheese
4 to 6 tablespoons honey
1/2 cup whipping cream, whipped
Fresh berries or sliced fruit

In a small saucepan, sprinkle gelatin over lemon juice and water to soften. Stir over low heat until gelatin dissolves; cool. In a medium-sized bowl, mix cheese and honey and stir in gelatin mixture. Fold in whipped cream. Layer mixture with fruit in parfait glasses or small bowls. Chill.
Makes 4 or 5 servings
16.9/13.5 grams protein per serving

Carob or Chocolate Early-Morning Pudding

2 cups milk
1/8 teaspoon salt (optional)
5 tablespoons cornstarch
1/4 to 1 cup Turbinado or granulated sugar or honey
1/3 cup carob or chocolate chips
1 egg, beaten (optional)
1 cup cottage cheese
1 taspoon vanilla extract

In a saucepan, mix 1/3 cup milk, salt and cornstarch, blending until smooth. Add sugar or honey to taste and carob or chocolate chips. Scald remaining milk and add to other ingredients. Cook over medium heat, stirring constantly, until mixture is thick and loses its starchy flavor, about 5 minutes. If adding an egg, add some hot pudding to egg, then add egg to pudding and cook about half a minute; remove from heat. Press cottage cheese through a sieve or puree in a blender or food processor; add to saucepan with vanilla and mix well. Pour into 5 custard cups and chill well.
Makes 5 servings
10 grams protein per serving

High-Protein Fruit Bavarian

This dessert includes orange juice, cottage cheese, wheat germ and nuts for a good supply of protein, vitamins and minerals. A nice change from eggs and much more nutritious than cold cereal or toast and coffee.

1 cup milk
2 tablespoons (2 envelopes) unflavored
  gelatin
1/2 cup honey
3 cups cottage cheese
One 6-ounce can frozen orange juice concentrate, thawed
1/4 cup wheat germ
1/2 cup chopped nuts or unsalted sunflower
  seeds (optional)
1 cup whipping cream, whipped

Pour milk into a large saucepan. Sprinkle gelatin over milk to soften. Place over low heat and stir till gelatin is dissolved. Remove from heat and stir in honey. Press cottage cheese through a sieve or puree in a blender or food processor. Stir cottage cheese into gelatin mixture. Add orange juice concentrate, wheat germ and nuts; blend well. Fold in whipped cream. Turn into a 6-cup serving dish or 8 custard cups, tin muffin cups or paper cups. Chill 4 to 6 hours.
Makes 8 servings
14.5 grams protein per serving

Cheese Dessert, Hindu Style

1/3 cup slivered blanched almonds
1 cup cottage cheese
1 cup ricotta cheese
1/4 cup packed light-brown sugar
Grated rind of 1 lemon
1 to 2 tablespoons lemon juice
1/4 teaspoon ground cardamom

In a dry skillet over medium heat, stir almonds until lightly toasted; set aside. Press cheeses through a sieve, then blend in sugar, or puree cheeses with sugar in a blender or food proces-sor until smooth. Add lemon rind, lemon juice, cardamom and 1/4 cup almonds and mix well. Pour into 4 serving dishes or custard cups and chill 1 hour or overnight. Garnish with remaining almonds.
Makes 4 servings
15 grams protein per serving

Breakfast Bread Pudding

These bread puddings are much better and more nutritious than toast and coffee—they really keep you going all morning long. Wheat germ and dry milk contribute extra protein to an already nourishing, change-of-pace breakfast.

2/3 cup non-instant nonfat dry milk
3 cups milk
4 slices whole-wheat bread, crusts removed
1/3 to 1/2 cup honey or packed brown sugar
2 tablespoons butter or safflower margarine
1 teaspoon vanilla extract
3 eggs, beaten
1/2 cup raisins or currants
1/4 teaspoon ground nutmeg
2 tablespoons wheat germ
Milk, half-and-half or Whipped Ricotta Topping,
   page 178

In a mixing bowl, gradually sprinkle dry milk over liquid milk while beating with a whisk; or pour liquid milk into a blender, cover and turn on blender, then uncover and sprinkle in dry milk, not allowing mixture to foam. In a saucepan, scald milk mixture and stir in honey or sugar, butter or margarine, vanilla, eggs and raisins. Cut bread into cubes and place in a mixing bowl; pour milk mixture over and mix well. Pour into a buttered baking dish. Sprinkle with nutmeg and wheat germ. Place dish in a shallow baking pan and add hot water to baking pan to a depth of 1 inch. Bake in a preheated 350°F oven 45 to 50 minutes, or until a knife inserted near center comes out clean. Serve warm or cold with milk, half-and-half or ricotta topping.
Makes 6 servings
10.3 grams protein per serving

CAROB BREAKFAST BREAD PUDDING Add 1/4 cup carob powder to scalded milk in preceding recipe.

Apple Bread Pudding

This reminds me of something Grandma would make. *So* nourishing.

4 slices whole-wheat bread, crusts removed
2 cups milk
1/2 cup non-instant nonfat dry milk
4 eggs
1/3 cup packed brown sugar or honey
1/2 teaspoon ground cinnamon
1/4 teaspoon ground nutmeg
Dash salt
1 medium apple, peeled, cored and diced
1/3 cup raisins
Whipped Ricotta Topping, page 178 (optional)

Toast bread on a baking sheet in a preheated 350°F oven until golden, about 10 minutes. Cut in 1/2-inch cubes. Turn into a buttered 8-1/4-inch round baking dish. Place milk in a saucepan and gradually sprinkle dry milk over it while beating with a whisk, blending thoroughly; or place liquid milk in a blender, cover and turn on blender, then uncover and sprinkle in dry milk but do not let it foam. Scald milk mixture and add to bread cubes in baking dish; let stand 15 minutes. Beat together eggs, sugar or honey, cinnamon, nutmeg and salt until light. Add apple and raisins and stir into bread mixture. Place baking dish in a larger shallow baking pan and add hot water to larger pan to a depth of 1 inch. Bake in a preheated 350°F oven 30 to 35 minutes or until a knife inserted near center comes out clean. Serve warm or cold, with ricotta topping, if you like.
Makes 6 servings
11.3 grams protein per serving

BANANA BREAD PUDDING Follow directions for preceding recipe, omitting apples and substituting 1 cup mashed banana (2 large or 3 small bananas) to egg mixture. Omit cinnamon and nutmeg and add 1/4 teaspoon grated lemon rind.

Extra-Nutritious Rice Pudding

I love this with tea in the morning—I keep it stored in the refrigerator and ready to eat.

5-1/2 cups milk
1 cup brown rice
Pinch salt
2 tablespoons packed brown sugar
3 eggs, beaten
1/4 cup honey
1/4 teaspoon ground cinnamon
1/4 teaspoon ground nutmeg
1 cup raisins or chopped dates

In a saucepan, bring 2-1/2 cups milk to a simmer. Add rice, salt and sugar. Stir once, cover and simmer over very low heat about 1 hour or until rice is tender and most of liquid is absorbed. Blend remaining milk well with eggs, honey, cinnamon and nutmeg. Stir into rice and add raisins or dates. Pour into an oiled 1-quart casserole or 6 custard cups. Bake in a preheated 325°F oven for 30 minutes, or until set.
Makes 6 to 8 servings
12.9/19.7 grams protein per serving

Baked Pumpkin Custard

Pumpkin provides fiber and vitamin A to this high-protein custard. Don't wait till Thanksgiving to enjoy this.

3 eggs, beaten
1 cup mashed cooked pumpkin
1/3 cup packed brown sugar
One 14-ounce can evaporated milk, or 1/2 cup non-instant nonfat dry milk mixed with 1-3/4 milk (see method)
1/4 teaspoon ground allspice
1/4 teaspoon grated orange rind
1/2 teaspoon ground cinnamon
Whipped Ricotta Topping, page 178 (optional)

Combine all ingredients except whipped ricotta topping, mixing well. (If using dry milk, sprinkle it gradually over liquid milk while beating with a whisk; or pour liquid milk in a blender, cover and turn on blender, then uncover and sprinkle in dry milk, not allowing mixture to foam.) Pour into six 6-ounce custard cups. Place in a shallow baking pan and pour hot water around cups to a depth of 1 inch. Bake in a preheated 325°F oven until a knife inserted near center comes out clean. Serve warm or chilled. Garnish with ricotta topping, if desired, and sprinkle with extra cinnamon.
Makes 6 servings
11 grams protein per serving

Baked Breakfast Custard

This is a good snack anytime. It takes about 10 minutes to put together.

1/2 cup non-instant nonfat dry milk
2 cups milk
3 eggs, beaten
1/4 cup Turbinado or granulated sugar or honey
Dash salt (optional)
1 teaspoon vanilla extract, or 1/2 teaspoon almond extract
Ground nutmeg

Gradually sprinkle dry milk over liquid milk while beating with a wire whisk; or place liquid milk in a blender, cover blender, turn on motor, uncover and sprinkle in dry milk but do not allow mixture to foam. Add eggs, sugar or honey, salt and flavoring and mix well (if adding honey to blender, it should first be warmed). Pour into four or five 6-ounce custard cups. Sprinkle with nutmeg. Place cups in a shallow pan and pour hot water to a 1/2-inch level around cups. Bake in a preheated 350°F oven for 35 minutes, or until a knife inserted 1/2 inch from center of custard comes out clean; be careful not to overbake.
Makes 4 to 5 servings
12.5/10 grams protein per serving

HIGHEST-PROTEIN BAKED CUSTARD Follow the preceding recipe, adding 1/2 to 1 cup pureed cottage cheese, bakers' (hoop) cheese or ricotta cheese to milk mixture (press cheese through a sieve or puree in a blender or food processor, or prepare entire recipe in a blender). Add an extra tablespoon of sugar or honey, if you like.
18/24 grams protein per serving

Apple Custard

This is better than creme caramel. Dry milk and wheat germ add extra protein.

2 medium Golden Delicious apples, peeled and
   cored
1 tablespoon butter or safflower margarine
1/4 teaspoon ground cardamom or cinnamon
1/2 cup wheat germ mixed with 1/4 cup brown
   sugar and 1 tablespoon soft butter or safflower
   margarine
3 eggs
1/3 cup packed brown sugar or honey
1/2 cup non-instant nonfat dry milk
2-1/2 cups milk
1/2 teaspoon vanilla extract

Cut apples into 1/4-inch-thick slices. In a frying pan with a cover, melt butter or margarine. Add apples and turn over heat to coat. Sprinkle cardamom or cinnamon over apples, cover and cook over medium heat until apples are tender, about 5 minutes. Lift apples from pan with a slotted spoon and distribute evenly in a shallow greased baking dish about 8 inches in diameter or 8 inches square. Sprinkle with wheat germ mixture. In a bowl beat eggs and sugar or honey with a fork until blended. Stir in liquid milk and vanilla until smoothly blended; gradually sprinkle dry milk over this mixture while beating with a whisk, blending thoroughly; pour over apples. Place custard inside a larger baking pan and add boiling water to a depth of about 3/4 inch. Bake in a preheated 325°F oven for 45 minutes or until a knife inserted near center comes out clean. Remove from water bath and chill thoroughly, about 3 hours.
Makes 6 to 8 servings
12/9 grams protein per serving

PIES AND COBBLERS

All of the pies in this chapter have high-protein fillings in combination with high-protein crusts. Some of them contain fruit, too, for extra nutrition. The cobblers are both healthy and easy—serve them with ricotta toppings for extra protein.

Note: Pies can be made into portable tarts by using small foil pie plates. Prepare cobblers ahead and warm them up when you're ready to eat, or prepare fruit mixture and mix wet and dry ingredients for topping separately ahead of time, then mix and bake just before serving. Freeze cobblers in foil-covered small foil pie plates or individual foil muffin cups for later use as portable breakfasts. Reheat in a preheated 350°F oven for 15 minutes or until heated through.

Breakfast Pumpkin Pie

After discussing nutrition and then making pumpkin pies for Thanksgiving, one of my students decided that pumpkin pie was "pretty good for you." He was right. I decided it could be made even better for breakfast. This pie has a lot of vitamin A, as well as protein, B vitamins and iron. It takes just a few minutes to assemble.

1/2 recipe Flaky Wheat Germ Pastry, page 176, or No-Roll Whole-Wheat Pastry, page 177, or 1 recipe Praline Crust, page 177
1/2 cup cottage cheese or ricotta cheese
1-1/2 cups milk
1/2 cup non-instant nonfat dry milk
3 eggs, beaten
1/2 to 3/4 cup packed brown sugar or honey
1-1/2 cups mashed cooked pumpkin
1-1/2 teaspoons ground cinnamon
1/2 teaspoon ground nutmeg
1/2 teaspoon ground ginger
1/4 teaspoon ground allspice
1/4 teaspoon ground cloves
1/2 teaspoon salt
1 egg white (optional)
Whipped Ricotta Topping, page 178 (optional)

Prepare one 9- or 10-inch pie shell and bake in a preheated 400°F oven for 4 minutes. Press cottage cheese or ricotta cheese through a sieve, or puree in a blender or food processor. Place milk in a bowl and gradually sprinkle dry milk over while beating with a whisk, blending thoroughly; or place milk in a blender, cover and turn on blender, then uncover and sprinkle in dry milk, not allowing it to foam. In a large bowl, combine cheese with liquid and dry milks, eggs, sugar or honey, pumpkin, spices and salt; mix until smooth. Lightly brush pie shell with egg white and fill with pumpkin mixture. Bake in a preheated 400°F oven 55 to 60 minutes, or until a knife inserted near center comes out clean. Cool in pan on a rack. Serve garnished with ricotta topping, if you like.
Makes 6 to 8 servings
15.3/11.4 grams protein per serving

Good Morning Orange Chiffon Pie

This pie is dedicated to Tony McNeely, who helped toward its perfection by testing it twice. He was a great guinea pig in class because he never ate breakfast at home.

One 9- or 10-inch Granola Crumb Crust, page 175
1/4 cup honey
3 eggs, separated
2 tablespoons (2 envelopes) unflavored gelatin
1/4 teaspoon salt
3 tablespoons Turbinado or granulated sugar
1/3 cup boiling water
One 6-ounce can frozen orange concentrate
1 cup cottage cheese or ricotta cheese
1/2 cup whipping cream, whipped
Orange slices (optional)

Prepare granola crust and cool. In a small bowl beat honey and egg yolks together. In a saucepan, mix gelatin, salt and 2 tablespoons sugar very well. Add boiling water, stirring to dissolve gelatin. Add eggs and honey to this mixture. Cook over low heat, stirring constantly, until mixture thickens slightly. Remove from heat and stir in orange juice until well blended. Press cottage cheese or ricotta cheese through a sieve, or puree in a blender or food processor. Beat cheese into orange juice mixture and place in the freezer until almost set. Beat egg whites until soft peaks form; add remaining sugar 1/2 teaspoon at a time

and beat until stiff. Fold egg whites into orange mixture and then fold in whipped cream. Pour filling into crust. Chill until firm, at least three hours. You may want to garnish your creation with orange slices.
Makes 6 to 8 servings
15.8/11.9 grams protein per serving

Creamy Cheese-and-Fruit Yogurt Pie

This takes about eight minutes to prepare if you have your frozen high-protein crumb crust ready. My students named this "Breakfast Skippers' Pie" for all the breakfast skippers in class who wolfed it down. It even converted some of them into health-awareness people.

1 Granola Crumb Crust or Nutty Bran Crumb Crust, page 175
1 tablespoon (1 envelope) unflavored gelatin
1/4 cup water
1/4 to 1/3 cup honey (or less)
1-1/4 cups cottage cheese or ricotta cheese
16 ounces natural fruit-flavored yogurt

Prepare pie crust and set aside. In a saucepan, sprinkle gelatin over water and allow to soften for about 5 minutes. Add honey and cook over low heat until gelatin is dissolved; cool. Press cottage cheese or ricotta cheese through a sieve or puree in a blender or food processor until smooth. Blend in yogurt and gelatin mixture; pour into crust and refrigerate about 3 hours or overnight.
Makes 6 to 8 servings
14.9/11.2 grams protein per serving

Berry Cobbler

I felt the first version of this was a total disaster, but my cousins ate it anyway. This version lives up to my culinary standards.

Topping
1/2 cup stirred unbleached all-purpose flour
1/3 cup stirred whole-wheat flour or whole-wheat
    pastry flour
1/4 cup non-instant nonfat dry milk, or 2 table-
    spoons high-protein powder
1/3 cup wheat germ
1/4 teaspoon salt
1 tablespoon baking powder
1 egg, beaten
1/4 cup milk
1 tablespon safflower or corn oil
1/3 cup honey
1 teaspoon vanilla extract
1/2 cup small-curd cottage cheese

4 cups fresh or frozen unsweetened blueberries
    or blackberries
1/3 to 1/2 cup honey
2 tablespoons cornstarch
1/4 cup wheat germ
1 tablespoon butter or safflower margarine,
    melted
2 teaspoons lemon juice
Whipped Ricotta Topping, page 178

To make the topping, mix flours, dry milk or protein powder, wheat germ, salt and baking powder. In another bowl mix egg, milk, oil, honey, vanilla and cheese. Combine wet ingredients with dry ingredients just until moistened.

In a saucepan, mix berries, honey, cornstarch and wheat germ and stir over medium heat until thickened and clear. Stir in butter or margarine and lemon juice. Pour into an oiled 8-inch-square baking dish. Drop topping in 9 mounds onto hot berry mixture. Bake in a preheated 375°F oven for about 30 minutes, or until lightly browned. Serve warm or cool, with whipped ricotta topping.
Makes 9 servings
10.1 grams protein per serving

Peach Cobbler

4 cups sliced peaches (5 to 6 peaches)
1-1/2 tablespoons cornstarch
1/4 cup wheat germ
1 or 2 tablespoons butter or safflower margarine,
    melted
1/2 to 3/4 cup honey
1 tablespoon lemon juice
1/2 teaspoon almond extract
Topping for Berry Cobbler, preceding
Whipped Ricotta Topping, page 178

Arrange sliced peaches in an oiled 8 × 8-inch baking pan; sprinkle with cornstarch and wheat germ and stir to coat. Mix butter, honey, lemon juice and almond extract and spread over fruit. Place in a preheated 300°F oven until hot while preparing topping. Prepare topping as directed in Berry Cobbler recipe and place in 9 mounds on hot fruit. Increase oven heat to 375°F and bake for about 30 minutes, or until lightly browned. Serve warm or cooled, with ricotta topping.
Makes 9 servings
10 grams protein per serving

APPLE COBBLER Follow preceding recipe, substituting 4 cups sliced apples (3 to 5 apples) for peaches and 2 tablespoons whole-wheat flour for cornstarch.

Apple Crisp

Apple Crisp is a good thing to make on Sunday—so you can eat the leftovers for breakfast during the week. The rolled oats, wheat germ and nuts combine with the soy flour and dry milk or protein powder to make complete protein. The bran, apples and raisins add fiber, vitamins and minerals to this wholesome dessert.

4 cups sliced apples (3 to 5 apples)
1/4 cup raisins
1/4 cup chopped nuts
1 teaspoon ground cinnamon
1/4 teaspoon ground nutmeg
3/4 cup rolled oats
1/4 cup unprocessed wheat bran (optional)
1/4 cup toasted wheat germ
1/4 cup soy flour
1/4 cup non-instant nonfat dry milk, or 2 tablespoons high-protein powder
1/2 cup safflower or corn oil
1/2 cup honey
Whipped Ricotta Topping, page 178 (optional)

Place apples in an oiled 9 × 9-inch baking dish. Combine raisins, nuts, cinnamon and nutmeg and sprinkle evenly over apples. Combine oats, bran, wheat germ, soy flour and dry milk or protein powder. Add oil and honey to oat mixture and mix until well combined. Distribute oat mixture evenly over apples and bake in a preheated 350°F oven for 30 minutes or until lightly browned. Serve warm or cooled with ricotta topping, if you like.
Makes 8 servings
6 grams protein per serving

HIGH-PROTEIN CAKES

The cakes in this chapter may be eaten as desserts, but they are also high enough in protein to be eaten as light meals or high-nutrient snacks. They are easily portable for a breakfast-on-the-go, and all of them may be frozen.

High-Protein Pound Cake

This delicious cake contains a whole pound of cottage cheese.

1 cup stirred whole-wheat flour
1-1/2 cups stirred unbleached flour
1/2 cup wheat germ
1/4 cup non-instant nonfat dry milk
3 teaspoons baking powder
1-1/2 teaspoons grated lemon peel
1/4 pound butter or safflower margarine, at room temperature

2/3 cup Turbinado or granulated sugar
2/3 cup honey
1-1/2 teaspoons vanilla or almond extract
3 eggs
2 cups small-curd cottage cheese
1/4 cup milk

Combine flours, wheat germ, dry milk, baking powder and lemon peel; set aside. With an electric mixer or in a food processor, cream butter and sugar together until very fluffy. Add honey a little at a time while mixing until mixture is smooth and light; add vanilla. Beat in eggs one at a time, beating after each addition. (It is extremely important to get the butter-egg mixture very light and fluffy, as the air you beat in will help to leaven this cake.) Beat in cottage cheese and milk until light and fluffy. Add cheese mixture to dry ingredients, mixing thoroughly. Pour into a well-greased 10-inch tube pan or two 5 × 9-inch loaf pans. Bake in a preheated 350°F oven for 50 to 60 minutes or until a toothpick inserted into center comes out clean. Cool in pan on a rack.
Makes 14 to 16 servings
8.7/7.6 grams protein per serving

Poppy Seed Cake

No one ever believes this has cheese and wheat germ in it. The luscious glaze is made from dry milk and adds even more protein to the cake. This can be put together in about ten minutes.

One 2-ounce box poppy seeds
1/2 cup apple juice
1-1/4 cups ricotta cheese
3 eggs
1/4 cup safflower or corn oil
1-1/2 cups Turbinado or granulated sugar
1 teaspoon vanilla extract
1 cup stirred unbleached all-purpose flour
1 cup stirred whole-wheat flour
1/3 cup wheat germ
1/4 cup non-instant nonfat dry milk

2-1/4 teaspoons baking powder
Dash ground cinnamon
Dash ground nutmeg
1/4 teaspoon grated lemon rind
Lemon Quick Milk Glaze, page 183

In a saucepan, bring apple juice to a boil; stir in poppy seeds and remove pan from heat. Allow seeds to soak in juice for 1 hour. Add cheese, eggs, oil, sugar and vanilla and mix well. Combine flours, wheat germ, dry milk, baking powder, cinnamon, nutmeg and lemon rinds. Add wet ingredients and mix well. Pour into a greased and floured 10-inch bundt or tube pan and bake in a preheated 350°F oven 50 to 60 minutes, or until a toothpick inserted into center comes out clean. Cool in pan on a rack, then remove from pan and glaze with lemon glaze.
Makes 10 to 12 servings
11.6/9.7 grams protein per serving

Extra-Special Carrot Cake

I've always loved carrot cake, but have cringed at the thought of all that oil in the batter and the fat in the cream cheese frosting. Now here is a low-oil, high-protein cake that contributes plenty of good nutrition to my diet. The carrots in this recipe produce a moist cake high in fiber and rich in vitamin A and minerals. Wheat germ and nuts contribute protein, iron and B vitamins. A special ricotta frosting adds even more protein. I, and many people I know, prefer the less-sweet version of this cake (1-1/2 cups sugar) but 2 cups makes it more like the familiar cake we all know. Either way, it is much more nutritious than any carrot cake you can buy.

1 cup drained juice-pack crushed pineapple
1-1/2 to 2 cups packed brown sugar
4 cups grated carrots
1/2 cup raisins (optional)
Juice from pineapple plus enough water to make 1-1/3 cups
1-1/2 teaspoons ground cinnamon
1/2 teaspoon ground cloves
1/2 teaspoon ground nutmeg
1 teaspoon ground allspice
Dash ground ginger
2 eggs, beaten
2 tablespoons safflower or corn oil
1-1/2 cups stirred unbleached all-purpose flour
1 cup stirred whole-wheat pastry flour
1 cup wheat germ
2 teaspoons baking soda
1-1/2 teaspoons baking powder
1 teaspoon salt
1/2 cup or more chopped English or black walnuts
Ricotta Frosting, page 178
Walnut halves (optional)

Place pineapple in a sieve to drain; reserve juice. Simmer sugar, carrots, raisins, liquid and spices in a saucepan for 10 minutes. Allow to cool to room temperature, then mix in eggs, oil and pineapple. In a 9 × 12-inch cake pan, mix flours, wheat germ, baking soda, baking powder, salt and nuts until thoroughly combined. Add to wet ingredients and mix well. Grease cake pan and spread batter into pan. Bake in a preheated 350°F oven 30 to 40 minutes or until a toothpick inserted into center comes out clean. Cool in pan on a rack, then frost with ricotta frosting. If you like a layer cake, cut cake in half crosswise, and frost one of the layers, then place other layer on top and frost top. Decorate with walnut halves, if desired.
Makes 12 servings
12.6 grams protein per serving

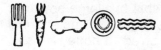

High-Protein Applesauce Cake

A delicious ready-when-you-are portable breakfast.

1-1/2 cups stirred whole-wheat pastry flour
3/4 cup stirred soy flour
1/2 cup non-instant nonfat dry milk
1/2 cup wheat germ
4 teaspoons baking powder
1 teaspoon salt
2 teaspoons ground cinnamon
1 cup packed brown sugar
1/2 cup safflower or corn oil
4 eggs
3/4 cup unsweetened applesauce
1 cup raisins, or 1/2 cup each raisins and
    chopped nuts
Fabulous Apple Juice Glaze, page 183 (optional)

Mix flours, dry milk, wheat germ, baking powder, salt and cinnamon together in an 8 × 12-inch baking pan. In a mixing bowl, beat oil and sugar together until smooth, then add eggs one at a time, beating after each one. Add one half of the dry ingredients, then one half of the applesauce, blending well. Add remaining dry ingredients, blending well. Mix in remaining applesauce, raisins and nuts. Grease baking pan and pour in batter. Bake in a preheated 350°F oven for 40 to 50 minutes, or until a toothpick inserted into center comes out clean. Cool in pan on a rack, then glaze with apple juice glaze, if you like.
Makes 12 servings
8.2 grams protein per serving

Spicy Banana Breakfast Bars

This is another great take-it-with-you-and-beat-the-traffic breakfast. It fights junk food cravings and, besides being delicious, it's portable, freezable and nourishing.

1 cup stirred whole-wheat pastry flour
1 cup stirred soy flour
1 cup non-instant nonfat dry milk
1/2 teaspoon salt
3 teaspoons baking powder
1 teaspoon ground cinnamon
1/2 cup chopped walnuts
1/4 cup chopped unsalted sunflower seeds
1/4 cup unhulled sesame seeds (optional)
1-1/2 cups mashed very ripe bananas
    (about 3 bananas)
2 eggs
1/2 cup safflower or corn oil
1/2 cup buttermilk
1 cup packed brown sugar

Mix flours, dry milk, salt, baking powder, cinnamon, nuts and seeds together in an 8 × 12-inch baking pan. In a large bowl, combine bananas, eggs, oil, buttermilk and sugar. Beat until well blended. Add dry ingredients and mix until just moistened. Grease baking pan and pour in batter. Bake in a preheated 350°F oven 35 to 45 minutes or until cake shrinks slightly from side of pan. Cool and cut into bars.
Makes 20 bars or 10 servings
5.6 grams protein per bar
11.2 grams protein per serving

CHEESECAKES

Cheesecakes are the desserts highest in protein if they are made with cottage cheese or ricotta cheese. Cream cheese has too much butterfat and far less protein. All of these recipes have adapted from really good cheesecake recipes. They are so good it's hard to convince yourself not to feel guilty after eating them. Most of them take only a few minutes to make.

Easy-as-Pie Cheesecake

This is my in-a-hurry version of cheesecake. I like to beat the traffic, so I take some to work and eat it when I get there.

One 9- or 10-inch Nutty Bran Crumb Crust, page 175
1 tablespoon (1 envelope) gelatin
1/2 cup or less Turbinado or granulated sugar or honey
2/3 cup boiling water
2-1/2 cups cottage cheese
2 ounces (1/4 cup) cream cheese, at room temperature
1 teaspoon vanilla extract
Fresh fruit or fruit glaze, following (optional)

Prepare crumb crust and chill. In a large bowl, mix gelatin and sugar; add boiling water and stir until gelatin is completely dissolved. (If honey is used, soak gelatin by sprinkling over 1/3 cup cold water. Allow to stand 5 minutes, then add honey and 1/3 cup boiling water, stirring until gelatin is completely dissolved.) Press cottage cheese through a sieve or puree in a blender or food processor; add to gelatin mixture with cream cheese and vanilla. Pour into prepared crust; chill until firm, about 2 hours. Top with fruit or fruit glaze, if desired.
Makes 8 servings
13.9 grams protein per serving

BLUEBERRY GLAZE Drain one 10-ounce package thawed frozen unsweetened blueberries, reserving juice. Mix 2 tablespoons honey or sugar with 2 tablespoons cornstarch, then mix into 1/2 cup reserved juice and cook, stirring, until mixture is thick; stir in 1 tablespoon lemon juice and blueberries. Cool thoroughly.

RED CHERRY GLAZE Drain one 16-ounce can of water-packed sour red cherries, reserving juice. Mix 1/4 cup honey or Turbinado or granulated sugar with 1 tablespoon cornstarch, then mix into 1/2 cup reserved juice and cook, stirring, until mixture is thick; stir in 1 tablespoon lemon juice and cherries. Cool thoroughly.

PINEAPPLE GLAZE Drain one 8-3/4-ounce can juice-packed crushed pineapple, reserving juice. Mix 1 tablespoon honey or sugar with 2 teaspoons cornstarch and mix into 1/2 cup reserved juice and cook, stirring, until mixture is thick; stir in 1 tablespoon lemon juice and crushed pineapple. Cool thoroughly.

Breakfast Cheesecake

People always ask me why I'm so slim, when I'm always eating so many goodies. This is one of my secrets: It's nutritious enough to be breakfast.

Cheesecake
One 9-inch high-protein crumb crust,
    pages 174-75
4 eggs
2 cups cottage cheese or bakers' (hoop) cheese
2 ounces (1/4 cup) cream cheese, at room
    temperature
1/2 teaspoon salt
1 teaspoon lemon juice
1/2 teaspoon vanilla extract
1/2 cup honey
Ground cinnamon

Topping
1-1/2 cups unflavored yogurt
1/2 teaspoon vanilla extract
2 tablespoons honey

Prepare crumb crust and chill. Put eggs into a blender or food processor and blend until whipped; add cottage or bakers' cheese 1/2 cup at a time, blending until smooth after each addition; add cream cheese and blend until smooth. Or, press cottage cheese through a sieve and beat together with eggs and cream cheese. Add salt, lemon juice, vanilla and honey to cheese mixture and mix well. Pour into pie crust. Dust with cinnamon and bake in a preheated 350°F oven for about 25 minutes. Stir together topping ingredients and pour over pie, then bake another 10 to 15 minutes, or until a knife inserted near center comes out clean. Cool pie on a rack for 1 hour, then chill several hours or overnight before serving.
Makes 8 servings
16.1 grams protein per serving

Italian Cheese Pie

This is one of my favorite things in the world. A famous northern Italian dessert, it is loaded with good nutrition and is perfect for breakfast, especially when served with fresh fruit.

1/2 recipe Flaky Wheat Germ Pastry, page 176, with 2 tablespoons Turbinado or granulated sugar and 1 teaspoon grated lemon rind added
2 cups cottage cheese
2 cups ricotta cheese
1/3 to 1/2 cup honey
3 eggs, beaten
1/2 teaspoon salt
1-1/2 teaspoons vanilla extract
1 tablespoon unbleached all-purpose flour
1 tablespoon golden raisins, rinsed and drained
1 tablespoon each candied citron and candied orange peel, or 1 teaspoon grated lemon rind and 1 tablespoon grated orange rind
2 tablespoons slivered blanched almonds or pine nuts

Place pastry in an 8-inch spring form pan or 10-inch pie pan; set aside. Press cottage cheese through a sieve or puree 1 cup at a time in a blender or food processor. Combine with ricotta cheese and stir in honey, eggs, salt, vanilla and flour. Mix in raisins and candied peels or grated rinds. Fill pastry crust and sprinkle with nuts. Bake in a preheated 350°F oven for 50 minutes, or until crust is golden and filling is firm. Cool in pan on a rack.
Makes 10 servings
14.2 grams protein per serving

Pumpkin Cheesecake

I made this for one of my mother's dinner parties, warning her that it was an experiment and that she should have some ice cream in reserve "just in case." For all I know she may still have the ice cream, since the cake was an enormous success and she has adopted the "if you're going to eat treats, why bother with unhealthy junk" attitude.

1 recipe high-protein crumb crust, pages 174-75
2-1/2 cups cottage cheese
One 3-ounce package cream cheese, at room temperature
3 eggs
1 cup mashed cooked pumpkin
3/4 cup packed brown sugar or honey
1-1/2 teaspoons vanilla extract
1/4 teaspoon ground ginger
1/4 teaspoon ground nutmeg
3/4 teaspoon ground cinnamon
Freshly ground nutmeg or whipped cream (optional)

Prepare crumb crust and press into a 9-inch spring form pan; bake and cool. Press cottage cheese through a sieve or puree in a blender or a food processor. Beat in the cream cheese. Separate 2 eggs and blend 2 yolks plus 1 whole egg into cheese mixture. Mix with pumpkin, sugar or honey, vanilla and spices. Beat 2 egg whites until they form stiff peaks. Fold into cheese mixture. Spoon into crust and bake in a preheated 325°F oven for about 50 minutes; cake may not seem quite firm. Cool in pan on a rack and refrigerate overnight. To serve, sprinkle with nutmeg or garnish with whipped cream, if desired.

Makes 8 to 10 servings
15.8/12.6 grams protein per serving

Carob or Chocolate Swirl Cheesecake

This is a fabulous cheesecake for chocolate addicts. Use three cups of cheese for a lighter cake that is higher in protein (17.9 grams per serving); use two cups of cheese for a more cake-like texture (14.4 grams per serving).

1 recipe High-Protein Graham Cracker Crumb
   Crust, pages 174-75, with 1 tablespoon cocoa
   added
3/4 cup carob or chocolate chips
3/4 to 1 cup Turbinado or granulated sugar or
   honey
2 to 3 cups cottage cheese
1/2 cup unflavored yogurt
2 teaspoons vanilla extract
4 eggs

Prepare crust and press into a 9-inch spring form pan or 10-inch pie pan; bake and cool. In a saucepan over hot water combine chips and 1/4 cup sugar or honey. Heat until melted and smooth. Remove from heat and set aside. Press cottage cheese through a sieve, or puree in a blender or food processor (use larger amount of cheese if you prefer a lighter cake). Gradually beat in 1/2 to 3/4 cup sugar or honey. Mix in yogurt and vanilla extract. Add eggs one at a time, beating well after each addition. Divide batter in half. Stir melted chocolate mixture into half of batter. Pour into crust, then pour plain layer over chocolate layer. With a knife, swirl batter layers together to marbleize. Bake in a preheated 325°F oven 50 to 60 minutes, or until only a 2-to 3-inch circle in center shakes. Cool in pan on a rack, then refrigerate until ready to serve.

Makes 8 servings
14.4/17.9 grams protein per serving

Ready-When-You-Are Meals and Salads
(Your Own Storable Fast Foods)

Working parents and harried housepersons are often too exhausted after a demanding day to plan and cook nutritious meals. The family dinner hour and three square meals a day have all but vanished in many homes, along with embroidered aprons and the icebox. Because of differing schedules and hunger patterns, homes with children often have as many mealtimes as family members. Fast foods and "take out" foods have become a desperate solution to this problem. Colorful plastic eateries beckon to us from the boulevards with their tempting but nutritionally poor products. We give in to the empty calories because we're in a hurry. But this situation can easily be changed.

Why take out a taco or burger stuffed with additives, fillers and chemicals when you can take out your own delicious, nourishing goodies without leaving the house? The fast food items in these recipes are designed to compete with commercial fast foods because they are satisfying, instantly available and often portable. They maximize good nutrition and minimize the number of hours spent in the kitchen.

Vegetables are usually ignored by the fast food world. Still, we know they are important contributors of dietary fiber, vitamins and minerals. In this chapter you'll find many ingenious ways to incorporate vegetables into sandwiches and other delicious ready-to-eat foods. The All-Week Salads will tempt you away from junk foods because they are all ready to eat without fuss. For other vegetable dishes, see the hot vegetable appetizers, vegetable dips and marinated vegetables in the "Make a Meal of Appetizers" chapter, following.

This chapter includes alternatives to the same old sandwiches, many of them using complementary-protein ingredients to reduce the need for meat. The turnovers with cottage cheese pastry, the Pizza Rustica, the Deep-Dish Pizza, the vegetarian pies, quick quiches and the other mealtime pies are all divine-tasting alternatives. These have all been adapted from traditional portable meals from other cultures. The foods some of my foreign students brought for lunch inspired many of these recipes. For other sandwich ideas, see the spreads and cold-cut loaves in the next chapter, "Make a Meal of Appetizers."

SANDWICHES

These sandwiches are designed to use small amounts of meat and to incorporate complementary proteins; many contain vegetables as well. Sandwiches that do not contain vegetables can be accompanied by an All-Week Salad (see pages 70 to 75) to complete your meal.

Note: To reheat sandwiches, wrap in aluminum foil and place in a 350°F oven until heated through.

Vegetable Heroes

If you want to make this a vegetarian dish, omit the salami and use twice as much cheese.

1 small cauliflower, broken into florets, or one 10-ounce package frozen cauliflower
3/4 pound Brussels sprouts, or one 10-ounce package frozen Brussels sprouts
1 small bunch broccoli or one 9-ounce package frozen broccoli, separated into florets
1/4 pound butter or safflower margarine, at room temperature
1/2 cup wheat germ
2 teaspoons prepared mustard
1/4 cup finely chopped green onion
6 burger buns made from Easy High-Protein Freezer Dough, pages 172-73
2 medium tomatoes, thinly sliced
24 slices salami
6 slices provolone cheese, halved

Steam vegetables over boiling water until crisp-tender. Beat butter or margarine, wheat germ and mustard together; stir in green onion. Cut a 1-inch slice from top of buns or rolls. Hollow out bottom sections of rolls, leaving 1/2-inch-thick shells (save remaining bread to make crumbs for other uses). Spread insides of shells and undersides of tops of rolls with mustard butter. Fill rolls with vegetables. Top with tomato slices, salami and cheese. Replace tops of rolls. Wrap each roll in aluminum foil and place on a shallow baking pan. Bake in a preheated 350°F oven for 25 minutes.
Makes 6 servings
22 grams protein per serving

Baked Wellington Sandwich

This fun-to-make, fun-to-eat dish has ingredients from each of the four basic food groups. A great portable lunch or supper that freezes well, too.

1 round loaf French bread, 9 to 10 inches in
    diameter (1-1/2 pounds)
1/2 pound spinach, chopped and steamed, or
    half a 10-ounce package frozen chopped
    spinach, thawed
3 eggs, beaten
1 cup small-curd cottage cheese
1/2 cup wheat germ
1/2 teaspoon dried basil, crushed
1/2 teaspoon dried oregano, crushed
1/4 teaspoon ground black pepper
1 teaspoon salt
2 garlic cloves, minced
1/4 cup minced parsley
1/2 cup minced onion
1/2 cup grated carrot
1 pound very lean ground beef or ground turkey
1 cup grated Monterey Jack cheese
3 tablespoons butter or safflower margarine,
    melted

Using a long serrated knife, slice bread in half horizontally. Pull soft bread out of both halves, leaving 1/2-inch-thick shells. Process enough soft bread in a blender or food processor to make 3/4 cup crumbs (save remaining bread for other uses). Place bread crumbs in a large bowl. Drain off 1/4 cup juice from spinach and add it to bread crumbs. Squeeze remaining moisture out of spinach. Add beaten eggs and cottage cheese to bread mixture. Mix well and allow to stand for 5 minutes. Next add wheat germ, spices, salt, pepper, garlic, parsley, onion, carrot, spinach, meat and cheese. Mix together well. Coat insides of bread shells with half of the butter or margarine. Pack meat mixture into bottom half of bread shell. Press top half firmly into place. Coat loaf lightly with butter or margarine. Securely wrap loaf in a double thickness of aluminum foil. Place on a baking sheet and bake in a preheated 350°F oven for 2 hours. Remove from oven. Loosen foil to allow steam to escape and let stand for 10 minutes. Cut into wedges to serve.
Makes 8 servings
23.2 grams protein per serving

Baked Cheese Sandwiches

One 7-ounce Edam cheese
8 slices firm whole-grain bread, crusts removed
1 cup milk, heated
1 tablespoon butter or safflower margarine,
  melted
Grated Parmesan cheese
Paprika

Cut Edam cheese lengthwise into 4 slices about
1/4-inch thick and 3-1/2 inches in diameter (use
end pieces for grating at another time); set aside.
Place bread slices on a large platter or in a baking
pan. Pour milk over bread and, when absorbed,
cover 4 bread slices with a cheese slice. Cover
with remaining bread slices and, with a spatula,
place on a well-greased baking pan. Brush tops
with melted butter or margarine, sprinkle with
desired amount of Parmesan cheese and lightly
with paprika. Bake in a preheated 450°F oven for
12 to 15 minutes, or until sandwiches are browned
and cheese is melted. Serve hot.
Makes 4 servings
21.9 grams protein per serving

BAKED HAM AND CHEESE SANDWICHES
Follow the above recipe, using four 1-ounce
slices of any type of natural cheese and adding 1
slice of boiled ham to each sandwich.
20.9 grams protein per serving

BAKED CHICKEN SANDWICHES In a saucepan, cover and cook 1 skinned whole chicken
breast in about 1/4 cup simmering salted water
for 8 to 10 minutes. Cool chicken, remove bones
and chop meat. Combine chicken with 1/4 cup
chopped parsley or drained cooked chopped
spinach, 2 to 3 tablespoons safflower mayonnaise
and 1/2 cup grated Cheddar cheese. Follow
directions for Baked Cheese Sandwiches, above,
replacing sliced cheese with chicken mixture.
23.3 grams protein per serving

BAKED TUNA MELTS Drain one 6-1/2-ounce
can of tuna and combine with 1/4 cup chopped
parsley or drained cooked chopped spinach, 1 or
2 minced green onions and 3 tablespoons safflower mayonnaise. Follow directions for Baked
Cheese Sandwiches, using 10 bread slices and
1-1/4 cups milk. Replace Edam cheese slices
with tuna mixture and a thin slice of Swiss or
Monterey Jack cheese.
Makes 5 servings
23 grams protein per serving

Giant Chicken and Cheese Picnic Sandwich

This giant baked "sandwich" is easy to put together using your own or fortified commercial frozen bread dough.

1/3 recipe Easy High-Protein Freezer Dough,
    pages 172-73, or 1 recipe Fortified Frozen
    Bread Dough, page 174
2 eggs, beaten
2 cups grated Monterey Jack or Cheddar cheese
    (8 ounces)
3 cups chopped cooked chicken (about 2 whole
    chicken breasts)
1/4 cup chopped parsley
4 tablespoons chopped canned peeled green
    chilies
1/4 teaspoon onion powder
3/4 teaspoon salt
1/4 teaspoon paprika
1 egg, slightly beaten, mixed with 1 tablespoon
    water
1 teaspoon poppy seeds (optional)

Divide dough in half. Cover and let rest 10 minutes. On a lightly floured surface roll one portion into a 13-inch circle. Place on a greased 12-inch pizza pan. Combine eggs, cheese, chicken, parsley, chilies, onion powder, salt and paprika. Spread over dough in pan. Roll remaining dough into a 13-inch circle. Place over filling; trim and flute edges. Prick top crust with a fork. Cover lightly with aluminum foil. Bake in a preheated 400°F oven for 25 minutes. Remove sandwich from oven and remove foil. Brush top with egg-water mixture; sprinkle with poppy seeds. Return to oven and continue baking uncovered for 15 to 20 minutes, or until lightly browned. Remove and cool on a wire rack. Cut into wedges to serve.
Makes 8 servings
25.5 grams protein per serving

SAVORY PIES

Most of these savory pies are good either hot or at room temperature. They are designed with portability in mind and they are great eaten out of hand. Wrap them in aluminum foil to warm up when you want something to eat without cooking, or bring them along for lunch.

Note: Freeze individual servings wrapped in aluminum foil. Reheat in a 350°F oven until heated through.

Deep-Dish Pizza Pie

Pizza lovers can get their vegetables in this pizza. I like this served at room temperature for lunch. Bring some in a lunch bag.

Crust
1-1/2 cups Healthy Biscuit Mix, page 172
About 1/2 cup milk

Filling
1 pound zucchini, thinly sliced
1/2 medium onion, chopped (about 1/3 cup)
1 garlic clove, minced
3 tablespoons safflower or corn oil
1/2 teaspoon dried basil, crushed
1/4 teaspoon dried rosemary, crushed
3/4 teaspoon dried oregano, crushed
1/2 teaspoon salt
2 teaspoons minced fresh parsley
2 eggs
One 8-ounce can tomato sauce
1 cup grated mozzarella cheese
1/4 cup grated Parmesan cheese
1/2 pound hot Italian sausage, or 1/4 pound
   thinly sliced pepperoni

To make the crust, in a mixing bowl combine biscuit mix and enough milk to make a soft dough. Form dough into a ball and place in an ungreased 9- or 10-inch pie pan or an 8-inch round or square cake pan. Press out to form a crust.

To make the filling, in a frying pan saute zucchini, onion and garlic in oil. Add herbs, salt and parsley. Spread zucchini and spice mixture evenly over crust. Beat eggs with 1/4 cup tomato sauce and pour over zucchini. If using Italian sausage remove from casings and saute in a frying pan, then sprinkle over top of pizza. With pepperoni, place slices evenly over top of pizza. Bake in a preheated 325°F oven for 15 minutes, then pour on remaining tomato sauce, sprinkle with cheese and bake another 25 minutes.
Makes 6 servings
19.1 grams protein per serving

SPINACH DEEP-DISH PIZZA Follow the preceding recipe, using 1 pound fresh spinach, chopped, steamed and squeezed dry; or one 10-ounce package frozen chopped spinach, thawed and squeezed dry, in place of zucchini.

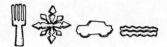

Pizza Rustica

No tomato sauce in this unique pizza! A fabulous dish that is good served at room temperature, so it makes great lunches. The spinach adds vitamins and fiber.

Filling
1 pound spinach, chopped, steamed and squeezed dry, or one 10-ounce package frozen chopped spinach, thawed and squeezed dry
2 cups ricotta or cottage cheese
1 cup grated mozzarella cheese
1/4 cup grated provolone cheese
1/4 cup grated Parmesan cheese
3 ounces Italian salami or ham, chopped
2 eggs, lightly beaten
1/2 teaspoon salt
1/4 teaspoon ground nutmeg
1/8 teaspoon ground black pepper

Crust
1 recipe Flaky Wheat Germ Pastry, page 176, made with 1 extra egg yolk and only 3 tablespoons water
1 egg white
1 tablespoon water

Combine filling ingredients in a medium-sized bowl; set aside. Prepare Flaky Wheat Germ Pastry and add egg yolk. Roll out two thirds of dough to fit bottom and sides of a 9 × 13-inch baking pan. Pour filling in shell. Roll out remaining dough, cover filling, seal edges and cut vents to allow steam to escape. Beat egg white with water and brush over top of pie. Bake in a preheated 375°F oven 50 to 60 minutes, or until filling is set and crust is browned.
Makes 12 to 15 servings
15.5/12.4 grams protein per serving

YEAST DOUGH PIZZA RUSTICA Follow directions for Pizza Rustica, replacing wheat-germ pastry with 2/3 recipe Easy High-Protein Freezer Dough, page 172-73, or 1-1/2 loaves Fortified Frozen Bread Dough, page 174.

Vegetarian Pie
with Rice Crust No. 1

The cheese in this pie complements the protein in the rice, wheat germ, nuts and seeds. This was such a hit that I made up two versions. It's good cold, so take some for lunch or reheat it for a ready-when-you-are meal.

Rice Crust
1-2/3 cups minced onions
1-1/2 tablespoons butter or safflower margarine
1 cup brown rice
1 teaspoon salt
2-1/2 cups chicken broth, vegetable broth or
    water
3 eggs, beaten
1/3 cup wheat germ
1/2 cup grated Parmesan cheese

Filling
1 large garlic clove, minced
1/3 cup reserved sauteed onions
1 tablespoon butter or safflower margarine
1 cup chopped mushrooms
2 large tomatoes, chopped
    (about 1-1/2 cups)
1/2 teaspoon dried oregano, crushed
1/2 teaspoon dried rosemary, crushed
1/2 teaspoon dried basil, crushed
1/2 teaspoon salt
1 pound spinach, chopped, steamed and
    squeezed dry, or one 10-ounce package frozen
    chopped spinach, thawed and squeezed dry

1/3 cup chopped walnuts
3 tablespoons unsalted sunflower seeds
1 cup cottage cheese
1 cup grated Swiss, brick or Monterey Jack
    cheese
4 eggs, beaten

Ground nutmeg
Grated Parmesan cheese

To make the crust, in a medium saucepan saute onion in butter until tender. Remove 1-1/3 cups onion and reserve for filling. Add rice, salt and broth or water to onions in pan. Cover and simmer 45 minutes, or until all water is absorbed. Toss rice with eggs, wheat germ and cheese. Pat rice mixture into bottom and partially up sides of a greased 11 X 13-inch baking pan to form a "crust." Cool.

To make the filling, saute garlic in butter or margarine until tender. Add reserved sauteed onions and mushrooms and saute about 1 minute. Add tomatoes and seasonings and cook mixture about 5 minutes. (If there is a lot of juice from tomatoes, turn up heat to high and cook mixture until most of juice evaporates.) Stir in spinach, nuts, seeds and cheeses. Stir eggs into vegetable mixture. Spread mixture into rice crust. Sprinkle with nutmeg and a little Parmesan cheese. Bake in a preheated 350°F oven for 50 minutes, or until filling is firm. Remove from oven and allow pie to set for 15 minutes before cutting into squares.
Makes 10 servings
11 grams protein per serving

Vegetarian Pie
with Rice Crust No. 2

A most delicious and unique way to eat vegetables
—and get complete non-meat protein.

Rice Crust
3/4 cup minced onions
2 tablespoons butter or safflower margarine
1 cup brown rice
1 teaspoon salt
1/4 teaspoon dried oregano, crushed
2-1/2 cups chicken broth, vegetable broth or
   water
1/3 cup wheat germ
3 tablespoons unhulled sesame seeds
3 eggs, beaten
1 cup grated Monterey Jack cheese
2 tablespoons grated Parmesan cheese
   (optional)

Filling
3 medium zucchini, grated (about 3 cups)
3/4 cup grated carrot
1/2 cup reserved sauteed onions
1 medium tomato, chopped
One 4-ounce can diced peeled green chilies,
   chopped
3/4 teaspoon dried oregano, crushed
1/2 teaspoon ground cumin
1 garlic clove, crushed, or 1/8 teaspoon garlic
   powder

3/4 teaspoon salt
Dash ground black pepper
1/4 cup unsalted sunflower seeds
1 cup cottage cheese
3 eggs, beaten

1 cup grated Cheddar or Monterey Jack
   cheese

To make the crust, in a medium saucepan,
saute onion in butter or margarine until tender. Remove a scant 1/2 cup onion for filling.
Add rice, salt, oregano and broth or water to
the saucepan. Cover and simmer about 45
minutes, or until all liquid is absorbed. Toss
cooked rice mixture with wheat germ, sesame
seeds, eggs, Cheddar or Monterey Jack cheese
and optional Parmesan cheese. Pat rice mixture
into bottom and partially up sides of a greased 11
X 13-inch baking pan to form a "crust." Cool.

   To make the filling, combine zucchini, carrot,
reserved sauteed onions, tomato and green chilies with herbs, garlic, salt, pepper, sunflower
seeds, cottage cheese and eggs. Spread over
rice crust. Bake in a preheated 400°F oven 10
minutes. Lower heat to 350°F and continue baking
35 minutes, or until pie is set and vegetables are
tender. Sprinkle with grated Cheddar or Jack
cheese and bake for another 10 to 15 minutes, or
until cheese is melted and bubbly. Remove from
oven and allow pie to set for 15 minutes before
cutting into squares.
Makes 10 servings
13.5 grams protein per serving

Vegetable Custard Pie

This no-crust pie is always very well received. People who hesitate to eat eggplant have no hesitation about eating this.

1/4 cup safflower or corn oil
1 small eggplant, peeled and cut into 1/2-Inch cubes
1 onion, chopped
1 garlic clove, minced or crushed
3 large mushrooms, sliced
1 small zucchini, sliced
3/4 teaspoon dried basil, crushed
3/4 teaspoon dried oregano, crushed
1/2 teaspoon salt
1/8 teaspoon ground black pepper
3 large tomatoes, chopped (about 1-1/4 pounds)
4 eggs
1/2 cup grated Parmesan cheese
2 cups grated mozzarella cheese (8 ounces)
1/2 cup wheat germ
Paprika

In a large frying pan, heat oil over medium to medium-low heat. Add eggplant, onion and garlic. Cook, stirring often, until vegetables are tender, about 10 minutes. Add mushrooms, zucchini, basil, oregano, salt and pepper. Cook, stirring until mushrooms are tender, about 7 minutes. Add tomatoes to pan and simmer rapidly, stirring often, until all liquid has evaporated, about 7 minutes. Cool. Lightly beat eggs with 1/4 cup Parmesan cheese, then stir into vegetable mixture. Pour half of vegetable mixture into a well-buttered 9-inch pie pan (1-1/4 inches deep), an 8 × 8-inch baking dish or 6 individual pie tins. Top with 1 cup mozzarella cheese, 1/4 cup wheat germ and remaining vegetable mixture. Sprinkle with remaining cheeses and wheat germ, then lightly with paprika. Bake in a preheated 400°F oven (375°F for glass dishes) for 25 minutes (18 to 20 minutes for individual tins), or until puffed and browned. Cool on a rack for 10 minutes. Cut into wedges or squares or spoon out portions.
Makes 6 to 8 servings
23.7/17.8 grams protein per serving

Quick Spinach Quiche

This quiche and the other quick quiches following form a top crust as they bake. They are very easy to put together, and their well-balanced ingredients make them a complete meal.

Filling
1/2 cup minced onion
1 small garlic clove, minced
1-1/2 tablespoons butter or safflower margarine
1 cup chopped mushrooms
1 pound spinach, chopped, steamed and squeezed dry, or one 10-ounce package frozen chopped spinach, thawed and squeezed dry
1-1/2 cups grated Swiss cheese (6 ounces)
1/2 cup small-curd cottage cheese
3/4 teaspoon salt
Scant 1/4 teaspoon ground nutmeg
1/8 teaspoon ground black pepper

Crust
2 cups milk
4 eggs
2/3 cup Healthy Biscuit Mix, page 172
2 tablespoons grated Parmesan cheese

To make the filling, saute onion and garlic in butter or margarine until tender. Add mushrooms and saute until tender, about 3 minutes. Remove from heat. Add spinach, cheeses, salt and spices to mushrooms and onion. Stir well, making sure to separate any clumps of spinach; mixture should be uniform. Pat into a greased 10-inch quiche pan.

To make the crust, beat together milk, eggs, biscuit mix and Parmesan cheese or blend in a blender or food processor until smooth. Place quiche pan on a baking sheet in the oven. Pour crust mixture over spinach mixture in quiche pan. Bake in a preheated 400°F oven for 25 minutes. Reduce heat to 350°F and continue baking until center is just barely firm, about 20 to 25 minutes. Remove from oven and allow quiche to stand about 20 minutes before cutting into wedges. Serve warm or cooled.
Makes 6 to 8 servings
20.4/15.3 grams protein per serving

Quick Tuna Quiche

This goes together in a few minutes—it's much more interesting than a boring tuna sandwich, and it contains both vegetables and cottage cheese.

Filling
1/3 cup minced onion
1 tablespoon butter or safflower margarine
2/3 cup shelled green peas
1 medium tomato, chopped
One 7-ounce can tuna, drained
2/3 cup small-curd cottage cheese
3/4 cup grated Cheddar cheese
2 tablespoons chopped parsley
1/4 teaspoon dried dillweed, crushed
1/4 teaspoon dried basil, crushed
1/4 teaspoon ground nutmeg
1/2 teaspoon salt

Crust
1-1/2 cups milk
3 eggs
1/2 cup Healthy Biscuit Mix, page 172

To make the filling, saute onion in butter or margarine until tender; remove from heat. Stir in peas, tomato, tuna, cheeses, parsley, dillweed, basil, nutmeg and salt. Pat tuna mixture into a greased 10-inch quiche pan.

To make the crust, beat milk, eggs and biscuit mix together lightly or blend in a blender or food processor just enough to combine. Place quiche pan on a baking sheet in the oven and pour milk mixture over top. Bake in a preheated 400°F oven for 25 minutes. Reduce heat to 350°F and continue baking until quiche is set, about 25 minutes. Remove from oven and let quiche stand about 15 minutes before cutting into wedges.
Makes 6 to 8 servings
24.3/18.2 grams protein per serving

Quick Mexican Quiche

Filling
1/2 pound ground beef or turkey
1/2 cup minced onion
2 tablespoons safflower or corn oil
1 cup fresh or frozen corn kernels
One 4-ounce can diced peeled green chilies, drained
1-1/4 cups grated Cheddar or Monterey Jack cheese (5 ounces)
3/4 cup canned enchilada sauce
1/4 teaspoon dried oregano, crushed
1/2 teaspoon salt

Crust
1 cup milk
3 eggs
1/2 cup Healthy Biscuit Mix, page 172

To make the filling, saute meat and onion together in oil until onion is tender and meat is browned. Remove from heat and stir in corn, chilies, cheese, 1/4 cup enchilada sauce, oregano and salt. Spread in a greased 10-inch quiche pan.

To make the crust, beat together milk, remaining enchilada sauce, eggs and biscuit mix or blend in a blender or food processor until smooth. Place quiche pan on a baking sheet in the oven and pour milk mixture over top. Bake in a preheated 400°F oven for 25 minutes; reduce oven heat to 350°F and continue baking until quiche is firm, about 25 minutes. Remove from oven and cool about 10 minutes before cutting into wedges.

Makes 8 servings
15.6 grams protein per serving

Quick Garden Quiche

Another great way to get both protein and vegetables in a do-ahead, portable meal.

Filling
1/2 cup chopped onion
2 garlic cloves, minced
1-1/2 cups finely chopped zucchini
1 tablespoon safflower or corn oil
1 medium tomato, chopped
2 tablespoons chopped parsley
1/4 teaspoon dried thyme, crushed
1/4 teaspoon dried oregano, crushed
1/2 teaspoon dried basil, crushed

Dash of ground allspice
3/4 teaspoon salt
2/3 cup small-curd cottage cheese
1 cup grated Cheddar cheese

Crust
1-1/2 cups milk
3 eggs
1/2 cup Healthy Biscuit Mix, page 172

To make the filling, in a medium skillet, saute onion and garlic in oil until just tender. Add zucchini and stir constantly, cooking 1 minute. Add tomato and cook until tender, about 1 minute more. Mix in spices and cheeses and pat into a greased 10-inch quiche pan.

To make the crust, beat together milk, eggs and biscuit mix or blend in a blender or food processor until smooth. Place quiche pan on a baking sheet in the oven, then pour crust mixture over vegetables. Bake in a preheated 400°F oven 25 minutes. Reduce heat to 350°F and continue baking until center is just barely firm, about 20 to 25 minutes. Remove from oven and allow quiche to stand about 20 minutes before cutting into wedges.

Makes 6 servings
14.9 grams protein per serving

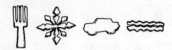

Portable Meat Pies

These are good to have in the freezer. You can freeze them baked or unbaked. Unbaked frozen pies may be baked without thawing.

Filling
1 whole chicken breast (about 3/4 pound)
1/2 pound bulk pork sausage (non-nitrate, if possible)
1 medium onion, chopped
1 large garlic clove, minced or crushed
1/3 cup sour cream mixed with 1 teaspoon unbleached all-purpose flour
One 7-ounce can diced peeled green chilies, drained
1 cup grated sharp Cheddar cheese

Pastry
3 cups Healthy Biscuit Mix, page 172
2/3 cup water or milk
1 egg yolk mixed with 1 tablespoon water

To make the filling, place chicken breast in a small pan with water to cover. Bring to boiling; reduce heat, cover and simmer 15 minutes, or until just tender. Cool, discard skin and bones and shred meat; set aside. Brown sausage in a frying pan over medium heat. Add onion and garlic and cook, stirring, until onion is limp. Remove from heat. Stir in chicken, sour cream mixture, chilies and cheese until blended (cover and chill if made ahead).

To make the pastry, stir together biscuit mix and water or milk to form a soft dough. Divide dough into thirds; roll one third at a time on a lightly floured board to make a 10-inch square; cut into 4 equal 5-inch squares. Place 1/4 cup filling on each square; fold corner to corner over filling to form a triangle. Roll and pinch edges to seal. Roll, cut and fill remaining dough in the same manner. Place assembled meat pies an inch apart on lightly greased baking sheets; make several slashes in top of each and brush top with part of egg yolk mixture. Bake in a preheated 350°F oven for 20 minutes, or until golden brown (about 30 minutes if frozen); cool on racks.
Makes 12 pies
15.2 grams protein per pie

Beef and Mushroom Turnovers

There is complete protein in both the filling and crust of these turnovers. You can bake them and store them in the freezer to reheat when you want; turnovers can also be frozen unbaked.

Cottage Cheese Pastry
1/2 pound butter or safflower margarine, at room temperature
1-1/4 cups small-curd cottage cheese
3 cups stirred whole-wheat pastry flour and 1/2 cup wheat germ, or 1-1/2 cups stirred unbleached all-purpose flour, 1-1/2 cups stirred whole-wheat flour, and 1/2 cup wheat germ

Filling
2 pounds lean ground beef
1-1/4 teaspoons salt
1 cup chopped onion
1 cup minced mushrooms
1 teaspoon dried dillweed, crushed
1/4 teaspoon ground black pepper
2/3 cup sour cream

To make the pastry, with an electric mixer or a food processor beat together butter and cottage cheese until well blended and creamy. Add flour and wheat germ and beat until thoroughly combined. Use immediately or cover and store in refrigerator for up to 5 days. (If chilled, let dough come to room temperature before using.)

To make the filling, crumble ground beef in a frying pan over medium heat; add salt and onion and cook, stirring, until beef is browned and onion is tender. Stir in mushrooms, dillweed, pepper and sour cream. Blend well; set aside. On a floured pastry cloth or board, roll out half the cottage cheese pastry into a 12 × 16-inch rectangle about 1/8 inch thick. Cut dough into twelve 4-inch squares. Spoon about 2 tablespoons of filling onto 1 corner of each square; bring opposite corner over top to enclose filling. With a fork, press open edges together to seal. Roll out second half of dough, fill and form into turnovers, as above. Place turnovers about 1 inch apart on ungreased baking sheets. Bake in a preheated

350°F oven for 20 to 30 minutes, or until pastry is lightly browned (25 to 35 minutes for frozen uncooked pastries). Serve warm. Or cool completely on racks, wrap airtight and freeze. To reheat, bake unwrapped frozen cooked pastries, in a preheated 350°F oven for 10 minutes.
Makes 24 turnovers
12 grams protein per turnover

CHEESE TURNOVERS In a medium-sized bowl, beat together the following ingredients until smooth: 2 cups grated Muenster or sharp Cheddar cheese, 1 cup dry cottage cheese or bakers' (hoop) cheese, 4 mashed hard-cooked egg yolks, 1 drained 4-ounce can chopped peeled green chilies (optional), 2 teaspoons minced fresh coriander or parsley, 1 teaspoon dried marjoram, 1 teaspoon celery salt and a dash of Tabasco sauce. Refrigerate, covered, at least 1 hour. Follow the above recipe, substituting cheese filling for beef-mushroom filling.
8.3 grams protein per turnover

CHICKEN TURNOVERS Follow recipe for Beef-Mushroom Turnovers, substituting filling for Giant Chicken and Cheese Sandwich, page 55.
10.5 grams protein per turnover

Savory Nut Turnovers

These taste very meaty.

1 cup water
1/4 teaspoon salt
1/3 cup brown rice
1/4 cup unsalted cashews
1/4 cup unsalted almonds
1/4 cup unsalted peanuts
1/3 cup unsalted sunflower seeds
1 egg
1 onion, coarsely chopped
1/4 cup toasted wheat germ
1/4 cup minced fresh parsley
1/4 teaspoon dried sage, crushed
1/4 teaspoon dried thyme, crushed
1/3 cup grated Cheddar cheese
1 recipe Cottage Cheese Pastry, page 65

In a saucepan, bring water with salt to a boil, add rice and stir once. Reduce heat, cover and simmer very slowly for about 45 minutes, or until rice is tender and liquid is absorbed. Chop cashews, almonds and peanuts or coarsely grind them in a blender in two batches. Place nuts in a bowl and stir in sunflower seeds. Place egg in a blender or food processor, add onion a little at a time and blend until smooth. Combine this mixture with nut-seed mixture and mix well. Prepare pastry and roll out, fill and bake as for Beef and Mushroom Turnovers, preceding.
Makes 24 turnovers
6.8 grams protein per turnover

Spinach Turnovers

This is a cousin of *spanakopeta*, the delicious Greek spinach pie. It's loaded with iron, and the wheat and cheese provide protein.

1 small onion, minced (about 1/2 cup)
3 green onions, minced
1 tablespoon butter
1/4 cup minced parsley
1-1/4 teaspoons dried dillweed, crushed
1/4 teaspoon salt
2 eggs
1 pound spinach, chopped, steamed and squeezed dry, or one 10-ounce package frozen chopped spinach, thawed and squeezed dry
8 ounces feta cheese, crumbled
1/3 cup grated Parmesan cheese
1/2 recipe Cottage Cheese Pastry, page 65

In a frying pan, saute onions in butter until tender. Stir in parsley, dillweed and salt. In a large bowl, beat eggs and add onion-herb mixture. Add spinach and cheeses and mix thoroughly. Prepare pastry and roll out, fill and bake as for Beef-Mushroom Turnovers, page 65.
Makes 12 turnovers
10.2 grams protein per turnover

HOT HIGH-PROTEIN DISHES

All of the following dishes contain complete protein—and all of them can be frozen and reheated for a quick hot meal.

Falafel Patties

This popular Middle Eastern staple contains no meat but you won't miss it: The protein in the garbanzo beans is complemented by the wheat germ and the dry milk. These patties are lower in calories than traditional falafel because they are baked or broiled rather than deep-fried. They can be frozen cooked or uncooked. The sesame tahini may be found in Middle Eastern markets or some supermarkets.

2 cups cooked garbanzo beans
1/2 cup parsley sprigs
1/4 cup sesame tahini
2 garlic cloves, crushed
1/4 cup non-instant nonfat dry milk
1/4 cup wheat germ
1 slice whole-wheat bread, crumbled
1 egg beaten with 1 tablespoon water
1/2 teaspoon dry mustard
1/2 teaspoon chili powder

1 teaspoon ground cumin
Celery salt to taste
Salt
Ground black pepper
1 teaspoon Worcestershire sauce
Whole-wheat or bran pita bread (optional)
Chopped lettuce
Chopped tomato
Yogurt Sauce, following

Puree garbanzos and parsley in a blender or food processor. Mix tahini, garlic, milk, wheat germ, crumbled bread, egg-water mixture, spices and Worcestershire together with pureed beans. Drop mounds from a large spoon (about 3 tablespoons falafel mixture) onto an oiled baking pan and flatten to form patties. Brush with oil. Bake in a preheated 350°F oven 15 minutes or broil a few minutes on each side, basting with more oil, if needed. Serve alone or in warm pita bread, accompanied with chopped lettuce, chopped tomato and yogurt sauce.
Makes 6 servings
13.6 grams protein per serving

YOGURT SAUCE Combine 1 cup unflavored yogurt with 1/3 cup safflower mayonnaise and 1/8 teaspoon each celery seed and ground coriander; blend until smooth.

FALAFEL DOGS Follow the directions for Falafel Patties, rolling the mixture into sausage shapes instead of patties. Bake or broil as directed and serve in warm whole-wheat pita bread or buns made from Easy High-Protein Freezer Dough, pages 172-73.

Tuna Florentine

1 medium onion, chopped (about 1/2 cup)
6 tablespoons butter or safflower margarine
1/4 cup unbleached all-purpose flour
1/2 teaspoon salt
Dash ground nutmeg
2 cups milk
1-1/2 cups grated Swiss cheese (6 ounces)
Two 7-ounce cans tuna, drained and flaked
2 pounds spinach, chopped, steamed and
    squeezed dry, or two 10-ounce packages
    frozen chopped spinach, thawed and
    squeezed dry
1/4 cup dry whole-wheat bread crumbs
1/4 cup wheat germ
1/4 cup grated Parmesan cheese

In a medium saucepan, saute onion in butter until tender but not brown. Stir in flour, salt and nutmeg. Cook, stirring constantly, just until bubbly. Stir in milk. Continue cooking and stirring until sauce thickens and bubbles for 1 minute; remove from heat. Stir in Swiss cheese, just until melted; add tuna. Spread spinach evenly in a lightly greased 9 X 11-inch baking dish or 8 individual pie pans or casserole dishes. Spoon tuna-cheese mixture over. Combine bread crumbs, wheat germ and Parmesan cheese and spread evenly over top of casserole. Bake in a preheated 350°F oven 25 minutes, or until golden. Cool 10 to 15 minutes and cut into squares to serve.
Makes 8 servings
26.5 grams protein per serving

Kugel Squares

Milk and cheese complement the protein in the potatoes, the wheat germ adds protein and B vitamins, and the carrot contributes vitamin A and fiber. These are delicious hot or cold.

6 medium boiling potatoes, peeled
2 to 3 carrots, peeled
1 large onion
1 garlic clove, minced
2 eggs, beaten
3 tablespoons safflower or corn oil
2 teaspoons salt
1/4 cup soft whole-wheat bread crumbs
1/4 cup wheat germ
1/2 cup non-instant nonfat dry milk
1-1/2 cups grated Cheddar cheese (6 ounces)

Grate potatoes, carrots and onion into a colander and allow to sit 20 minutes; press out excess liquid with a large spoon. Add garlic, eggs and oil to potato mixture and mix well. Combine salt, bread crumbs, wheat germ and dry milk and add to potato mixture. Spread evenly in 2 oiled 8 X 8-inch cake pans. Bake in a preheated 350°F oven for 50 to 60 minutes, or until a toothpick inserted in center comes out clean. Sprinkle cheese over top and bake 5 minutes longer, or until cheese is completely melted. Cool slightly and cut into squares; serve hot or cooled.
Makes 12 squares
8.1 grams protein per square

Zucchini Flips

Vegetable pancakes with a chicken or turkey filling—try them also with Tomato Sauce, page 109. Zucchini flips may be frozen filled or unfilled.

Chicken or Turkey Sauce
1/2 cup non-instant nonfat dry milk
1-1/2 cups chicken broth
1/3 cup minced onion
3 tablespoons butter or safflower margarine
3 tablespoons unbleached all-purpose flour
2 cups cooked chicken meat, or 3/4 pound
  ground turkey, sauteed
Salt and ground black pepper

Pancakes
3 medium zucchini, shredded (about 2 cups)
2 eggs, beaten
1/4 cup whole-wheat flour
3 tablespoons wheat germ
2 tablespoons grated Parmesan cheese
1 teaspoon minced parsley
1 teaspoon minced chives
Dash salt
Dash ground black pepper

To make the sauce, sprinkle dry milk gradually over chicken broth while beating with a whisk; blend well. Or place broth in a blender, cover and turn on blender, uncover and sprinkle in dry milk; do not let mixture foam. In a saucepan, saute onion in butter or margarine until tender but not brown. Add flour and blend well; cook 1 minute. Add chicken broth and milk mixture. Cook, stirring over medium heat about 1 minute, or until mixture is thick. Mix in chicken or turkey. Season to taste with salt and pepper. Set aside and keep warm.

To make the pancakes, place zucchini in a colander and drain for 20 minutes. Press out excess moisture with a spoon. Combine eggs, flour, wheat germ, cheese, parsley, chives, salt and pepper. Add zucchini and mix well. Drop 1/4 cup batter onto a greased griddle or skillet and flatten slightly; cook until browned. Turn and brown other side. Remove and keep warm. Repeat to make a total of 8 pancakes. Place a large spoonful of sauce on 1 side of each pancake, fold over and place in a baking dish seam side down; repeat with remaining pancakes and pour remaining sauce over all. Place in a preheated 350°F oven 5 to 10 minutes or until heated through.
Makes 4 servings
32.9 grams protein per serving

ALL-WEEK SALADS

I love salads but I'm often tempted not to eat them when I think of dragging all those ingredients out of the refrigerator, washing and cutting them, etc. If I do these salads once a week, I always have something good to grab quickly. When I'm tired and don't feel like preparing anything, there they are. The light steaming of the vegetables helps the dressing to permeate them, making them oh so flavorful. These are better than raw vegetables merely coated on the outside with dressing.

All-Week Garden Salad

1/2 pound green beans, trimmed
2 carrots, cut into sticks
1 cup broccoli florets
1 cup cauliflower florets
1 small zucchini, cut into sticks
1 tomato, cut into wedges
1 medium cucumber, peeled, seeded and cut into sticks
1 small onion, sliced and separated into rings

Italian Marinade
2/3 cup safflower or corn oil
1/4 cup vinegar
2 tablespoons lemon juice
1 teaspoon dried oregano, crushed
1/2 teaspoon honey
1 teaspoon salt
1/4 teaspoon ground black pepper
1 small garlic clove, minced or crushed

Steam beans and carrots for 2 minutes. Add broccoli and cauliflower to steamer and continue steaming 1 minute longer. Add zucchini and continue steaming about 1-1/2 minutes longer. Remove vegetables from steaming basket immediately and combine with remaining vegetables. In a jar, combine all marinade ingredients and shake well. Pour over vegetables and mix well. Place in a glass or ceramic bowl, cover and refrigerate for at least 8 hours, stirring occasionally.
Makes about 8 servings
Protein count negligible

Note: If you wish to use frozen vegetables, don't steam them, just thaw.

All-Week Parmesan Salad Bowl

1/2 pound green beans, or 3 small zucchini
2 cups broccoli or cauliflower florets
2/3 cup cooked garbanzo beans
6 medium mushrooms, sliced
1/2 green bell pepper, seeded, deribbed and
 chopped
1 small onion, chopped

Marinade
2/3 cup safflower or corn oil
1/3 cup wine vinegar
1 teaspoon salt
1/2 teaspoon dried oregano, crushed
1/4 teaspoon dried thyme, crushed
1 garlic clove, crushed
1/4 cup grated Parmesan cheese

Tomato wedges or cherry tomatoes

Cut beans into thirds or cut zucchini in half crosswise, then into thin sticks. Steam beans or zucchini and broccoli or cauliflower about 5 minutes,
or until crisp-tender. In a large glass or ceramic
bowl, combine steamed and raw vegetables. In a
jar, combine all marinade ingredients and shake
well. Pour over vegetables, cover and refrigerate
until well chilled. Serve with tomato wedges or
cherry tomatoes.
Makes 6 to 8 servings
6.5/4.9 grams protein per serving

All-Week Colorful Vegetable Bowl

2 medium boiling potatoes
1 cup diced or sliced carrots
1 cup shelled green peas
1 fresh or canned pimiento, chopped
1/4 cup minced onion
2 tablespoons minced parsley

French Marinade
1/4 cup safflower or corn oil
2 tablespoons vinegar
1/4 teaspoon salt
Dash ground black pepper
1/4 teaspoon dried basil, crushed
Pinch dry mustard
Chopped lettuce (optional)

In a covered saucepan, boil potatoes in their
jackets until tender but still firm, about 35 to 40
minutes; peel and dice while they are warm. (You
should have about 1 cup diced potatoes.) Steam
carrots and peas lightly, about 5 minutes. While
they are still warm, combine potatoes, carrots
and peas with pimientos, onion and parsley in a
glass or ceramic bowl. Combine marinade ingredients in a jar, shake well and pour over vegetables. Cover and chill well. Serve alone or over
lettuce.
Makes 8 servings
Protein count negligible

All-Week Dill Salad Bowl

This delicious combination of flavors is great to have on hand when you get the munching crazies. Low in calories, high in fiber and nutrients, and delicious for a salad or snack. This will keep up to two weeks in the refrigerator.

1/2 pound carrots, peeled and cut into sticks
1/2 pound green beans, cut into thirds
2 cups broccoli florets
2 cups cauliflower florets
1/3 cup chopped onion
4 garlic cloves, cut in half
1/2 bay leaf
1 sprig fresh dill, or 2 teaspoons dried dillweed, crushed
2 teaspoons mustard seed
3 to 4 allspice berries, or a pinch of ground allspice
3/4 teaspoon salt

Marinade
2 cups water
1 cup cider vinegar
1/2 cup honey or Turbinado or granulated sugar
1/2 cup safflower or corn oil

Steam vegetables over boiling water until crisp-tender, about 5 minutes. Place vegetables in a large glass or ceramic bowl and add onion, garlic, herbs, spices and salt. To make the marinade, in a saucepan combine water, vinegar and honey or sugar; boil 1 minute. Mix in oil and pour over vegetables. Cover and marinate in the refrigerator overnight.
Makes about 10 servings
Protein count negligible

Two-Week Bean Salad

Always a good stand-by. Good plain or as a topping for lettuce and tomato salad. The dressing from the beans will also season the salad.

1-1/2 pounds green beans, cut into 2-inch sections and steamed, or two 10-ounce packages frozen cut green beans, thawed
One 10-ounce package frozen cut wax beans, thawed, or one 16-ounce can cut wax beans
2 cups cooked or one 15-ounce can dark red kidney beans or garbanzo beans
1/2 red onion, sliced
1/2 cup chopped green bell pepper

Marinade
1/2 cup honey
2/3 cup vinegar
1/3 cup safflower or corn oil
1/2 cup sliced red onion
1 garlic clove, pierced with a toothpick
1 teaspoon salt
1/4 teaspoon ground black pepper

If using canned beans, drain (save bean water to use in soup or in cooking rice—it has half the vitamins from the beans). In a large glass or ceramic dish, combine beans and add onion and green pepper. To make the marinade, in a bowl beat together honey, vinegar, vegetable oil, onion, garlic, salt and pepper; pour over vegetables and toss. Cover and chill overnight. Before serving, toss to coat beans with marinade and remove toothpick with garlic.

Makes 12 servings
4.5 grams protein per serving

Your Own All-Week Salad

Just pick your favorite marinade and some compatible vegetables.

Marinades
Italian Marinade, page 70
All-Week Parmesan Salad Bowl Marinade, page 71
Two-Week Bean Salad Marinade, pages 72-73
All-Week Dill Salad Bowl Marinade, page 72
French Marinade (All-Week Colorful Vegetable Bowl), page 71

Vegetables
Broccoli
Cauliflower
Green beans
Wax beans
Brussels sprouts
Zucchini
Summer squash
Asparagus
Beets
Peas
Artichoke hearts
Radishes*
Green onions*
Green pepper strips*
Cucumber slices*
Onions*
Leeks
Potatoes
Carrots
Corn
Garbanzo beans, cooked
Kidney beans, cooked
Soy beans, cooked

Steam the vegetables (vegetables with an asterisk are used raw) lightly for 2 to 3 minutes. They should be slightly softened but still crisp. Use 3/4 cup marinade for about 6 cups of vegetables, and pour the marinade over the vegetables while they are still warm. Place in a glass or ceramic dish, cover and refrigerate. If the marinade doesn't cover the the whole salad, stir it once a day. If you wish to use frozen vegetables, don't steam them, just thaw.
Protein count negligible

All-Week Fruity Salad

Dressing
1/2 cup cottage cheese
1/3 cup ricotta cheese
1/2 cup unflavored yogurt
1-1/2 teaspoons ground cinnamon
1/4 teaspoon ground ginger
1/4 teaspoon ground cardamom
1/8 teaspoon ground cloves
1/2 teaspoon ground nutmeg
1 to 2 tablespoons honey

2 apples, cut into 1/2-inch dice
1 orange, cut into 1/2-inch dice
1 pear, cut into 1/2-inch dice
1 cup 1-inch-square cubes canteloupe,
  honeydew or Persion melon
1 large or 2 small bananas, sliced
1/3 cup toasted wheat germ

To make the dressing, press cottage cheese through a sieve and blend with ricotta cheese and yogurt, or puree cottage cheese, ricotta cheese and yogurt together in a blender. Add spices. Stir in honey. In a large bowl, combine fruit and toss gently. Pour cheese-yogurt mixture over; sprinkle with wheat germ. Toss again, cover and refrigerate.
Makes 6 to 8 servings
6.5/4.9 grams protein per serving

Cold All-Week Green-Salad Soup

5 cups chicken broth (preferably homemade)
1/4 cup chopped parsley
2 cups chopped green beans
2 cups chopped zucchini
2 cups chopped romaine lettuce
1 cup chopped celery
1/2 cup chopped green onions
2 cups shelled green peas, or one 10-ounce
  package frozen green peas (unthawed)
1 cup unflavored yogurt
Salt
Ground black pepper
Chopped parsley

In a saucepan, combine broth, parsley and vegetables; simmer, partially covered, 15 to 20 minutes, or until tender. Place all of the liquid from vegetables and half the vegetables into a blender about 1 cup at a time, blending until smooth. Place pureed vegetables in a large bowl and add unpureed vegetables (or, if you like a smooth soup, all vegetables may be pureed). Stir in yogurt and season with salt and pepper. Cover and chill thoroughly. Garnish with chopped parsley to serve.
Makes 8 to 10 servings
Protein count negligible

All-Week Gazpacho

This delicious soup-salad from Spain improves with age. It will keep up to six days in the refrigerator. A blender or food processor comes in handy here—just be careful not to overblend the vegetables.

2 cups chicken stock (preferably homemade)
One 16-ounce can tomatoes
1/4 cup parsley sprigs
1-1/2 cups chopped cucumber
3/4 cup diced celery
1-1/4 cups chopped red onion
1 cup chopped green bell pepper
1/4 cup chopped green onions
2 garlic cloves, minced or crushed
1/2 teaspoon dried basil, crushed
1/2 teaspoon dried tarragon, crushed
3 tablespoons lemon juice
3 tablespoons safflower or corn oil
1 teaspoon chili powder
Salt to taste
Chopped tomato or minced parsley (optional)

Combine 1/2 cup broth, tomatoes, parsley and half of the cucumbers, celery, red onion and bell pepper in a blender or food processor. Blend or process until not quite pureed. Pour into a glass or ceramic bowl and add remaining remaining chopped vegetables, green onions, garlic, herbs, lemon juice, oil, chili powder and salt. Mix well, cover and chill overnight. Garnish with tomato and parsley to serve, if desired.
Makes about 8 servings
Protein count negligible

All-Week Ratatouille

This seems to get better as the week goes by. Serve cold or warmed.

2 medium onions, coarsely chopped (about 1-1/2 cups)
2 garlic cloves, minced
3 tablespoons olive oil
2 small zucchini, cut into 1/2-inch slices
2 tomatoes, peeled, seeded and diced
1 small eggplant, chopped
1 green bell pepper, chopped
1/4 cup parsley sprigs
1 bay leaf
2 teaspoons salt
Dash ground black pepper
3 slices bacon (non-nitrate if possible)

In a Dutch oven or large, heavy saucepan, cook onion and garlic in oil until tender but not brown. Add zucchini, tomatoes, eggplant, green pepper, parsley, bay leaf, salt and pepper. Bring to a boil; cover and simmer 30 minutes, stirring occasionally. Fry bacon until crisp; drain and crumble. Add to vegetables and simmer, uncovered, for 10 minutes. Remove bay leaf. Cover and store in the refrigerator.
Makes 8 servings
Protein count negligible

Make a Meal of Appetizers
(High-Nutrient Snacks
and Hors d'Oeuvre)

Junk food makes frequent appearances at parties and social gatherings. But why serve it when there are so many fabulous-tasting nutritious alternatives? You won't even have to bother with dinner when you serve a variety of complementary-protein snacks and hors d'oeuvre made from the recipes in this chapter. But don't wait until you entertain to try them out: When you're not in the mood to cook, you'll be glad you have some of these high-nutrient morsels around for unexpected visitors or anyone who gets the munchies. Most of these appetizers are storable and may be made in advance to avoid last-minute fuss. Any of these dishes may be served as appetizers, as part of a buffet or as the main course of a meal.

If you are looking for some creative ways to have do-ahead nutritious meals on hand, you'll find lots of ideas in this chapter. Instead of a salad, why not serve a vegetable appetizer? A week's supply of marinated or raw vegetables may be prepared ahead and kept on hand. The vegetable dips provide an interesting way to include more vegetables (and fiber) in your diet. And the high-protein dips with vegetables can be meals in themselves.

Addicts of crunchy foods can enjoy the snack mixes knowing they are eating a balance of complementary-protein ingredients—something you won't find in any purchased snacks (not even those from a health food store). Of course, these crunchy treats are portable, and for meal-skippers, they're an enormous improvement over junk food.

And health-conscious snackers will appreciate the no-nitrate, no-preservative cold-cut loaves and spreads. Some are like meat but contain no meat and make elegant appetizers and brown-bag lunches.

Note: To freeze recipes marked with a snowflake symbol, wrap in aluminum foil; to reheat, place wrapped portions in a 350°F oven until heated through.

CRUNCHY SNACK MIXES

These help you beat the potato chips-cheese puff syndrome. You can serve them at parties, they travel well in brown bags for lunch, and they're just plain healthier to have around than no-nutrient, no-protein, preservative-filled junk food.

Try these "crunch" recipes, even if you're not usually a cereal snack fan. They're deliciously different, and they contain complete protein, which is missing in most crunchy snack mixes (including trail mix and gorp). The cheese or soy products in these nibbles complement the protein in the cereal and nuts.

Spicy Nut Mix

Nuts and soy nuts are combined to make complete protein. This can be made with salted nuts, but the salt in the recipe must be omitted.

1-1/4 cups raw cashews or peanuts
3/4 cup unsalted soy nuts
1 cup raw sunflower or unhulled pumpkin seeds
   or a mixture of the two
2 tablespoons safflower or corn oil
1-1/2 teaspoons chili powder
1/8 teaspoon garlic powder
1-1/4 teaspoons salt
1 teaspoon Worcestershire sauce

Combine nuts and seeds in a large bowl. Place oil and seasonings in a jar with a lid, cover and shake; sprinkle over nut and seed mixture and toss to coat. Spread evenly in a baking pan and bake in a preheated 300°F oven for 20 minutes, or until nuts are toasted. Cool. Store refrigerated in covered jars or cans.
Makes 3 cups
35.7 grams protein per cup

GARLIC SPICY NUT MIX Omit seasonings in above recipe and substitute 1-1/4 teaspoons salt and 3/4 teaspoon each garlic powder and paprika.

MEXICAN SPICY NUT MIX Omit seasonings in the Spicy Nut Mix and substitute 2 teaspoons chili powder, 3/4 teaspoon ground cumin, 1/4 teaspoon garlic powder, and 1 teaspoon each ground coriander and salt; add a dash of cayenne pepper or Tabasco sauce.

ORIENTAL SPICY NUT MIX Follow the Spicy Nut Mix recipe, using 4 teaspoons safflower or corn oil and 2 teaspoons Oriental sesame oil, or use 2 tablespoons peanut oil. Omit seasonings and substitute 2 teaspoons soy sauce, 1/8 teaspoon garlic powder, 1/4 teaspoon ground ginger, 3/4 teaspoon sugar and 1/2 teaspoon salt.

CURRY SPICY NUT MIX Follow Spicy Nut Mix recipe, omitting seasonings and substituting 2 teaspoons curry powder, 1/8 teaspoon garlic powder, 1/4 teaspoon onion powder, 1/4 teaspoon ground coriander (optional) and 1-1/4 teaspoon salt.

Fiesta Crunch

Since I work and live in a multicultural setting, I made a taste treat drawn from several ethnic backgrounds.

4 cups natural puffed rice or wheat cereal
1 cup raw almonds
1 cup raw hulled pumpkin seeds
1 cup raw sunflower seeds
3/4 cup grated Parmesan cheese
1/4 cup safflower or corn oil
1/3 cup water
4 teaspoons chili powder
1/2 teaspoon onion powder
1 teaspoon ground coriander
1/2 teaspoon garlic powder
1 teaspoon dried oregano, finely crushed
2 teaspoons salt
Dash Tabasco sauce or cayenne

In a large bowl, mix cereal, nuts and seeds. Sprinkle with cheese and shake bowl to distribute. In a jar with a lid, mix oil, water and spices. Cover jar and shake well. Pour over nut mixture and stir to coat very well. Spread into two rimmed baking sheets and bake in a preheated 350°F oven for 20 to 25 minutes until toasted. Cool before serving. Store refrigerated in covered cans or jars.
Makes 7-1/4 cups
16.6 grams protein per cup

Oriental Sesame Crunch

4 cups natural puffed rice or wheat cereal
1-1/4 cups raw cashews or almonds
1 cup raw sunflower seeds, hulled pumpkin
  seeds or unsalted soy nuts
1/2 cup unhulled sesame seeds
1/4 cup soy flour
3 tablespoons safflower or corn oil plus 1 tablespoon Oriental sesame oil, or 4 tablespoons
  peanut oil
4 tablespoons soy sauce
1/4 cup water
2 tablespoons honey
1-3/4 teaspoons salt
1/2 teaspoon onion powder
1/2 teaspoon garlic powder
3/8 teaspoon ground ginger

In a large bowl, mix together cereal, nuts, seeds and flour. In a jar with a lid, combine oil, soy sauce, water, honey and seasonings. Shake well to mix. Pour over nut mixture and toss to coat very evenly. Spread on 2 rimmed baking sheets and bake in a preheated 350°F oven about 20 minutes, or until lightly toasted; cool. Store refrigerated in covered cans or jars.
Makes about 7 cups
11.3 grams protein per cup

Toasted Pumpkin Seeds

Pumpkin seeds have the highest and most complete protein of all nuts and seeds. The cheese and sesame seeds provide complementary protein and add a delicious touch.

2 cups raw hulled pumpkin seeds
1/4 cup unhulled sesame seeds
1 tablespoon butter or safflower margarine, melted
Salt to taste
1 tablespoon Worcestershire sauce
2 tablespoons grated Parmesan or Romano cheese

Combine all ingredients and spread on a rimmed cookie sheet. Bake in a preheated 375°F oven until lightly toasted, stirring frequently. Cool. Store refrigerated in covered jars or cans.
Makes about 2 cups
47 grams protein per cup

Oat Nuts

1/2 cup unsalted soy nuts
1/2 cup raw almonds
1/4 cup unhulled sesame seeds
1/4 cup raw hulled pumpkin seeds or raw sunflower seeds
1-1/2 cups rolled oats
1/4 cup untoasted wheat germ
6 tablespoons butter or safflower margarine
1/4 cup soy sauce
1 teaspoon honey
1/4 teaspoon onion powder
1/8 teaspoon garlic powder
1/2 teaspoon paprika
1 teaspoon salt

Combine soy nuts, almonds, sesame seeds, pumpkin seeds or sunflower seeds, rolled oats and wheat germ in a baking dish. Melt butter or margarine in a saucepan and add remaining ingredients. Pour over nut mixture. Mix well. Place in a 9 × 13-inch baking pan, cover, and bake in a preheated 225°F oven for 1 hour. Remove cover and bake 45 minutes to 1 hour longer, stirring occasionally. Cool. Store refrigerated in covered cans or jars.
Makes 3 cups
21.5 grams protein per cup

Continental Crunch

Parmesan cheese complements the nuts and seeds in this delicious snack.

4 cups natural puffed rice or wheat cereal
1-1/2 cups raw cashews or almonds
1 cup raw sunflower seeds or hulled pumpkin
  seeds
3/4 cup grated Parmesan or Romano cheese
4 tablespoons safflower or corn oil, heated
1/3 cup water
1/2 teaspoon garlic powder
1/2 teaspoon onion powder
1-1/2 teaspoons paprika
1/4 teaspoon dried oregano, crushed
2 teaspoons salt
Dash cayenne

In a large bowl, mix cereal, nuts and seeds. Sprinkle with cheese and shake bowl to distribute. In a jar with a lid, mix oil, water and spices. Cover jar and shake well. Pour over nut mixture and stir to coat evenly. Spread into 2 rimmed baking sheets and bake in a preheated 350°F oven for 20 minutes or until toasted. Cool before serving. Store refrigerated in covered cans or jars.
Makes 6-1/2 cups
16 grams protein per cup

BAKED SAVORY SNACKS

Here is a selection of crackers and crisps to replace potato chips and other high-calorie, low-nutrient munchies. To recrisp these snacks, heat them on baking sheets in a preheated 350°F oven for about 6 minutes, then let them cool at room temperature.

Quick Crackers

Slice 6 whole-wheat or bran pita breads in half to make 2 disks of each bread. Cut each disk into 6 wedges. Arrange wedges, without overlapping, on baking sheets. Bake in a preheated 250°F oven for about 10 minutes or until completely dried out.
Makes 6 dozen
Protein count negligible

Amazing All-Protein Crunchies

If you find it hard to resist salty snacks, this is the treat for you. These crunchy treats are made from whole-wheat flour, cheese and flavorings—*that's all!* They do not contain the large amounts of oil and the preservatives found in most commercial crunchy treats. Imagine, it's as though you are eating a cheese sandwich! I have suggested different cheeses for the sake of variety (farmers' cheese contains half the calories of Swiss or Cheddar). This recipe may be divided in half.

1-1/2 cups stirred whole-wheat pastry flour
1-1/2 teaspoons salt
2 cups grated farmers', Swiss or Cheddar cheese (8 ounces)
4 teaspoons vegetable shortening or safflower margarine
4 tablespoons ice water
Grated Parmesan cheese or unhulled sesame seeds
1 egg white, slightly beaten

Cut flour, salt, cheese, and shortening together with a pastry blender or a food processor. Sprinkle water over mixture and mix in with a fork. Form the pastry into 2 balls. Chill. On waxed paper, roll out one half of the pastry into a 10 X 12-inch oblong. On another sheet of waxed paper, sprinkle Parmesan cheese or sesame seeds or both, a little larger than size of pastry. Brush dough with beaten egg white. Invert dough onto second paper and peel away first piece of waxed paper. (If dough is too sticky, chill on a cookie sheet a few minutes.) Brush reverse side of dough with beaten egg white and sprinkle with more cheese and/or seeds. Cut the dough into 3/4 X 2-1/2-inch strips. Place individual pieces slightly apart on a lightly greased baking sheet. Bake in a preheated 375°F oven for 10 to 12 minutes or until lightly browned and crisp. Cool, then store in a covered can or jar in the freezer or refrigerator.
**Makes about 10 dozen or 10 servings
9.5 grams protein per dozen**

WELSH RAREBIT CRUNCHIES Follow the above recipe, using Cheddar cheese. Add 1 teaspoon Worcestershire sauce and 1 teaspoon dry mustard. Use sesame seeds to coat, omitting Parmesan cheese.

MEXICAN CRUNCHIES Use farmers', Cheddar or Monterey Jack cheese. Add 4 teaspoons chili powder and 1 teaspoon dried oregano, crushed.

GARLIC CRUNCHIES Use farmers', Swiss or Monterey Jack cheese. Add 3/4 teaspoon garlic powder. Roll dough in Parmesan cheese only, omitting sesame seeds.

ONION CRUNCHIES Add 3/4 teaspoon onion powder. Roll dough in a mixture of Parmesan cheese and sesame seeds.

ITALIAN CRUNCHIES Use farmers' cheese. Add 1/2 teaspoon garlic powder; 1/4 teaspoon dried rosemary, crushed; and 1/2 teaspoon each dried oregano and basil, crushed.

Cheese-Corn Crisps

2 tablespoons grated onion
4 tablespoons butter or safflower margarine
1-1/2 teaspoons salt
1 cup stone-ground yellow cornmeal
1-1/2 cups boiling water
1/2 cup grated Parmesan cheese
1/4 cup wheat germ
Poppy, unhulled sesame or chopped unsalted
   sunflower seeds

In a small saucepan, combine onion, butter, salt, cornmeal and boiling water. Cook the mixture over very low heat, stirring occasionally until cornmeal is thickened and forms a mound, about 5 minutes. Stir in cheese and wheat germ. Drop batter by 1/2 teaspoonfuls 1 inch apart onto 2 greased baking sheets. With a spatula, flatten each to a circle about 1-1/2 inches in diameter. (Dip spatula in flour if it sticks to the dough.) Sprinkle with seeds. Bake in a preheated 350°F oven for 18 to 20 minutes or until crisp throughout. Partially cool on a wire rack. Serve warm. Store covered, in the refrigerator.
Makes 4 dozen
13 grams protein per dozen

Savory Triangles

A delicious crackerlike treat you can put together in a few minutes.

1-1/2 cups rolled oats
1/2 cup stirred whole-wheat pastry flour
1/4 cup soy flour
3/4 cup wheat germ
1/3 cup unhulled sesame seeds
1/2 cup slivered blanched almonds
2 tablespoons Turbinado or granulated sugar
2-1/4 teaspoons salt
1/2 teaspoon onion powder
1-1/4 teaspoons dried oregano, crushed
3/4 teaspoon dried thyme, crushed
3 eggs
3/4 cup safflower or corn oil

In a large bowl stir together oats, flours, wheat germ, sesame seeds, almonds, sugar, salt, onion powder, oregano and thyme. With a fork beat together eggs and oil. Stir into oat mixture until well moistened. With a spatula, press and spread mixture in a greased 15 X 10-inch jelly roll pan. Bake in a preheated 400°F oven 20 minutes or until golden. Cut in 1-1/2-inch squares, then in triangles. Remove to a rack to cool. Store in an airtight container; these will keep about 2 weeks at room temperature, 1 to 2 months in the freezer.
Makes about 6-1/2 dozen
14.7 grams protein per dozen

Cheesettes

1-1/4 cups unhulled sesame seeds
1-1/2 cups grated Cheddar cheese (6 ounces)
1/2 cup sherry or water
1/4 teaspoon Worcestershire sauce
1 egg
2 teaspoons salt
1/4 teaspoon each onion powder, garlic powder
  and paprika
2 cups stirred whole-wheat pastry flour
3 tablespoons safflower or corn oil

Grind sesame seeds in a blender and set aside. Mix cheese, sherry or water, Worcestershire and egg until well blended. Stir in salt and seasonings, then add whole-wheat flour. Knead mixture lightly. Add oil and knead; then knead in the ground sesame seeds 1/3 cup at a time. Pinch off pieces of dough and roll them into balls about the size of a large marble. Place them on an unoiled baking sheet and flatten them. Bake in a preheated 400°F oven for 8 to 12 minutes, or until dry. Serve warm. Reheat in 325°F oven until warm throughout. Store covered, in the refrigerator.
Makes about 4 dozen
12.2 grams protein per dozen

Cheese-Yogurt Pastry Snacks

Unbaked rolls of dough may be frozen, but need to be slightly thawed before slicing and baking.

3/4 cup stirred whole-wheat flour
1-1/2 cups stirred unbleached all-purpose flour
1/3 cup wheat germ
1/2 pound butter or safflower margarine, at room
  temperature
1 cup unflavored yogurt
Seasoned salt
Ground black pepper
3 cups shredded Cheddar cheese (12 ounces)
Paprika

Combine flours, wheat germ and butter. Blend with a pastry blender or in a food processor until mixture resembles cornmeal. Mix in yogurt. Divide into 4 portions. Wrap in lightly floured waxed paper and chill. Roll out one portion at a time on a floured surface to a 12 × 6-inch rectangle. Sprinkle each rectangle with seasoned salt and pepper, then with 3/4 cup cheese. Starting with 12-inch side, roll up jelly roll style. Seal edge and ends. Place seam side down on an ungreased cookie sheet. Cut rolls halfway through at 1-inch intervals. Sprinkle with paprika. Bake in a preheated 350°F oven for 30 to 35 minutes or until golden; break or cut off scored sections and serve warm. Store covered, in the refrigerator.
Makes 4 rolls or 48 snacks
34.5 grams protein per roll,
2.9 grams protein per snack

Sesame Seed Logs

4 ounces cream cheese, at room temperature
4 tablespoons butter or safflower margarine, at
    room temperature
1 cup stirred whole-wheat pastry flour
1/2 cup minced or ground ham
1/2 teaspoon dry mustard
1/2 teaspoon paprika
2 tablespoons mayonnaise
1/3 cup unhulled sesame seeds
1/3 cup grated Parmesan cheese
Milk

Mix together cream cheese and butter or margarine until well blended. Stir in flour. Shape dough into a ball. Roll out on a lightly floured surface or between 2 sheets of wax paper to slightly larger than a 14-inch square; trim edges. Cut into 2-inch squares. Combine ham, mustard and paprika and mayonnaise and blend well. Spread 1/2 teaspoon of this mixture over each square and roll up jelly roll fashion. Combine sesame seeds and Parmesan cheese. Brush logs with milk and roll in seed-cheese mixture. Bake on lightly greased baking sheets in a preheated 375°F oven for 20 to 25 minutes, or until golden. Serve warm or at room temperature. Cover and store in the refrigerator or freeze.
Makes about 4 dozen
34.5 grams protein per dozen

Wheat-Sesame Cheese Wafers

These are divine! They go together very quickly and store in the freezer or refrigerator just like refrigerator cookies. Just slice and bake whenever you're ready.

2 cups grated sharp Cheddar cheese (8 ounces)
1/4 pound butter or safflower margarine, at room
    temperature
1-1/4 cups stirred whole-wheat pastry flour
1 teaspoon salt
1/2 cup unhulled sesame seeds, or 1/2 cup plus
    1 tablespoon unsalted sunflower seeds, finely
    chopped

Cream cheese and butter together. Add flour, salt and nuts or seeds and blend well. Form long rolls about the diameter of a silver dollar. Wrap in waxed paper and chill in refrigerator or freeze until ready to use. Slice thin. Bake in a preheated 375°F oven for 10 minutes on greased cookie sheets until crisp and golden. Cover and store in the refrigerator; serve at room temperature.
Makes 6 dozen
15.6 grams protein per dozen

Whole-Wheat Pretzels

1/2 cup milk
3 tablespoons honey
1 teaspoon salt
2 tablespoons butter or safflower margarine
1 tablespoon (1 envelope) active dry yeast
1/2 cup warm water (110°F to 115°F)
1/4 cup soy flour
1/2 cup stirred unbleached all-purpose flour
2-1/2 to 3 cups stirred whole-wheat flour
1 egg white mixed with 1 tablespoon water
Sesame seeds, poppy seeds or coarse salt

Scald milk. Add honey, salt and butter and place in a bowl. Cool to lukewarm. Sprinkle yeast over warm water; stir to dissolve. Add yeast, soy flour, all-purpose flour, and 1 cup whole-wheat flour to milk mixture. Beat 100 strokes by hand or with an electric mixer at low speed until smooth. Add remaining flour a little at a time until dough leaves the sides of bowl. Turn dough out onto a floured board. Knead until smooth and elastic, about 8 minutes. Place in a lightly oiled bowl; turn over to oil top. Cover and let rise in a warm place until doubled in bulk, about 45 minutes. Turn dough onto a floured board and roll to a 16 × 8-inch rectangle. From wide side, cut into 1/2-inch strips. Roll each strip under the hand to a pencil shape and tie or fold into pretzel shapes. Place a little apart on buttered baking sheets. Let rise in a warm place for about 20 minutes. Brush pretzels with egg white mixed with water. Sprinkle with seeds or salt. Bake in a preheated 400°F oven for 10 to 15 minutes or until brown and crisp. Cool on racks. Store refrigerated.
Makes about 32 pretzels
2 grams protein per pretzel

Complementary-Protein Sesame Crackers

1-1/2 cups stirred whole-wheat flour
1/4 cup soy flour
1/4 cup unhulled sesame seeds
1/8 teaspoon onion powder
1-1/4 teaspoons salt
1/3 cup safflower or corn oil
1/2 cup cold water (as needed)

Stir flours, seeds, onion powder and salt together, sprinkle oil over and blend well. Add enough water to dough to make it soft enough to roll out very easily. Form into 2 balls; roll each 1/8 inch thick between sheets of waxed paper. Cut into squares or sticks and place on an ungreased baking sheet. Prick crackers with tines of a fork. Bake in a preheated 350°F oven for about 8 minutes or until crisp and golden. Store refrigerated in a covered can or jar.
Makes 3 to 4 dozen
11.2/8.4 grams protein per dozen

VEGETABLE DIPS

Vegetables can be made into divine-tasting dips that are high in fiber and vitamins, low in calories—a novel but delicious way to get more vegetables into your diet. Vegetable dips such as Baba Ghanouj and Humus have been served in the Middle East for centuries. These, as well as other vegetable dips, are great salad substitutes for do-ahead family meals, especially when raw vegetables are used for the dipping.

Creamy Green Dip

This protein-rich dip is high in iron from the parsley and spinach. It always disappears fast.

1 cup cottage cheese
1 pound spinach, chopped, steamed and squeezed dry, or one 10-ounce package frozen chopped spinach, thawed and squeezed dry
6 green onions, minced, or 1/2 cup minced onion
1/2 cup packed parsley sprigs
1/2 cup safflower mayonnaise
1 teaspoon lime juice
1-1/4 teaspoons dried dillweed, crushed
1/4 teaspoon dried thyme, crushed
1/4 teaspoon dried basil, crushed
1/2 teaspoon salt

Puree cottage cheese in a blender or food processor. Add all remaining ingredients and blend until smooth and creamy. Cover and chill at least 1 day to blend flavors.
Makes about 3 cups
12.2 grams protein per cup

Zucchini Dip

1 cup firmly packed grated zucchini
Salt
1 tablespoon safflower mayonnaise
1/4 cup unflavored yogurt
2 small garlic cloves, minced or crushed
1/2 teaspoon honey
Salt to taste

Place the zucchini in a sieve, sprinkle with salt and let drain for 20 minutes. Press out excess moisture with a large spoon. (Be sure to do this, or mixture will be too runny.) Place zucchini in a blender or food processor along with remaining ingredients and blend until very well mixed. Cover and chill at least 1 day to blend the flavors; stir and salt to taste before serving.
Makes about 1 cup
Protein count negligible

Cucumber-Chili Dip

1 large cucumber, peeled, seeded and minced
1/2 teaspoon salt or to taste
One 3-ounce package cream cheese, at room
 temperature
2 tablespoons unflavored yogurt or sour cream
1 garlic clove, crushed
2 tablespoons chopped canned peeled green
 chilies
1/4 teaspoon onion powder
Tabasco sauce to taste

Place cucumber in a sieve, sprinkle with salt and
let drain at least 1 hour; press out excess moisture with a large spoon. Blend cream cheese and
yogurt or sour cream and stir in cucumber. Stir in
garlic, chilies, onion powder and Tabasco sauce.
Cover and chill. Test for seasoning before serving.
Makes about 1-1/3 cups
Protein count negligible

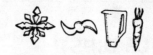

Baba Ghanouj
(Middle Eastern Eggplant Dip)

No one ever knows what this is. But they like it. It's
very nutritious and doesn't have many calories.
Sesame tahini can be found in Middle Eastern
markets and some supermarkets.

2 large eggplants
2 to 3 tablespoons lemon juice
1/2 teaspoon or more salt
2 tablespoons sesame tahini
1 garlic clove, crushed
2 tablespoons olive oil
1/4 cup chopped parsley
Raw vegetables, wedges of whole-wheat pita
 bread or Quick Crackers, page 81

Cut eggplants in half lengthwise and place them
cut side down on aluminum foil on a broiler pan.
Broil until skins are charred and eggplant is soft.
Cool. Meanwhile, mix lemon juice, salt, tahini, garlic and olive oil in a blender. Scoop out eggplant
pulp and add it to the blender; discard skin. Puree
eggplant until smooth, then pour into a serving
dish, sprinkle with parsley and chill. Serve with
vegetables for dipping or spread on pita bread or
crackers. Store covered and chilled.
Makes about 4 cups
Protein count negligible

Note: Thaw frozen Baba Ghanouj at room temperature and mix well if any separation occurs.

Moroccan Eggplant Dip

This dip is a simmered mixture of eggplant, tomato sauce, and green pepper. Serve it with pita bread or crackers, or with raw vegetables such as raw mushrooms, cucumber slices, carrot, zucchini or green pepper sticks.

1 large eggplant (about 1-1/2 pounds)
3 tablespoons olive oil
2 garlic cloves, minced or crushed
1 green pepper, seeded and chopped
One 8-ounce can tomato sauce
1 tablespoon ground cumin
1/4 teaspoon cayenne
2 teaspoons Turbinado or granulated sugar or
   honey
2 teaspoons salt
1/4 cup red wine vinegar
1/4 cup chopped fresh coriander (cilantro)
Raw vegetables, wedges of whole-wheat pita
   bread or Quick Crackers, page 81

Trim, peel and dice eggplant. In a large frying pan, heat oil over medium-high heat; add eggplant, garlic, and green pepper and saute until tender. Add tomato sauce, cumin, cayenne, sugar or honey, salt and vinegar. Cook, covered, over medium heat for 20 minutes. Uncover and boil mixture over high heat, stirring and mashing, until reduced to about 3 cups. Place in a glass or ceramic container, cover and chill at least 2 hours or overnight. Before serving, stir in coriander.
Makes about 3 cups
Protein count negligible

Humus

1/2 cup unhulled sesame seeds
2 tablespoons olive oil
2 cups cooked garbanzo beans
2 to 3 garlic cloves, crushed
Lemon juice to taste
Chopped parsley to taste
Raw vegetables, wedges of whole-wheat pita
   bread or Quick Crackers, page 81

Stir sesame seeds in an ungreased frying pan over medium heat until lightly toasted. Place sesame seeds in a blender with olive oil and blend until creamy. Drain garbanzos thoroughly and add to blender with garlic, lemon juice and a generous amount of parsley. Blend until mixture is very creamy. (In the Middle East, a little well is made in the center of the mixture when it is served and olive oil is placed in the well.)
Makes about 1-3/4 cups
30.4 grams protein per cup

HIGH-PROTEIN DIPS

Most sour cream- or mayonnaise-based dips have very few nutrients. The following dips are based on cheese or tofu and add lots of protein—and far fewer calories—to your dipping. A protein-rich dip and vegetables are all you need for a meal. If you're not dieting, you can have a high-protein dessert as well.

High-Protein Dip Base

1-1/4 cups cottage cheese
2 ounces cream cheese, at room temperature
2 tablespoons safflower mayonnaise

Place all ingredients in a blender or food processor and puree until smooth.
Makes about 1-1/2 cups
24.9 grams protein per cup

HERB DIP Crush 2 teaspoons dried dillweed and 1/4 teaspoon dried tarragon and add to dip base. Add 1 tablespoon chopped chives or green onion, 1/4 teaspoon paprika, 1 teaspoon chopped capers, 1/4 cup minced green onions, 1/4 cup minced parsley, a few drops of Tabasco sauce and 1/2 teaspoon celery salt; blend thoroughly. Cover and chill 24 hours, then add salt to taste.

GARLIC HERB DIP Add 1 small crushed garlic clove, or a scant 1/8 teaspoon garlic powder to Herb Dip along with herbs. Chill 24 hours; add salt to taste.

CURRY DIP To dip base add 1 tablespoon each honey, lemon juice and curry powder, 1/4 teaspoon onion powder, and a small crushed garlic clove or a scant 1/8 teaspoon garlic powder; blend well. Chill 24 hours, then add salt to taste.

BLUE CHEESE DIP Add 1 crushed garlic clove or 1/8 teaspoon garlic powder, 3 ounces crumbled blue cheese (about 1/3 cup), 1/2 teaspoon celery seed (optional) to basic mix and blend well; cream cheese may be omitted, if you like. Chill 24 hours and add salt to taste.
Makes about 2 cups
30.9 grams protein per cup

THOUSAND ISLANDS DIP Add 1/4 cup chili sauce, 3 tablespoons chopped green pepper, 1 tablespoon chopped onion, 1/4 cup chopped stuffed green olives and 2 tablespoons chopped sweet pickle or pickle relish to basic dip; blend well. Chill 24 hours and add salt to taste.
Makes about 2 cups
18.7 grams protein per cup

GUACAMOLE DIP Mash 1 large ripe avocado and add to basic dip along with 1 small crushed garlic clove or a scant 1/8 teaspoon garlic powder, 1-1/2 tablespoons minced onion and 4 teaspoons lemon or lime juice; blend well. Add Tabasco sauce to taste; chill 24 hours and add salt to taste.
Makes about 2-3/4 cups
13.6 grams protein per cup

CLAM DIP Prepare half a recipe High-Protein Dip Base. Drain one 8-ounce can minced clams and reserve juice. Blend clams, 2 tablespoons clam juice, 2 teaspoons lemon juice and one crushed garlic clove, or 1/8 teaspoon garlic powder into dip base; blend well. Chill 24 hours and add salt to taste.
Makes about 1-3/4 cups
27.1 grams protein per cup

CRAB DIP Drain one 6- or 8-ounce can crab meat and add to basic dip along with 1 tablespoon chopped chives or green onion and a little lemon juice; blend well. If desired, add 2 to 4 teaspoons curry powder, or 1 tablespoon soy sauce and 1/2 cup chopped water chestnuts. Chill 24 hours and add salt to taste.
Makes about 2-1/2 cups
31.7 grams protein per cup

Cheddar Dip

1 cup cottage cheese
2 teaspoons grated onion
1 teaspoon celery salt
1-1/2 cups grated very sharp Cheddar cheese
  (6 ounces)
1/4 teaspoon Worcestershire sauce
1/4 teaspoon dry mustard

Blend all ingredients together in a blender or food processor until smooth.
Makes about 2-1/2 cups
29.2 grams protein per cup

Veggie Fondue

This wonderful fondue contains broccoli and makes a nourishing lunch or light supper dish as well as a high-protein dip.

1-1/2 pounds broccoli, chopped and steamed, or one 10-ounce package frozen chopped broccoli, thawed
1/4 cup milk
1/2 teaspoon red pepper flakes
1 tablespoon whole-wheat flour
4 cups grated Cheddar or Swiss cheese
  (1 pound)
1/2 cup or more chopped pitted black olives, drained
Salt to taste
Raw vegetables or whole-wheat bread cubes

Place broccoli in a colander to drain off any excess moisture. Combine milk, red pepper and flour in a heavy saucepan or fondue pot. Add cheese. Cook over very low heat, stirring until all and cook over very low heat, stirring until all cheese is melted and mixture is smooth; do not boil. Stir in olives and broccoli and add salt to taste. Serve in a casserole dish, a fondue pot or warmed individual bowls.
Makes about 6 cups or 6 meal-sized servings
20.7 grams protein per cup or serving

Easy Cheese Fondue

Fondues make great party dips for teenagers. My students didn't like the flavor of traditional fondue, probably because of the wine, but they liked this one and the Veggie Fondue, preceding. Served with raw vegetables, these dishes are a great change from the same old salad routine. This is one of my cousin Isabel's recipes.

2-1/2 cups milk
1/3 cup non-instant nonfat dry milk
3 tablespoons butter or safflower margarine
1/4 teaspoon minced garlic
3 tablespoons unbleached all-purpose flour
1/2 teaspoon salt
1/8 teaspoon ground black pepper
4 cups grated Cheddar cheese (1 pound)
1 tablespoon prepared mustard
2 teaspoons Worcestershire sauce
Dash Tabasco sauce (optional)
Raw or cooked vegetables, whole-wheat bread
    cubes or apple slices

Place milk in a bowl and gradually sprinkle dry milk over while beating with a whisk; blend thoroughly. Or place milk in a blender, cover and turn on blender, then uncover and sprinkle in dry milk, not allowing mixture to foam. In a heavy medium-sized saucepan or fondue pot, melt butter over moderate heat. Stir in garlic and flour and cook just a few seconds, until foamy; add salt and pepper. Reduce heat to moderately low and add milk mixture to flour mixture gradually, beating constantly with a whisk. When all milk is added, cook mixture about 5 minutes, stirring occasionally, until thickened. Stir in cheese, mustard, Worcestershire sauce and Tabasco; heat a few minutes, without boiling, to melt cheese. Serve fondue in a casserole dish or fondue pot or in warmed individual bowls. Serve vegetables, bread cubes or apple slices attractively arranged on a platter.
Makes about 6-1/2 cups
22 grams protein per cup

Curried Tuna Tofu Dip

Some of my Oriental students were amused at what I did with tofu. Deceptively low in calories, this creamy appetizer and the following variations start with tofu (soybean curd) instead of sour cream or mayonnaise. One cup of mashed tofu equals about 150 calories, compared to about 454 for sour cream or about 1,600 for mayonnaise. And it is *very* high in protein. Look for tofu in the produce section of your supermarket or in Oriental markets. It's packaged in plastic cartons (usually four squares to a carton). Make dips a day ahead for best flavor.

12 ounces (1/2 carton) tofu
1/4 cup unflavored yogurt or sour cream
2 tablespoons safflower mayonnaise
1 teaspoon curry powder
1/4 teaspoon garlic powder
1/2 teaspoon salt
Pinch cayenne
4 green onions, thinly sliced
1/2 cup unsweetened flaked coconut
One 6-1/2 ounce can tuna, drained and flaked

Drain tofu and pat dry with paper towels. Puree in a blender or food processor with yogurt or sour cream and mayonnaise until very smooth. Turn into a bowl and add all remaining ingredients; mix well. Cover and refrigerate overnight to blend flavors.
Makes about 3 cups
107 grams protein per cup

CLAM TOFU DIP Drain and pat dry 12 ounces tofu, as in preceding recipe. Puree in a blender or food processor with 2 tablespoons mayonnaise and 3 tablespoons unflavored yogurt or sour cream. Add 2 teaspoons lemon juice, 1/2 teaspoon Worcestershire sauce, 1/2 teaspoon onion powder, 1/4 teaspoon garlic powder, 1-1/4 teaspoons salt and 2 tablespoons minced parsley. Drain two 6-1/2-ounce cans minced clams, reserving juice. Add clams and 2 tablespoons clam juice to tofu and season to taste with Tabasco sauce.
Makes about 3 cups
32.4 grams protein per cup

HERBED TOFU DIP Drain and pat dry 12 ounces tofu, as in recipe for Curried Tuna Tofu Dip. Puree in a blender with 2 tablespoons mayonnaise and 1/4 cup unflavored yogurt. Add 1-1/2 teaspoons celery salt, 1 tablespoon minced parsley, 1/2 cup minced green onions, 2 teaspoons Dijon mustard, 2 to 3 teaspoons prepared horseradish, 1/2 teaspoon dried dillweed, 1/4 teaspoon onion powder and 2 crushed garlic cloves or 1/4 teaspoon garlic powder and 2 tablespoons lemon juice.
Makes about 2 cups
26.2 grams protein per cup

MARINATED VEGETABLES

Everyone knows vegetables are healthy and low in calories, and more and more social gatherings are featuring raw vegetables in place of chips to dip. You can add wonderful flavor to vegetables by marinating or "pickling" them. They're much more delicious than plain old boring carrot sticks. Like the all-week salads in the "Ready-When-You-Are" chapter, these can be kept on hand for lunchboxes and snacks—marinated vegetables can be kept eight to ten days in the refrigerator.

Dilled Vegetable Sticks

1 pound green beans
1 pound carrots, peeled
2 teaspoons mustard seeds
2 teaspoons dried dillweed, crushed
4 garlic cloves, halved
2-1/2 cups water
1 cup vinegar
1/2 cup Turbinado or granulated sugar or honey
3 tablespoons safflower or corn oil

Steam beans 5 minutes or until crisp-tender; drain and place in a glass or ceramic dish. Cut carrots into thin sticks and steam about 3 minutes or until crisp-tender; drain. Add carrots to green beans and stir in dillweed, mustard and garlic. In a saucepan combine water, vinegar and sugar or honey; bring to a boil and pour over vegetables. Stir in oil. Cool, then cover and chill overnight.
Makes about 8 cups
Protein count negligible

MARINATED CAULIFLOWER Replace beans and carrots with 2 pounds fresh cauliflower or two 10-ounce packages frozen cauliflower, separated into florets. Steam fresh cauliflower 3 minutes, or until crisp-tender; do not cook frozen cauliflower, just thaw.

Marinated Raw Mushrooms

Serve as a salad or with toothpicks for appetizers. Make these a few days ahead for the best flavor.

1/2 pound very fresh mushrooms
3 tablespoons wine vinegar or lemon juice
1/3 cup safflower or corn oil
1/2 teaspoon dried tarragon or oregano, crushed
1/4 teaspoon salt
Ground black pepper to taste

Halve or quarter mushrooms and place in a glass or ceramic dish. Place remaining ingredients in a jar with a lid and shake to mix; pour over mushrooms and toss until thoroughly coated. Cover and refrigerate.
Makes about 3 cups
Protein count negligible

Minicarrots in a Dill Marinade

About 1 pound whole miniature carrots, peeled,
   or medium carrots peeled and cut into julienne
   strips
2 bay leaves
1/2 cup white vinegar
1/2 teaspoon salt
1/2 teaspoon mustard seeds
1/2 teaspoon dried dillweed, crushed
1/4 teaspoon dill seed
1/4 teaspoon red pepper flakes
1 garlic clove, minced
1/4 cup water
4 tablespoons Turbinado or granulated sugar or
   honey

Steam carrots for 10 to 12 minutes or until just
tender when pierced. Pack carrots in a clean pint
jar and tuck in bay leaves. In a small bowl, stir
together vinegar, salt, spices, garlic, water and
sugar or honey. Stir until sugar or honey is
dissolved. Pour over carrots, cover and refrigerate
for at least 2 days or up to 3 weeks.
Makes about 2 cups
Protein count negligible

Ginger-Minted Carrots

Mint-topped carrots marinated in a ginger-fla-
vored orange juice mixture.

2 pounds miniature carrots, peeled, or medium
   carrots, peeled and cut into 1/2 × 3-inch
   sticks, or two 10-ounce packages frozen
   baby carrots
1 cup orange juice
1 teaspoon grated fresh ginger
Dash each salt and ground black pepper
1 tablespoon chopped fresh mint

In a saucepan, combine carrots, orange juice,
ginger, salt and pepper. Cover and bring to a boil;
then reduce heat and simmer frozen carrots
about 2 minutes, fresh carrots about 7 minutes,
or until tender. Place carrots and their liquid in a
glass or ceramic container. Cover and chill at
least 6 hours or up to 10 days. To serve, drain
carrots and spoon into a bowl; garnish with mint.
Serve with wooden picks.
Makes about 4 cups
Protein count negligible

Marinated Artichoke Hearts

Also try steamed cauliflower or broccoli florets, Brussels sprouts, asparagus and green beans in this dish—be sure they are crisp-tender. Raw zucchini and bell pepper spears and raw mushrooms can also be used.

1/2 cup safflower or corn oil
3 tablespoons vinegar
3 tablespoons lemon juice
2 teaspoons salt
Dash ground black pepper
1/2 teaspoon Turbinado or granulated sugar
  or honey
1 garlic clove, crushed
One 15-ounce can artichoke hearts, drained, or
  one 10-ounce package frozen artichoke hearts
  hearts, thawed
Salad greens (optional)

In a jar with a lid combine all ingredients except the artichoke hearts and salad greens; shake well. Place the artichoke hearts in a glass or ceramic dish and pour marinade over. Cover and refrigerate overnight. To serve, drain and serve on salad greens or spear on toothpicks.
Makes about 2 cups
Protein count negligible

Marinated Brussels Sprouts or Broccoli

Marinated Brussels sprouts and broccoli take on a delightful dill flavor. This will keep for about two weeks.

10 ounces fresh or frozen Brussels sprouts, or
  1 pound broccoli, cut into florets, or one
  10-ounce package frozen broccoli florets
1/2 cup French Marinade, page 71, or Italian
  Marinade, page 70
1 small garlic clove, minced or crushed
2 tablespoons minced onion
1 tablespoon chopped parsley
1/2 teaspoon dried dillweed, crushed

Steam fresh Brussels sprouts or broccoli until crisp-tender; thaw frozen sprouts or broccoli but do not steam. Cut large Brussels sprouts in half. Combine marinade, garlic, onion, parsley and dillweed. Pour over sprouts or broccoli. Cover; marinate in a covered glass or ceramic dish in the refrigerator overnight or until ready to use. Drain and serve with toothpicks.
Makes about 2 cups
Protein count negligible

SPREADS

These spreads are good for everyday sandwiches as well as for party appetizers.

High-Protein Cheese Spread

1 cup grated Cheddar cheese
One 3-ounce package Neufchatel or cream
  cheese, at room temperature
2 tablespoons safflower mayonnaise
1 teaspoon lemon juice
1 teaspoon Worcestershire sauce
1/2 cup finely shredded carrot
1/2 cup finely shredded apple
1 tablespoon minced green pepper
1/4 cup minced celery
1/4 cup chopped walnuts
1 tablespoon wheat germ
Whole-wheat bread triangles

In a small bowl, combine cheeses, mayonnaise, lemon juice and Worcestershire. Beat until nearly smooth. Fold in carrot, apple, pepper, celery, walnuts and wheat germ. Cover and chill. Stir to blend ingredients before serving. Serve on bread triangles.
Makes 2 cups
22.2 grams protein per cup

Peanut-Ricotta Spread

Use as a sandwich or cracker spread, or to stuff celery (see recipe following).

3/4 cup ricotta cheese
1/4 cup creamy old-fashioned peanut butter
2 tablespoons light cream
1 tablespoon minced onion
1/2 teaspoon curry powder

In a small bowl, cream cheese and peanut butter until well blended. Blend in cream, onion and curry powder.
Makes about 1 cup
38 grams protein per cup

PEANUT-RICOTTA STUFFED CELERY Prepare Peanut-Ricotta Spread. Cut 8 celery stalks in half crosswise and fill with spread. Sprinkle 1/2 cup chopped salted peanuts over the filled stalks. Refrigerate 30 minutes before serving.
Makes 16 appetizers
3.6 grams protein per appetizer

Tuna Pate

This pate came from a friend, Mary Hughes, who teaches art at my school. People are always asking her for recipes, so I did too. This can be molded to serve as a party appetizer; left unmolded it makes a wonderful sandwich spread for lunch boxes.

One 8-ounce package Neufchatel cheese, at
    room temperature
2 tablespoons chili sauce
2 tablespoons minced parsley
1 tablespoon grated onion
1/2 teaspoon Tabasco sauce
Two 6-1/2-ounce cans tuna, drained

Blend cheese, chili sauce, parsley, onion and Tabasco; gradually stir in tuna. Beat till well blended. To mold, pack in an oiled 4-cup mold or a small bowl; chill thoroughly, at least 3 hours. At serving time, dip mold into hot water for a few seconds and invert on a serving plate.
Makes 16 appetizer servings
8.9 grams protein per serving

Chicken Liver Pate in a Jar

This unbaked pate is eaten like a spread. Just mix everything together and pack into a jar.

2 tablespoons butter or safflower margarine
1/2 pound chicken livers
1/4 cup chopped onion
2 eggs, hard-cooked
1 tablespoon minced parsley
Two 3-ounce packages Neufchatel or cream
    cheese, at room temperature
2 tablespoons Cognac, tomato juice or water
Scant 1/4 teaspoon ground allspice
1/8 teaspoon ground mace
Pinch dried thyme
3/4 teaspoon salt
1/8 teaspoon ground black pepper

Melt butter or margarine in a medium skillet. Add chicken livers and onions and cook over medium heat, stirring occasionally, until onion is tender and livers are firm but still pink inside, about 10 minutes. Combine livers and onions with eggs and grind in a meat grinder, or puree in batches in a blender or food processor. Beat Neufchatel or cream cheese until light and fluffy and add to liver mixture along with remaining ingredients. Pack into a mold or small baking dish, cover and refrigerate.
Makes about 2 cups
35.9 grams protein per cup

COLD-CUT LOAVES

These tasty meats are good for parties as well as for everyday snacking. Ordinary lunch meats found in markets are expensive and filled with nitrates and preservatives. These are much more healthful and delicious and will keep in the refrigerator about ten days. You may also freeze them.

Chicken Cold-Cut Loaf

For parties, slice Chicken Cold-Cut Loaf or Fancy Cold-Cut Loaf (following) thin, arrange on a platter and decorate with parsley and cherry tomatoes or radishes. Serve with your favorite whole-grain breads.

1-1/2 pounds chicken breasts, boned and
  skinned (reserve 2 skins), or ground turkey
1 pound non-lean hamburger
2-1/4 teaspoons salt
1/4 teaspoon ground black pepper
1/8 teaspoon ground cloves
1/8 teaspoon ground nutmeg
1/4 teaspoon ground allspice
1/4 teaspoon dried thyme, crushed
1/4 bay leaf, crushed
3 tablespoons port, Madeira, brandy or water
1/4 cup chopped parsley
2 large garlic cloves, crushed
3/4 cup minced onion
3 tablespoons butter or safflower margarine
1 cup milk
2/3 cup soft whole-wheat bread crumbs
3 eggs, beaten

Have your butcher grind the chicken or turkey and hamburger together as fine as possible, or grind them yourself in a meat grinder or food processor. Mix meats, salt and spices and herbs with port, Madeira, brandy or water; stir in parsley and garlic and refrigerate overnight, if possible. In a saucepan, saute onions in butter or margarine until tender but not brown. Add milk and bread crumbs. Cook over medium heat until thick. Mix eggs into ground meat mixture, then add milk mixture. For a very smooth-textured loaf, puree this mixture in a blender or food processor. Pour mixture into a well-greased loaf pan. Lay reserved chicken skins over top of loaf and cover loaf with aluminum foil. Set loaf pan inside a larger pan and add boiling water to one third the height of the loaf pan. Bake in a preheated 350°F oven for 1-1/2 hours or until loaf shrinks slightly from edge of pan. Remove pan from water bath. Weigh loaf down with several full tin cans and cool thoroughly, then chill overnight or 2 to 3 days before serving (aging improves flavor).
Makes 12 to 16 servings
14.5/10.9 grams protein per serving

FANCY COLD-CUT LOAF Prepare Chicken Cold-Cut Loaf and place half of loaf mixture in loaf pan; sprinkle with 1/2 cup pistachio nuts. Arrange 4 thin slices boiled ham over meat. Add rest of loaf mixture to pan and bake as directed.
17.9/13.4 grams protein per serving

Quick Meat Loaf

This is good for lunch, snacks or parties.

2-1/2 pounds lean ground beef
1/2 cup minced onion (optional)
1 pound spinach, chopped, steamed and
    squeezed dry, or one 10-ounce package frozen
    chopped spinach, thawed and squeezed dry
1-1/2 cups dry whole-wheat bread crumbs
1/2 cup wheat germ
1/2 cup water
One 8-ounce can tomato sauce
3 eggs
2 garlic cloves, minced or crushed
1/2 teaspoon dried basil, crushed
1/2 teaspoon dried oregano, crushed
1/4 teaspoon dried thyme or rosemary, crushed
1-1/2 teaspoons salt
1/2 teaspoon ground black pepper

In a large bowl, mix all ingredients well. Pack into
a 5 × 9-inch loaf pan. Bake in a preheated 375°F
oven 50 to 55 minutes, or until loaf is firm and
shrinks slightly from sides of pan. For easier
slicing, cover with aluminum foil. Weigh loaf down
with several full tin cans and refrigerate overnight.
Makes 10 servings
29 grams protein per serving

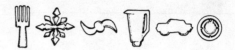

Country Pate

This smooth, mellow pate should be baked a day
or two in advance and served cold or at room temperature. Try it on dark, whole-grain pumpernickel.

2 slices bacon (non-nitrate if possible)
1 pound beef liver
1 pound boneless pork shoulder
1/4 pound pork fat (optional)
1 medium onion, quartered
1 medium garlic clove
3 or 6 tablespoons butter or safflower margarine
2/3 cup soft whole-wheat bread crumbs
3 teaspoons salt
2/3 teaspoon ground allspice
1/4 teaspoon ground cloves
1/2 teaspoon black pepper
2 cups milk
2 eggs

Simmer bacon slices in water for 10 minutes,
then rinse in cold water and drain. Trim any
membranes from liver. Grind liver, pork, optional
pork fat, onion and garlic twice through the fine
blade of a meat grinder or in a food processor.
Place in a large bowl. Melt butter or margarine
in a medium-sized saucepan, using the larger
amount if you have not used the pork fat earlier;
stir in crumbs, salt, allspice, cloves and pepper.
Gradually add milk. Cook, stirring constantly,
until sauce thickens and bubbles for 1 minute;
cool slightly. Stir hot sauce into ground liver-meat
mixture; add eggs and beat with a wooden spoon
until thoroughly mixed. For an extra-smooth tex-

ture, blend or process entire mixture again. Turn mixture into a greased shallow 6-cup baking dish. Top with blanched bacon slices and cover tightly with aluminum foil. Place dish in a larger pan; pour boiling water into outer pan to come halfway up the side of pate dish. Bake in a preheated 350°F oven for 1-1/2 hours or until juices run clear when pate is pierced with a knife. Remove dish from water bath. Weigh loaf down with several full tin cans. Cover and refrigerate overnight or 2 to 3 days (aging improves flavor).
Makes 12 to 14 servings
17.7/15.1 grams protein per serving

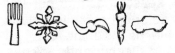

Meatless Pate or Sandwich Loaf

Vegetables and grains combine with dairy products in this nutritious meatless loaf. Brown rice, wheat germ, vegetables and walnuts are combined for complete protein. When my students read this recipe they are less than enthusiastic because it contains so many "weird" ingredients. When they taste it, though, they like it, and they always try to get other kids who are not part of the class to guess what's in it. This freezes well and can be served hot or cold—use it for sandwiches or cut into bite-sized squares for finger food appetizers.

3/4 cup salted water
1/3 cup brown rice
2 cups grated Cheddar cheese (8 ounces)
1 cup wheat germ
1 cup chopped walnuts
1 cup chopped mushrooms
1/2 cup grated green pepper
1/2 cup grated carrots
1 small garlic clove, minced
1 large onion, chopped
5 eggs, beaten
2 tablespoons soy sauce
2 tablespoons prepared mustard
1/2 teaspoon dried thyme, crushed
1/2 teaspoon dried marjoram, crushed
1/2 teaspoon dried sage, crushed
3/4 teaspoon salt
1/4 teaspoon ground black pepper

In a saucepan, bring salted water to a boil. Add rice, stir once, reduce heat, cover and cook 45 minutes, or until rice is tender and water is absorbed. Combine cooked rice, cheese, wheat germ, walnuts, mushrooms, green pepper, carrot, garlic and onion. Mix in eggs, soy sauce, prepared mustard, thyme, marjoram, sage, salt and pepper; firmly pat into a greased 5 × 9-inch loaf pan or 3 small loaf pans. Bake in a preheated 350°F oven for 55 minutes for the large pan and 40 minutes for small pans, or until browned. Let stand 15 minutes, then slice and lift out each portion with a spatula. Or, cover with aluminum foil, weigh down loaf with several full tin cans and chill overnight— this creates a firmer loaf that is easier to slice.
Makes 10 to 12 servings
15.1/12.6 grams protein

HOT VEGETABLE APPETIZERS

Here is an unexpected and delicious way to get vegetables into your diet. Many of these appetizers contain protein as well as the good nutrients in vegetables, and are delicious as light meals any time—they will convert diehard vegetable-haters into vegetable appreciators.

Note: Wrap individual servings in aluminum foil to freeze; reheat in a 300°F oven until heated through.

Easy Zucchini-Artichoke Squares

My cousin Isabel (who's known for her good cooking) gave me this recipe, which is always a great hit at social gatherings. You'll see more of Isabel's recipes in this book, because I raided her recipe files. Isabel's five children have all tasted and evaluated them. Anything that can survive that must be worth printing.

Two 6-1/2-ounce jars marinated artichoke hearts
4 eggs
1/8 teaspoon Tabasco sauce
1/8 teaspoon dried oregano, crushed
2 tablespoons minced parsley
4 cups grated Cheddar cheese (16 ounces)
1/4 cup whole-wheat bread crumbs
1 medium onion, minced
1 garlic clove, minced or crushed
1 cup grated or thinly sliced zucchini

Drain artichokes, reserving marinade; chop. In a large bowl, beat eggs, seasonings and parsley. Mix in cheese and bread crumbs. Saute onions and garlic in about 2 tablespoons of the reserved marinade until tender. Add zucchini and cook one minute. Stir onions, zucchini and artichoke hearts into cheese mixture. Turn into a greased 7-1/2 × 11-3/4-inch (2-quart) baking dish or two 8 × 8-inch cake pans. Bake in a preheated 350°F oven for 30 minutes, or until firm. Cool for 10 minutes before cutting into 1-inch squares (cut larger squares for a light meal). Remove from baking dish to serve.
**Makes about 50 appetizers
or 9 meal-sized servings
3 grams protein per appetizer,
16.8 grams protein per serving**

Florentine Squares

Get your iron, vitamin A and protein in these easy-to-assemble quichelike squares. Even spinach haters admit that "this is OK, even though it has spinach in it." I think it's delicious, but then, I like spinach enough to make this a meal.

1/3 cup grated Parmesan or Romano cheese
1/2 cup chopped green onions, including tops
3 tablespoons butter or safflower margarine
4 eggs
1 cup whole milk or half-and-half
2 pounds spinach, chopped, steamed and squeezed dry, or two 10-ounce packages frozen chopped spinach, thawed and squeezed dry
1 teaspoon salt
1/4 teaspoon ground nutmeg
1/8 teaspoon ground black pepper
1/2 cup dry whole-wheat bread crumbs
1 cup grated Swiss cheese

Grease a 7-1/2 ×11-3/4-inch (2-quart) baking dish. Sprinkle with 3 tablespoons grated cheese; set aside. Saute onions in butter until tender but not brown. Combine eggs and milk or half-and-half in a large bowl and beat well. Add spinach, onions, spices, bread crumbs and cheeses; blend well. Spread into prepared pan and bake in a preheated 350°F oven for 35 to 45 minutes, or until just barely firm. Remove and cool to room temperature. For appetizers, cut into 1-1/2-inch squares. Cut into 8 squares for a light meal.
Makes 36 appetizers or 8 meal-sized servings
2.8 grams protein per appetizer,
12.4 grams protein per serving

VARIATION Before cutting, sprinkle with 3/4 cup grated Swiss cheese and place under a broiler until melted.
3.4 grams protein per appetizer,
15.4 grams protein per serving

Zucchini Flan

This sumptuous flan was adapted from a gourmet recipe. It can be used as an appetizer or part of a meal. Sometimes I eat it for lunch or dinner.

2 tablespoons butter or safflower margarine
3 tablespoons chopped onion
1 tablespoon minced green onions
5 to 6 medium zucchini, thinly sliced or grated
1/2 teaspoon salt
Pinch ground black pepper
1 cup whole milk or half-and-half
3 eggs, lightly beaten
1/3 cup whole-wheat bread crumbs
1/4 cup grated Parmesan cheese
1/4 teaspoon ground nutmeg
1 cup grated Fontina, Swiss or Gruyere cheese

Melt butter or margarine in a large skillet and add the chopped onion and green onions. Cook, stirring, until onion is tender. Add zucchini and cook briefly, stirring occasionally, until crisp-tender. Sprinkle with salt and pepper. Spoon vegetables into 2 buttered 8 × 8-inch cake pans or an 11 × 13-inch baking dish. Blend milk or half-and-half, eggs, crumbs, Parmesan cheese and nutmeg. Pour mixture over zucchini. Sprinkle with Fontina, Swiss or Gruyere and bake 30 minutes, or until lightly set. Cool 10 minutes before cutting into 1/2-inch squares or 8 servings. Serve warm.
**Makes 50 appetizers
or 8 meal-sized servings
1.6 grams protein per appetizer,
9.7 grams protein per serving**

Vegetable Morsels

3 eggs, lightly beaten
2-1/2 teaspoons salt
1/8 teaspoon garlic powder
1/4 teaspoon onion powder
1-1/2 teaspoons ground cumin
1/4 teaspoon dried oregano, crushed
1/4 teaspoon ground black pepper
3 tablespoons unhulled sesame seeds
1/4 cup wheat germ
1/4 cup non-instant nonfat dry milk
3 tablespoons unbleached all-purpose flour
2 cups shredded carrots
1 pound spinach, chopped, steamed and squeezed dry, or one 10-ounce package frozen chopped spinach, thawed and squeezed dry
1-1/2 cups chopped cooked green beans, or one 10-ounce package frozen chopped green beans, thawed
2 teaspoons honey
1 cup unflavored yogurt

Stir together all ingredients except yogurt until well blended. Shape mixture into 1-inch balls; place 1 inch apart on well-greased rimmed baking pans. Bake uncovered in a preheated 450°F oven for 10 minutes, or until lightly browned. Serve warm with toothpicks for dipping in yogurt.
**Makes about 5 dozen
12.9 grams protein per dozen**

Note: Thaw frozen morsels, unwrap and place in a single layer in a shallow baking pan; place in a preheated 350°F oven until heated through.

Mushrooms Florentine

Vitamin- and mineral-rich mushrooms are stuffed with spinach-cheese filling.

24 medium mushrooms
1/4 cup minced green onions
2 tablespoons butter or safflower margarine
1/2 pound spinach, chopped, steamed and squeezed dry, or half of a 10-ounce package frozen chopped spinach, thawed and squeezed dry
4 tablespoons whole-wheat bread crumbs
1 egg, beaten
1/3 cup grated Parmesan cheese
1/4 teaspoon dried tarragon, crushed
1 teaspoon lemon juice
Dash ground nutmeg
Salt and ground black pepper to taste
Grated Parmesan cheese (optional)

Remove stems from mushrooms and reserve for another use. In a large saucepan, cook green onions in 1 tablespoon butter until tender. Remove from heat and stir in spinach, bread crumbs, Parmesan cheese, tarragon, lemon juice and nutmeg; add salt and pepper to taste. Lightly saute mushroom caps in remaining 1 tablespoon butter for 4 to 5 minutes until tender but still firm. Stuff mushrooms with filling and place in a lightly greased baking pan. Sprinkle with extra Parme-

san cheese, if desired. Bake in a preheated 350°F oven for about 15 minutes, or until golden.
**Makes 24 appetizers
or 4 meal-sized servings
1.5 grams protein per appetizer,
8.7 grams protein per serving**

ZUCCHINI FLORENTINE Substitute 4 medium halved zucchini for mushrooms. Hollow out zucchini, reserving pulp for another use. Stuff and bake; slice into bite-sized pieces to serve.

Artichoke-Ham Bites

You can dine on these alone.

One 14-ounce can artichoke hearts, or one 10-ounce package frozen halved artichoke hearts
1/2 cup French Marinade, page 71
1/8 teaspoon garlic powder
6 thin slices boiled ham

Drain canned artichoke hearts and cut in half, or steam frozen hearts until tender. In a glass or ceramic dish, combine dressing with garlic powder; add artichokes. Cover and refrigerate overnight, then drain. Cut ham into 1 X 4-inch strips and wrap 1 strip around each artichoke half; secure with a toothpick. Bake in a preheated 300°F oven for about 10 minutes.
**Makes 24 appetizers
or 4 meal-sized servings
2.1 grams protein per appetizer,
13 grams protein per serving**

HIGH-PROTEIN
HOT APPETIZERS

All of the following appetizers are high in complete protein, and all of them may be reheated. They are good choices for light meals, combined with a vegetable appetizer or salad and a high-protein dessert.

Ham-and-Cheese
Crustless Quichettes

One New Year's Eve, between the Rose Bowl and a dinner engagement, I threw these together to bring to a party as hors d'oeuvre. They were a hit and a sought-after recipe. For another party, I made a mushroom-spinach version because the idea struck me as interesting. (And I probably had some mushrooms that needed to be used up.) *Et voila!* Another success. For the book, I adapted some of my favorite quiche recipes to this easier method of preparation. Quichettes make a wonderful light meal, as well as delicious appetizers. Don't wait until you entertain to serve them. There's no crust to roll out so they're quite easy to assemble. They may be baked ahead and rewarmed in a 250°F oven.

1/2 cup chopped onion
1 tablespoon butter or safflower margarine
1 cup minced ham
2 cups grated sharp Cheddar or Swiss
  cheese (8 ounces)
1/2 pound spinach, chopped, steamed and
  squeezed dry, or half a 10-ounce package
  frozen chopped spinach, thawed and
  squeezed dry
2/3 cup whole-wheat cracker crumbs or dry
  whole-wheat bread crumbs
4 eggs, beaten
1-2/3 cups milk
1/2 teaspoon salt
Ground black pepper to taste

In a large saucepan, saute onion in butter until tender but not brown. Add ham, cheese, spinach and bread crumbs. In a bowl mix together eggs, milk, salt and pepper. Blend in ham and cheese mixture. Turn into a greased 9 × 13-inch pan and bake in a preheated 250°F oven until set, about 30 minutes. Cool to lukewarm in pan on a rack. Cut into forty-eight 1-1/2-inch squares or 9 large servings. Serve warm.
**Makes 48 appetizers
or 9 meal-sized servings
2.7 grams protein per appetizer,
14.2 grams protein per serving**

ITALIAN QUICHETTES Remove 5 ounces sweet Italian sausage from casings, crumble and saute with onion; drain off fat. Add 1-1/2 cups grated zucchini to pan and saute until tender. Omit ham and spinach from recipe and substitute 1-3/4 cups grated Swiss cheese and 1/4 cup grated Parmesan or Romano cheese for Cheddar or Swiss.

ASPARAGUS QUICHETTES Replace spinach with 1 cup steamed chopped asparagus (about 8 to 10 stalks), or three-quarters of a 10-ounce package of frozen asparagus, thawed and chopped.

MUSHROOM QUICHETTES Replace spinach with 8 ounces mushrooms, sliced and sauteed lightly in 2 tablespoons butter or safflower margarine.
2.6 grams protein per appetizer,
13.7 grams protein per serving

CHEESE QUICHETTES Omit ham and vegetable and increase grated Cheddar or Swiss cheese to 3-1/3 cups.
2.9 grams protein per appetizer,
15.7 grams protein per serving

Cheese-Potato Bites

4 medium potatoes, peeled and grated
1 cup grated Tilsit, brick, Swiss or Gruyere cheese
1 small onion, coarsely grated (about 1/4 cup)
3 eggs
2 tablespoons whole-wheat flour
6 tablespoons wheat germ
1 teaspoon salt
1/8 teaspoon ground black pepper
Safflower or corn oil to a depth of 1/4 inch
Applesauce

Place grated potatoes in a colander and let drain for 20 minutes; press out excess moisture with a large spoon. In a large bowl, mix potatoes, cheese, onion, eggs, flour, wheat germ, salt and pepper. In a large frying pan, drop potato mixture by tablespoonfuls into hot oil and flatten with the back of a spoon. Cook on both sides over medium-high heat until golden brown and crisp. Drain on paper towels. Serve warm with applesauce as a dip.
Makes about 4 dozen
18.6 grams protein per dozen

Note: To freeze, place cooked bites slightly apart on a plate and freeze solid. Remove from plate and wrap tightly in foil; store in freezer. To reheat, unwrap and place on a baking sheet in a preheated 350°F oven until heated through.

Protein-Stuffed Mushrooms

Cheese and whole wheat complement each other to make a complete protein—why eat meat? Good for lunch with a salad or as a healthy snack or light dinner.

12 large mushrooms
3 tablespoons olive oil or safflower or corn oil
1 cup grated Romano, Parmesan or Swiss
   cheese
1 cup soft whole-wheat bread crumbs
1 tablespoon minced parsley, preferably Italian
1/2 teaspoon dried basil, crushed
1 or 2 garlic cloves, minced or crushed
Salt and ground black pepper

Remove stems from mushroom caps. Chop stems and cook them in 1 tablespoon oil until they give up their juices, then cook until moisture evaporates. Let cool. Combine cooked stems with 2/3 cup of cheese and all remaining ingredients except mushroom caps and oil. Stuff caps with filling. Sprinkle with remaining cheese. Arrange mushrooms in a baking dish and add a little water to prevent sticking. Drizzle remaining oil evenly over mushrooms. Bake in a preheated 350°F oven 15 to 20 minutes, or until golden. If you prepare these ahead, they may be run under the broiler for a few seconds just before serving.
**Makes 12 appetizers
or 4 meal-sized servings
5.6 grams protein per appetizer,
16.8 grams protein per serving**

PROTEIN-STUFFED ZUCCHINI Follow above recipe, substituting 5 medium zucchini for the mushrooms. Trim zucchini and slice them in half lengthwise. Scoop out pulp and reserve. Steam zucchini 5 minutes. Chop pulp and cook as for mushroom stems, above. Stuff zucchini with pulp mixture, then bake and slice to serve.

Chili-Corn Squares

One Sunday, this recipe was tested by my cousin Isabel and her husband, five children, assorted in-laws and grandchildren. Everyone came to the conclusion that I should have made two batches, since it vanished in about five minutes.

1 cup stone-ground yellow corn meal
1/3 cup wheat germ
3/4 teaspoon salt
3 teaspoons baking powder
3/4 cup unflavored yogurt
Few drops Tabasco sauce
1/2 cup safflower or corn oil
3 eggs
2 cups fresh or thawed frozen corn kernels
2/3 cup small-curd cottage cheese
1/4 cup unbleached all-purpose flour
2 tablespoons honey
2-1/2 cups grated Cheddar cheese (10 ounces)
One 4-ounce can chopped peeled green chilies

In a mixing bowl, combine corn meal, wheat germ, salt and baking powder; set aside on waxed paper. In the same bowl, mix yogurt, Tabasco, oil and eggs. Mix in corn, cottage cheese, flour and honey. Blend well. Add corn meal mixture, mixing just enough to combine. Place half of the batter in a greased 8 × 8-inch pan. Spread on chilies and half of the cheese. Top with remaining batter and remaining cheese. Bake in a preheated 350°F oven 45 to 55 minutes, or until cheese is melted and cake is firm. Cool 15 minutes. Cut into twenty-five 1-1/2-inch squares or 8 large squares.

Makes 25 appetizers
or 8 meal-sized servings
5.8 grams protein per appetizer,
18.1 grams protein per serving

Un-Meatballs

These have all the protein you'd get from meat, and are great for light meals or after-school snacks. They're even good cold for munchies or lunchboxes. For parties, serve cocktail-sized un-meatballs with toothpicks.

Tomato Sauce
1/2 onion, minced
3 garlic cloves, minced, or 3/4 teaspoon garlic powder
2 tablespoons olive oil or safflower or corn oil
Two 8-ounce cans tomato sauce

1 tablespoon anchovy paste (optional but very good)
1/3 cup water
1/2 teaspoon dried oregano, crushed
1/2 teaspoon dried basil, crushed
1/4 teaspoon dried thyme or rosemary, crushed

Un-Meatballs
1-1/2 cups small-curd cottage cheese
4 eggs, beaten
1/2 cup coarsely chopped walnuts
1/2 cup chopped unsalted sunflower seeds
1/2 cup wheat germ
1/2 teaspoon seasoned salt
1 cup grated sharp Cheddar cheese
2 cups whole-wheat croutons or dried chopped whole-wheat bread
1/2 cup chopped onion
1 garlic clove, minced
1 teaspoon dried basil, crushed
1/2 teaspoon dried oregano, crushed
1/2 teaspoon dried sage, crushed
Pinch of dried thyme

To prepare the sauce, saute onion and garlic in oil until tender. Add remaining ingredients, blend well and simmer 30 minutes or more. To make the un-meatballs, in a large bowl combine all ingredients and mix well. Shape tablespoons of mixture into balls (use heaping teaspoonfuls for cocktail-sized un-meatballs). Arrange in a lightly greased 8 × 8-inch baking dish; spoon Tomato Sauce evenly over top. Bake uncovered in a preheated 350°F oven for 30 to 35 minutes, or until heated through and bubbly.

Makes 16 appetizer servings
or 8 meal-sized servings
9.8/19.6 grams protein per serving

Delicious Vegetable Desserts

Pumpkin pie and carrot cake have long been popular desserts. I suspect, however, that their popularity is more a result of their taste than of their food value. You'll be surprised to find how many cakes, cookies, pies and other mouthwatering desserts can be made using vegetables. When I serve them at parties, people rarely associate them with "health food." But the special desserts and treats in this chapter have much more than good flavor. These recipes incorporate complementary proteins and other important nutrients along with vegetables.

Of course you can't get all the vegetables you need in a dessert, but vegetables do add health-giving substances to treats that would normally be empty calories. Vegetables are complex carbohydrates that break down more slowly than simple sugars, their energy entering the bloodstream at a more gradual rate. Vegetables also contain fiber (cellulose), which exercises the digestive tract and helps you to absorb and maximize the nutrients in your foods. Last but not least, vegetables are a rich source of vitamins and minerals.

With the addition of whole-grain flour, wheat germ, dry milk, soy flour and nuts and seeds, these desserts are excellent sources of complete protein.

Check the "Have Some Dessert for Breakfast" chapter for these extra-high-protein vegetable desserts: Pumpkin Cheesecake, Breakfast Pumpkin Pie, Baked Pumpkin Custard and Extra-Special Carrot Cake.

CAKES AND PIES

Zucchini and Carrot Cake

If you like carrot cake or zucchini cake you'll love this. Both vegetables add fiber, vitamins and minerals. Soy nuts, dry milk and wheat germ complement the flour.

1 cup grated zucchini
3 eggs
1-1/4 cups packed brown sugar
2/3 cup safflower or corn oil
3/4 cup stirred whole-wheat flour
1-1/4 cups stirred unbleached all-purpose flour
1/4 cup non-instant nonfat dry milk
1/4 cup wheat germ
2 teaspoons baking powder
2 teaspoons baking soda
1-1/4 teaspoons ground cinnamon
1/4 teaspoon ground allspice
1 cup grated carrots
1/4 cup chopped walnuts
1/4 cup chopped unsalted soy nuts
Creamy Cheese Frosting, page 179, or Ricotta
    Frosting, page 178

Place zucchini in a sieve to drain for 20 minutes; press out excess moisture with a large spoon. In a large bowl, beat eggs and sugar together until foamy. Beat in oil gradually. Combine flours, dry milk, wheat germ, baking powder, baking soda, cinnamon and allspice; mix thoroughly and blend into egg mixture. Stir in vegetables and nuts. Pour into a well-greased 9 × 11-inch baking pan or a 5 × 9-inch loaf pan. Bake in a preheated 350°F oven 40 minutes or until a toothpick inserted in center of cake comes out clean. Cool in pan on a rack. Frost when cool.
Makes 15 to 18 servings
8/6.7 grams protein per serving

Date-Nut Zucchini Torte

This is a rich and substantial cake.

2/3 cup stirred whole-wheat flour
1/3 cup non-instant nonfat dry milk
1/4 cup wheat germ
2-1/2 teaspoons baking powder
1 teaspoon ground cinnamon
1/2 teaspoon salt
2 eggs
1 cup packed brown sugar
1 tablespoon safflower or corn oil
1 teaspoon vanilla extract
2 cups grated zucchini
1 cup chopped dates
1/3 cup chopped walnuts
3 tablespoons chopped unsalted soy nuts
Whipped Ricotta Topping, page 178 (optional)

Combine flour, dry milk, wheat germ, baking powder, cinnamon and salt. Beat together eggs, brown sugar, oil and vanilla. Stir in zucchini, dates and nuts. Pour into a greased 9 × 9-inch cake pan. Bake in a preheated 350°F oven for 60 minutes or until top is dry and cake shrinks very slightly from sides of pan. Let cool in pan on a rack for 1 hour before serving. Cut into squares and serve with ricotta topping, if desired.
Makes 9 to 12 servings
7/5.3 grams protein per serving

Carrot Custard Pie

This is always a very successful party dessert. No one knows it's healthy—but you will after examining the ingredients in this recipe.

1 recipe Nutty Bran Crumb Crust, page 175, with
   3/4 teaspoon ground ginger added
1 pound carrots, peeled and halved
One 4-ounce package Neufchatel cheese, at
   room temperature
One 8-ounce can crushed pineapple
1/2 cup non-instant nonfat dry milk
2 tablespoons packed brown sugar

3 eggs
1/2 teaspoon salt
1 teaspoon ground cinnamon
1 teaspoon ground nutmeg
One 14-ounce can sweetened condensed milk
1 teaspoon vanilla extract
Sweetened whipped cream and very thinly sliced
   raw carrots (optional)

Prepare the crumb crust in a 10-inch pie pan or a 9-inch springform pan; set aside. Steam carrots or cook them in a covered pan in 1 inch of boiling water just until tender; drain and cool. Drain juice from crushed pineapple and pour juice into a blender or food processor; add carrots and Neufchatel cheese and puree until smooth. Combine with dry milk, brown sugar, eggs, salt, spices and crushed pineapple, using the food processor or an electric mixer. Add condensed milk and vanilla, blending until smooth. Turn into prepared crust and bake in a preheated 375°F oven 45 to 55 minutes, or until a knife inserted in center of pie comes out clean. Cool thoroughly on a rack, then refrigerate. Before serving, loosen springform pan and remove sides. Decorate with rosettes of whipped cream and sliced carrots, if desired.
Makes 8 to 10 servings
13.6/10.9 grams protein per serving

CARROT CUSTARD CUPS Pour filling into 6 to 8 buttered custard cups and bake in a preheated 375°F oven for 25 to 30 minutes, or until a knife inserted in center of custard comes out clean.
Makes 6 to 8 servings
18.1/13.6 grams protein per serving

Honey and Pumpkin Cake

Pumpkin adds vitamin A and fiber to an already healthy cake.

1 cup stirred whole-wheat flour
3/4 cup stirred unbleached all-purpose flour
1/2 cup non-instant nonfat dry milk
1/3 cup wheat germ
2 teaspoons baking soda
1/4 teaspoon salt
1/4 teaspoon ground mace
1/4 teaspoon ground allspice
1/4 teaspoon ground cloves
1/2 teaspoon ground nutmeg
1/2 teaspoon ground cinnamon
1/2 teaspoon ground ginger
1/3 cup safflower or corn oil
1/4 cup molasses
3/4 cup honey
3 eggs
2/3 cup mashed cooked pumpkin
1/2 cup unflavored yogurt or buttermilk
Ricotta Frosting, page 178, or Creamy Cheese
    Frosting, page 179

Combine flours, dry milk, wheat germ, baking soda, salt and spices. With an electric mixer or in a food processor, beat oil, molasses and honey together until light. Add eggs one at a time and continue beating. Beat in pumpkin and yogurt or buttermilk. Blend in dry ingredients thoroughly. Pour into an oiled 8 × 12-inch cake pan and bake in a preheated 350°F oven for 45 to 50 minutes, or until a toothpick inserted in center of cake comes out clean. Cool in pan on a rack, then frost.
Makes 15 servings
8.4 grams protein per serving

Tomato-Spice Cake

The surprising ingredients in this recipe make a wonderfully delicious cake.

1-1/3 cups stirred whole-wheat flour
2 cups stirred unbleached all-purpose flour
1/3 cup stirred soy flour
1/2 cup wheat germ
3/4 cup non-instant nonfat dry milk
1-1/2 cups packed brown sugar
2-1/2 teaspoons baking soda
2-1/2 teaspoons ground cinnamon
1 teaspoon ground nutmeg
1 teaspoon ground cloves
1-1/2 teaspoons salt
1/4 pound butter or safflower margarine
6 medium tomatoes, peeled and seeded (about
    2 pounds)
1 cup honey, warmed
2 teaspoons vanilla extract
1/2 cup chopped walnuts
Milk-and-Honey Glaze, page 182 (optional)

In a large bowl, combine flours, wheat germ, dry milk, sugar, baking soda, cinnamon, nutmeg, cloves and salt. Cut in butter or margarine with a pastry blender. In a blender or food processor, puree tomatoes until smooth (there should be 2-1/2 cups of pureed tomatoes). Mix in honey and vanilla. Combine tomato mixture and dry ingredients. With an electric mixer at low speed, beat this mixture until just mixed. Increase speed to high and beat 2 minutes or until mixture is smooth, occasionally scraping bowl with a rubber spatula. Sprinkle half the nuts into bottom of a 9-inch tube pan or bundt pan. Pour in batter and sprinkle with remaining nuts. Bake in a preheated 350°F oven 65 to 70 minutes, or until a toothpick inserted in center of cake comes out clean. Cool in pan on a rack for 10 minutes, then remove from pan and serve cake warm or completely cooled. Glaze, if desired.
Makes 12 to 16 servings
9.1/6.8 grams protein per serving

Zucchini Spice Pie

1/2 recipe No-Roll Whole-Wheat Pastry, page
    177, or Flaky Wheat Germ Pastry, page 176
1-1/2 cups grated zucchini
1/2 teaspoon salt
3/4 cup packed brown sugar
1-1/2 cups evaporated milk
2 eggs
2 tablespoons molasses
1 tablespoon unbleached all-purpose flour
1-1/2 teaspoons ground cinnamon
1 teaspoon ground ginger
1/2 teaspoon ground cloves
1/4 teaspoon ground nutmeg
Honey Ricotta Topping, page 178

Prepare a 9-inch unbaked pie crust and set aside. Place zucchini in a colander and sprinkle with salt; let drain for 30 minutes, then press out excess moisture with a large spoon. In a blender or food processor, blend all ingredients except ricotta topping at high speed for at least 1 minute. Pour into prepared pie crust and bake in a preheated 450°F oven for 10 minutes, then lower heat to 350°F and bake 45 minutes longer. Cool on a rack. Serve with ricotta topping.
Makes 8 servings
8.9 grams protein per serving

ZUCCHINI PRALINE PIE Prepare 1 Praline Crust, page 177; bake and cool as directed. Fill and bake as directed for Zucchini Spice Pie.
9.8 grams per serving

Pumpkin or Sweet Potato Chiffon Pie

1 recipe Praline Crust, page 177
1 tablespoon (1 envelope) unflavored gelatin
1/4 cup apple juice or water
1/2 cup milk
1/4 cup non-instant nonfat dry milk
2 tablespoons honey
2 tablespoons molasses
1/2 teaspoon ground ginger
1/2 teaspoon ground allspice
1/2 teaspoon ground cinnamon
1/4 teaspoon ground nutmeg
1/4 teaspoon salt
1-1/4 cups mashed cooked pumpkin or sweet
    potato
3 eggs, separated
1/8 teaspoon cream of tartar
5 tablespoons Turbinado or granulated sugar
Chopped nuts (optional)

Prepare the pie crust and set aside to cool. Sprinkle gelatin over juice or water in a small saucepan. Warm mixture and stir until gelatin is dissolved. Place milk in a bowl and sprinkle dry milk over gradually while beating with a whisk; blend thoroughly; or, place milk in a blender, cover and turn on blender, uncover and sprinkle in dry milk, not allowing it to foam. In a large saucepan, combine milk mixture, honey, molasses, spices, salt and pumpkin or sweet potato. Bring to the boiling point, then remove from heat. Add a small amount of hot mixture to egg yolks, blend well and add egg yolks and gelatin mixture to hot mixture in pan. Chill about 1 hour, or until partially set. Beat egg whites until soft peaks form. Add cream of tartar, then sprinkle in sugar 1 teaspoon at a time while beating to stiff peaks. Fold into chilled pumpkin or sweet potato mixture. Turn into cooled pie crust. Decorate with nuts, if desired. Chill thoroughly.

Makes 8 servings
11.7 grams protein per serving

PUDDINGS, MOUSSES AND ICE CREAMS

Steamed Pumpkin Pudding

This is a delicious autumn dessert.

1 cup stirred whole-wheat flour
3/4 cup stirred unbleached all-purpose flour
1/2 cup wheat germ
1/2 cup non-instant nonfat dry milk
1-1/2 teaspoons baking powder
1/4 teaspoon baking soda
1/2 teaspoon salt
1/2 teaspoon ground cinnamon
1/2 teaspoon ground nutmeg
1/2 teaspoon ground ginger
1/4 pound butter or safflower margarine, at room temperature
3/4 cup packed brown sugar
1/4 cup granulated sugar
1/4 cup molasses
1 teaspoon vanilla extract
1/2 cup unflavored yogurt
2 eggs
1 cup mashed cooked pumpkin
1/2 cup chopped walnuts
1/3 cup chopped unsalted soy nuts
1 tablespoon grated lemon rind
Brandy Dessert Sauce, page 179 (optional)

Combine flours, wheat germ, dry milk, baking powder, baking soda, salt and spices. With an electric mixer or in a food processor, cream butter and sugars until fluffy. Beat in molasses, vanilla, yogurt. Add eggs, one at a time, beating well after each addition. Blend in pumpkin, dry ingredients, nuts and lemon rind. Turn into a well-greased 8-cup mold or an oiled 10-inch bundt pan. Cover tightly with foil, place on a rack in a large pot and add water to halfway up outside of mold. Cover, bring to a boil, then reduce to a simmer; cook for 2 hours. Remove from kettle and let stand for 10 minutes. Loosen pudding with a knife and invert onto a plate, shaking mold to dislodge pudding. Serve warm with dessert sauce.
Makes 12 to 16 servings
8.1/6 grams protein per serving

Pumpkin Mousse

2 tablespoons (2 envelopes) unflavored gelatin
1/3 cup cold water
1 cup honey
2 cups buttermilk
2/3 cup non-instant nonfat dry milk
1 cup mashed cooked pumpkin
1/2 teaspoon ground cinnamon
Pinch ground allspice
Pinch ground cloves
Pinch ground nutmeg
Pinch ground ginger
1 teaspoon grated lemon rind
3/4 cup chopped walnuts
1 cup whipping cream, whipped

Sprinkle gelatin over water in a large saucepan. Add honey and 1 cup buttermilk. Stir over low heat until gelatin is completely dissolved. Stir in pumpkin, spices and lemon rind. Place remaining 1 cup buttermilk in a bowl and sprinkle dry milk over gradually while beating with a whisk, blending thoroughly; or place buttermilk in a blender, cover and turn on blender, then uncover and sprinkle in dry milk, but do not let this mixture foam. Blend this mixture into pumpkin mixture and chill until thickened. Fold in nuts and whipped cream. Turn into a wet 6-cup mold or bundt pan. Chill until firm. To unmold, dip mold in hot water for a few seconds and invert onto a plate.
Makes 10 to 12 servings
6.9/5.7 grams protein per serving

Pumpkin Ice Cream

1 cup mashed cooked pumpkin
1 cup non-instant nonfat dry milk
1/2 teaspoon vanilla extract
3/4 teaspoon ground cinnamon
1/8 teaspoon ground allspice
1/8 teaspoon ground cloves
1/8 teaspoon ground nutmeg
Pinch ground ginger
4 teaspoons unbleached all-purpose flour
1/2 cup Turbinado or granulated sugar
3/4 cup milk
1 egg, separated
1/2 cup whipping cream

Blend pumpkin, dry milk, vanilla and spice with an electric mixer or in a blender or food processor. In a large saucepan, combine flour, 1/4 cup sugar and milk. Cook and stir over medium heat until the mixture boils and is thick. Beat in egg yolk and cook half a minute more. Stir in pumpkin mixture, then remove from heat and chill thoroughly. When mixture is chilled, beat egg white till soft peaks form. Add sugar a little at a time, continuing to beat until stiff. Beat cream and fold egg white and cream into chilled pumpkin mixture. Freeze in a covered container until firm. To freeze in a machine, blend unwhipped cream into pumpkin mixture, beat egg white and fold it in, then freeze as directed by manufacturer.
Makes about 1 quart or 6 to 8 servings
8.2/6.1 grams protein per serving

COOKIES

Carrot and Raisin Chews

A very nutritious cookie—besides the fiber and the vitamins in the carrots, raisins, nuts and oats, there's soy flour, wheat germ, nonfat milk and whole-wheat flour for complete protein.

1 cup stirred whole-wheat pastry flour
1/4 cup soy flour
2/3 cup wheat germ
1/2 cup non-instant nonfat dry milk
1-1/2 teaspoons baking powder
1/2 teaspoon salt
1 teaspoon ground cinnamon
1/4 teaspoon ground nutmeg
1/4 teaspoon ground cloves
1/2 pound butter or safflower margarine, at room temperature
1 cup packed brown sugar or honey
2 eggs
1 teaspoon vanilla extract
1-1/2 cups rolled oats
2 cups shredded carrots
3/4 cup raisins
3/4 cup chopped nuts or unsalted sunflower seeds

Combine flours, wheat germ, dry milk, baking powder, salt, cinnamon, nutmeg and cloves. With an electric mixer or in a food processor, beat together butter and sugar until light and fluffy. Blend in eggs and vanilla. Stir in oats, carrots, dry ingredients and raisins and nuts or seeds. Drop batter by rounded teaspoonfuls 1-1/2 inches apart onto greased cookie sheets. Bake in a preheated 350°F oven for 12 to 15 minutes or until cookies are firm to the touch; cool on racks. Store in a loosely covered container.
Makes about 5 dozen
23.3 grams protein per dozen

Vitamin-Rich Pumpkin Bars

This recipe is a favorite of my high school classes.

1 cup stirred unbleached all-purpose flour
3/4 cup stirred whole-wheat flour
1/2 cup wheat germ
1/2 cup non-instant nonfat dry milk
2 teaspoons baking powder
1 teaspoon baking soda
1 teaspoon salt
1 teaspoon ground cinnamon
4 eggs
1 cup safflower or corn oil
1-2/3 cups packed brown sugar
One 16-ounce can pumpkin
Creamy Cheese Frosting, page 179

Stir together flours, wheat germ, dry milk, baking powder, soda, salt and cinnamon. With an electric mixer or in a food processor, beat eggs, oil, sugar and pumpkin until light and fluffy. Add flour mixture to pumpkin mixture and mix thoroughly. Spread batter in an ungreased 15 × 10 × 1-inch baking pan. Bake in a preheated 350°F oven for 25 to 30 minutes or until top springs back when lightly touched. Cool in pan on rack. Frost and cut into bars.
Makes 35 bars
4.1 grams protein per bar

Zucchini Almond Squares

These bars are light and delicious. They use no butter and very little flour.

1-1/2 cups grated zucchini
1 teaspoon almond extract
1/3 cup stirred whole-wheat flour
1/3 cup wheat germ
1 teaspoon baking powder
1/4 teaspoon salt
1/4 cup chopped unsalted soy nuts
1/3 cup chopped almonds
2 egg whites
1/2 cup packed brown sugar

Place zucchini in a sieve and sprinkle with almond extract; let drain for 20 minutes, then press out excess moisture with a large spoon. Mix together flour, wheat germ, baking powder, salt, soy nuts and almonds. Beat egg whites until foamy; add sugar a little at a time while beating whites to stiff peaks. Fold in dry ingredients, then fold in zucchini. Spoon into a greased 8 × 8-inch pan. Bake in a preheated 350°F oven for 40 minutes. Cool in pan on a rack. Cut into squares to serve.
Makes 9 to 12 servings
4.5/3.4 grams protein per serving

Honey Zucchini Cookies

1 cup grated zucchini
2/3 cup stirred whole-wheat flour
2/3 cup stirred unbleached all-purpose flour
1/4 cup soy flour
1/4 cup wheat germ
1/3 cup rolled oats
1/2 cup non-instant nonfat dry milk
1/2 teaspoon salt
1 teaspoon baking soda
1 teaspoon ground cinnamon
1/2 teaspoon ground cloves
1/2 teaspoon ground nutmeg
1/4 pound butter or safflower margarine, at room temperature
3/4 cup honey
1 egg
1-1/2 cups chopped walnuts, or 1 cup chopped walnuts and 1/2 cup chopped unsalted soy nuts
1-1/2 cups raisins, chopped dates or carob or chocolate chips
2/3 cup unsweetened shredded coconut (optional)

Place zucchini in a sieve to drain for 20 minutes; press out excess moisture with a large spoon. Combine flours, wheat germ, rolled oats, dry milk, salt, baking soda, cinnamon, cloves and nutmeg. With an electric mixer or in a food processor, beat together butter or margarine, honey, egg and drained zucchini for 3 minutes, or until creamy. Fold in dry ingredients, nuts and raisins, dates or chips and optional coconut. Drop by heaping spoonfuls 1-1/2 inches apart onto oiled cookie sheets. Bake in a preheated 325°F oven for 15 minutes or until cookies are golden and firm to the touch. Cool on racks.
Makes 6 dozen
16.7 grams protein per dozen

Complementary-Protein Cakes, Cookies and Candies

Dessert, whether at a meal or in between meals, is a custom most people have not learned to live without. At the same time, we are a nation concerned with good nutrition and weight watching. Fresh fruit is probably the most ideal dessert, but it does not often appear at birthdays, office parties or holiday dinners. Most people like to treat themselves to a dessert now and then. They may develop feelings of deprivation if they are asked to deny themselves this traditional pleasure.

Any sweetened food is less than ideal. For example, you get just about the same nutrients in a fresh apple as in a piece of apple pie, but the pie, of course, has far more calories. If you ate three or four apples, they would amount to the same number of calories as the pie, but you would be getting three times the fiber and nutrients as in that single piece of pie. (Anyway, who eats three or four apples?)

The recipes in this chapter, along with the other sweets in this book, can help you "have your cake and eat it too." They are so full of essential nutrients that you can substitute them for part of a meal or eat them as a wholesome snack without a trace of guilt. The complete protein in these desserts allows you to eat less meat, dairy products and breads or cereals when you include them as part of your meal. You and your family will be satisfied and well nourished without consuming too many extra calories. These recipes have been tested by families, friends and high school students and have passed the flavor test. You will find some of your old favorites, plus some new and unusual desserts.

Other desserts in this book are the cakes, pies, cookies, puddings and frozen desserts in the "Delicious Vegetable Desserts" section, preceding, and the extra-high-protein desserts in the "Have Some Dessert for Breakfast" chapter.

CAKES

All the cakes in this chapter are made from complementary-protein ingredients—and all of them are delicious. Following are cakes found in other chapters:

"Have Some Dessert for Breakfast"
Extra-Special Carrot Cake
High-Protein Pound Cake
Poppy Seed Cake
Spicy Banana Breakfast Bars
High-Protein Applesauce Cake
Breakfast Cheesecake
Easy-As-Pie Cheesecake
Italian Cheese Pie
Carob or Chocolate Swirl Cheesecake
Pumpkin Cheesecake

"Delicious Vegetable Desserts"
Tomato-Spice Cake
Zucchini and Carrot Cake
Date-Nut Zucchini Torte
Honey and Pumpkin Cake

Quick Apple Cake

This is a cross between a cake and a pie—with no crust to roll out.

1 egg
2 tablespoons safflower or corn oil
3/4 cup honey
1/3 cup stirred unbleached all-purpose flour
1 teaspoon baking powder
1/2 cup wheat germ
1/4 teaspoon salt
1 teaspoon ground cinnamon
1/3 cup non-instant nonfat dry milk
1-3/4 cups chopped apples
1/2 cup walnuts or almonds, chopped, or a mixture of half walnuts or almonds and half unsalted soy nuts, chopped
Whipped Ricotta Topping, page 178, or high-protein vanilla ice cream, pages 158-59 (optional)

In a large mixing bowl, beat egg and oil until light, then beat in honey until well blended. Combine flour with baking powder, wheat germ, salt, cinnamon and dry milk; stir into egg mixture until well mixed, then stir in apples and nuts. Spoon into a well-greased 8- or 9-inch pie pan and smooth top with a spatula. Bake in a preheated 350°F oven for 35 to 45 minutes, or until top is browned and pie springs back when lightly touched near center. Serve warm or cool. To reheat, place uncovered in a preheated 350°F oven for about 10 minutes.
Makes 8 servings

Fresh Apple Cake

This wonderfully wholesome cake is loaded with fresh apples, which give it lots of fiber. Wheat germ, soy nuts, and soy flour contribute extra protein and complement the protein in the flour and nuts.

2/3 cup stirred unbleached all-purpose flour
2/3 cup stirred whole-wheat flour
1/3 cup stirred soy flour
2/3 cup wheat germ
2 teaspoons baking soda
2 teaspoons ground cinnamon
1/4 teaspoon salt
1 cup chopped unsalted soy nuts
1 cup chopped walnuts
1/2 cup safflower or corn oil
1 cup packed brown sugar
1 cup honey
4 eggs
1-1/2 teaspoons vanilla extract
5 cups finely chopped peeled tart apples
Wheat germ or whole-wheat bread crumbs
Milk-and-Honey Glaze, page 182, or Fabulous
  Apple Juice Glaze, page 183

In a large bowl, combine flours, wheat germ, baking soda, cinnamon, salt and nuts. With an electric mixer or in a food processor, cream oil and sugar. Add honey in thirds, beating after each addition. Beat in eggs and vanilla. Add wet ingredients and apples to dry ingredients and mix well. Turn into a well-greased 10-inch bundt or tube pan heavily coated with wheat germ or whole-wheat bread crumbs. Bake in a preheated 350°F oven for 60 to 65 minutes, or until a toothpick inserted in the cake comes out clean. Cool in pan on a rack for 15 minutes, then invert onto a plate. Cool and glaze.
Makes 12 to 14 servings
11.6/8.7 grams protein per serving

CAROB OR CHOCOLATE FRESH APPLE CAKE Follow recipe for Fresh Apple Cake, reducing cinnamon to 1 teaspoon and adding 1/2 cup carob powder or cocoa to dry ingredients.

Banana-Oat Cupcakes

1/2 cup stirred whole-wheat flour
3/4 cup stirred unbleached all-purpose flour
1/4 cup soy flour
1/4 cup non-instant nonfat dry milk
1/3 cup wheat germ
1-1/4 teaspoons baking powder
1-1/2 teaspoons baking soda
3/4 teaspoon salt
1/4 pound butter or safflower margarine, at
    room temperature
3/4 cup packed brown sugar
1/2 cup honey
3 eggs
3 medium bananas, mashed (about 1 cup)
2/3 cup rolled oats
1/2 cup chopped nuts or unsalted soy nuts
    (optional)

Combine flours, dry milk, wheat germ, baking powder, baking soda and salt. With an electric mixer or in a food processor, cream butter or margarine with sugar until light and fluffy. Add honey and continue beating. Beat in eggs, one at a time. Beat in bananas. Blend in dry ingredients and add oats and nuts, stirring just to mix. Fill 24 muffin cups lined with paper baking cups two-thirds full with batter. Bake in a preheated 375°F oven for 18 to 20 minutes, or until a toothpick inserted in a cupcake comes out clean. Remove from pans and cool on wire racks.
Makes 24 cupcakes
3.7 grams protein per cupcake

BANANA OAT CAKE Bake batter for Banana Oat Cupcakes in a greased 9 × 9-inch cake pan in a preheated 375°F oven for 30 to 35 minutes. Test for doneness as above.
Makes 12 servings
7.5 grams protein per serving

German Carob Cake

This cake is good either plain or filled and frosted. The coconut-pecan frosting and filling creates a healthful version of German chocolate cake and adds 3.3 grams of protein per serving.

2-1/4 cups stirred whole-wheat pastry flour
1/3 cup stirred soy flour
1/3 cup non-instant nonfat dry milk
1/2 cup carob powder
1/2 teaspoon salt
1/2 teaspoon baking soda
1 teaspoon baking powder
1/4 pound butter or safflower margarine, at room
    temperature
1-1/3 cups honey
2 eggs
1 teaspoon vanilla extract
2/3 cup milk
Coconut-Pecan Frosting and Filling, page 182
    (optional)

Combine flours, dry milk, carob powder, salt, baking soda and baking powder and mix thoroughly. With an electric mixer or in a food processor cream butter or margarine until fluffy. Add honey very gradually, beating until thick and creamy. Add one fourth of the dry ingredients to creamed butter mixture and mix until smooth and well blended. Beat in eggs, one at a time. Beat in vanilla. Add remaining dry ingredients in thirds alternately with milk, beating well after each addition. Pour batter into a greased and lightly floured 7-1/2 × 12-inch baking pan or 2 greased, waxed paper-lined 8-inch round cake pans. Bake large pan in a preheated 350°F oven for 40 to 45 minutes, layers for 30 to 35 minutes, or until a toothpick inserted in cake comes out clean. Cool on racks.

Makes 12 servings
6.1 grams protein per serving

Peanut Butter Cake

1 cup stirred unbleached all-purpose flour
1 cup stirred whole-wheat flour
1/2 cup non-instant nonfat dry milk
1/4 cup wheat germ
4 teaspoons baking powder
3/4 teaspoon salt
3/4 cup chunky old-fashioned peanut butter
1/4 pound butter or safflower margarine, at room
   temperature
1-1/2 cups packed brown sugar
1-1/2 teaspoons vanilla extract
3 eggs
1 cup milk
Wheat germ or whole-wheat bread crumbs
Carob or Chocolate Quick Milk Glaze, page 183
   (optional)
About 1/4 cup chopped salted roasted peanuts
   (optional)

In a large bowl, stir together flours, dry milk, wheat germ, baking powder and salt. With an electric mixer or in a food processor, cream peanut butter and butter or margarine until fluffy. Beat in sugar until very fluffy; add vanilla. Beat in eggs, one at a time, beating well after each addition. Stir in flour mixture alternately with milk, beginning and ending with flour mixture. Pour into a well-greased 10-inch tube pan or a 9 × 13-inch pan heavily coated with wheat germ or bread crumbs. Bake in a preheated 350°F oven for 40 to 45 minutes, or until a toothpick inserted in cake comes out clean. Cool in pan on a rack for 10 minutes, then turn out on a rack to cool completely. Decorate with carob or chocolate glaze and peanuts, if desired. Cool in pan on a rack. Cut into squares.

Makes 15 to 18 servings
9/7.5 grams protein per serving

Orange Sponge Cake

2/3 cup stirred unbleached all-purpose flour
2/3 cup stirred soy flour
1/2 teaspoon baking powder
1/2 teaspoon salt
1/2 cup packed brown sugar
1 cup Turbinado or granulated sugar
6 eggs, separated
1 teaspoon cream of tartar
1 teaspoon lemon juice
1 teaspoon grated lemon rind (optional)
1 tablespoon grated orange rind
1 tablespoon thawed frozen orange juice
   concentrate
2 tablespoons water
Orange Milk-and-Honey Glaze, page 182

Stir together flours, baking powder, salt, brown sugar and 1/2 cup sugar. Beat egg whites with cream of tartar until soft peaks form. Gradually add remaining 1/2 cup sugar, beating until stiff peaks form. In a large bowl, beat egg yolks until thick and lemon colored. Beat in rinds, juices and water. By hand, stir flour mixture into egg yolks; beat for 30 seconds. Fold in egg whites just until blended. Pour into a 10-inch ungreased tube pan. Bake in a preheated 375°F oven for 45 to 50 minutes, or until cake shrinks slightly from sides of pan. Remove from the oven and invert pan on a funnel or bottle until cool, at least 1 hour, before removing from pan; glaze when cool.
Makes 12 servings
6.8 grams protein per serving

Orange Cream-Filled Bundt Cake

This nutritious cake is filled with a high-protein cheese filling. The lemon and carob or chocolate versions following are also delicious.

Filling
One 8-ounce package Neufchatel cheese, at
   room temperature
1/2 cup dry cottage cheese or bakers' (hoop)
   cheese
2 tablespoons honey
2 eggs, separated (reserve whites)
2 teaspoons grated orange rind
1/2 teaspoon salt
1/2 teaspoon vanilla extract

Cake
2/3 cup boiling water
1 cup rolled oats
1/2 cup stirred unbleached all-purpose flour
1/4 cup whole-wheat flour
2/3 cup wheat germ
1-1/4 teaspoons baking powder
1/2 teaspoon baking soda
1/2 teaspoon salt
1/2 cup chopped nuts
1 tablespoon grated orange rind
1/4 pound butter or safflower margarine, at room
   temperature
2/3 cup Turbinado or granulated sugar
3/4 cup honey
2 eggs
2 egg whites

1/4 cup thawed frozen orange juice concentrate
1/2 cup unflavored yogurt
1 teaspoon vanilla extract

2 to 3 tablespoons wheat germ

To make the filling, beat filling ingredients until smooth with an electric mixer or in a food processor, then place in the freezer while mixing the cake.

To make cake, pour boiling water over oats and allow them to soak. Mix flours, wheat germ, baking powder, baking soda, salt, nuts and orange rind. With an electric mixer or in a food processor, cream together butter or margarine and sugar until light and fluffy. Add honey in a fine stream, beating continuously. Add eggs and whites one at a time, beating after each addition. Stir in orange juice, yogurt and vanilla. Add oat mixture and stir well. Fold in dry ingredients. Pour one half of the batter into a 10-inch bundt or tube pan that has been well-greased and sprinkled on the sides and bottom with 2 to 3 tablespoons wheat germ. Spread cheese filling in a circle or ring over batter. Spread remaining batter carefully over filling. Bake in a preheated 350°F oven for 50 to 60 minutes, or until a toothpick inserted in the cake comes out clean. Cool on a rack for 15 minutes, then invert cake onto a plate and remove from pan.
Makes 12 to 16 servings
11.3/8.5 grams protein per serving

LEMON CREAM-FILLED BUNDT CAKE To make the filling, follow the directions for filling in Orange Cream-Filled Bundt Cake, substituting 2 teaspoons grated lemon rind for the orange rind. To make the cake, follow the directions for the Orange Cream-Filled Bundt Cake, replacing boiling water with 1/2 cup boiling water and 1/4 cup lemon juice and increasing baking powder to 1-1/2 teaspoons. Substitute lemon rind for orange rind and 2/3 cup unflavored yogurt for orange juice concentrate and yogurt.

CAROB OR CHOCOLATE CREAM-FILLED BUNDT CAKE To make the filling, follow directions for filling in Orange Cream-Filled Bundt Cake. Omit orange rind and add an additional 1/2 teaspoon vanilla extract and 1/2 cup carob or chocolate chips. To make the cake, follow the directions for Orange Cream-Filled Bundt Cake, increasing boiling water to 3/4 cup and baking powder to 1-1/2 teaspoons. Substitute 1/2 cup carob powder or cocoa for orange rind and 2/3 cup unflavored yogurt for orange juice concentrate and yogurt.

Oatmeal Gingerbread

Delicious with Whipped Ricotta Topping or a high-protein vanilla ice cream or ice milk.

1/2 cup stirred whole-wheat flour
1/2 cup stirred unbleached all-purpose flour
2/3 cup wheat germ
1/2 cup non-instant nonfat dry milk
1 cup rolled oats
1-1/4 teaspoons ground ginger
1/2 teaspoon ground cloves
1 teaspoon ground cinnamon
1/2 teaspoon salt
1 teaspoon baking soda
4 tablespoons butter or safflower margarine
3/4 cup honey
1/3 cup molasses
1 egg
2/3 cup unflavored yogurt
Whipped Ricotta Topping, page 178, or high-
  protein vanilla ice cream, pages 158-59
  (optional)

Combine flours, wheat germ, dry milk, oats, ginger, cloves, cinnamon, salt and baking soda. Cut in butter or margarine with a pastry blender or food processor until it is evenly distributed. Remove from processor, if used. With an electric mixer or food processor, beat honey, molasses, egg and yogurt together. Mix in dry ingredients. Pour into a greased 9 × 9-inch pan. Bake in a preheated 350°F oven for 35 minutes, or until a toothpick inserted in cake comes out clean (be careful not to

overbake or gingerbread will be dry). Cool in pan for 15 minutes, then remove and cool on a rack.
Makes 9 to 12 servings
8.8/6.6 grams protein per serving

Wheaty Gingerbread

1 cup stirred whole-wheat pastry flour
2/3 cup non-instant nonfat dry milk
1/2 cup wheat germ
1-1/2 teaspoons ground ginger
1/2 teaspoon ground cloves
1 teaspoon ground cinnamon
1 teaspoon baking soda
1/2 teaspoon salt
1 egg, beaten
1/3 cup safflower or corn oil
2/3 cup molasses
1/3 cup honey
2/3 cup water
Unflavored yogurt with honey to taste, or lemon
  yogurt (optional)

Combine flour, dry milk, wheat germ, ginger, cloves, cinnamon, baking soda and salt. Combine egg, oil, molasses, honey and water. Combine wet and dry ingredients with only a few strokes. Grease an 8 × 8-inch or 9 × 9-inch cake pan and dust with flour. Pour batter into pan and bake in a preheated 350°F oven for 45 to 50 minutes for an 8-inch pan or 40 to 45 minutes for a 9-inch pan, or until a toothpick inserted in center comes out clean; be careful not to overbake. Cut into squares and serve topped with yogurt, if you like.
Makes 9 to 12 servings
6.9/5.2 grams protein per serving

COOKIES

The aroma of freshly baked cookies is a wonderful pleasure. But raiding the cookie jar has always been associated with guilt, and now that we are learning more about nutrition, we feel even more guilty about eating cookies. This collection of complementary-protein cookie recipes will satisfy cookie lovers without compromising their health. These cookies make handy snacks at home or away and can add food value to a light meal.

Don't forget these cookies in the "Delicious Vegetable Desserts" section: Honey Zucchini Cookies, Carrot and Raisin Chews, Vitamin-Rich Pumpkin Bars and Zucchini Almond Squares.

Easy Mix-in-the-Pan Brownies

There always seem to be a lot of brownie addicts around, both in and out of high school. I'm one of them, so I'm always looking for healthy brownie recipes. Here's my collection of easy, mix-in-the-pan, protein-rich brownies and brownie-like recipes. Some use cheese, others wheat germ and dry milk for their complementary protein ingredients, and they are every bit as chocolaty and fudgy as the empty-calorie kind.

Healthy Hi-Pro Brownies

1/4 pound butter or safflower margarine
Two 1-ounce squares unsweetened chocolate
1/4 cup whole-wheat pastry flour
3/4 cup wheat germ
1/2 cup non-instant nonfat dry milk
1/2 teaspoon baking powder
1/4 teaspoon salt
1/2 cup chopped walnuts or unsalted sunflower seeds
2/3 cup honey
1/3 cup Turbinado or granulated sugar
2 eggs
2 teaspoons vanilla extract

In a large saucepan, over very low heat, melt butter or margarine and chocolate together; cool slightly. In an 8 X 8-inch baking pan, combine flour, wheat germ, dry milk, baking powder, salt and nuts. Beat honey into cooled chocolate mixture. Beat in sugar. Beat in eggs, one at a time. Mix in vanilla. Stir dry ingredients into mixture in saucepan, mixing just enough to moisten. Grease the pan and spread in batter. Bake in a preheated 350°F oven 25 to 30 minutes; brownies will be slightly soft in center and dry on sides. Cool in pan on a rack for 30 minutes before cutting into squares.
Makes 12 to 16 brownies
6/4.5 grams protein per brownie

Apple Brownies

Apple adds fiber, vitamins and minerals to these delicious brownies.

1/4 pound butter or safflower margarine
2/3 cup packed brown sugar
Two 1-ounce squares unsweetened chocolate
1/2 cup stirred whole-wheat pastry flour
1/3 cup wheat germ
1/4 cup non-instant nonfat dry milk
1 teaspoon baking powder
1/2 teaspoon salt
1/2 teaspoon ground cinnamon
1/2 teaspoon ground mace
1/2 cup chopped nuts or unsalted sunflower
   seeds
1/3 cup honey
1/3 cup dry cottage cheese or bakers' (hoop)
   cheese (optional)
1/2 teaspoon vanilla extract
2 eggs, beaten
1-1/2 cups finely grated apple

In a large saucepan, melt butter, sugar and chocolate together over low heat; cool slightly. In a 9 X 9-inch baking pan, mix flour, wheat germ, dry milk, baking powder, salt, cinnamon, mace and nuts or seeds. Add honey to cooled chocolate mixture and mix well. If using dry cottage cheese, press it through a sieve or puree in a blender. Add cheese and vanilla to chocolate mixture. Add eggs one at a time, beating well after each addition. Mix in apple. Add dry ingredients, blending just enough to moisten. Grease baking pan and spread batter in it. Bake in a preheated 350°F oven for 35 to 40 minutes. Brownies will be slightly gooey in center and dry on sides. Cool in pan 30 minutes, then cut into squares.
Makes 12 to 16 brownies
5.2/4 grams protein per brownie

Honey Carob Brownies

1/4 pound butter or safflower margarine
1/2 cup carob powder
1 cup honey
1/2 cup stirred whole-wheat pastry flour
1/2 cup toasted wheat germ
1/4 cup non-instant nonfat dry milk
1 teaspoon baking powder
1/4 teaspoon salt
1/2 cup chopped walnuts
2 eggs, beaten
1 teaspoon vanilla extract

Melt butter in a large saucepan over low heat. Add carob powder and honey; blend and remove from heat. Cool slightly. In an 8 X 8-inch baking pan, mix flour, wheat germ, dry milk, baking powder, salt and nuts. Beat eggs into carob mixture one at a time, beating well after each. Mix in vanilla. Add dry ingredients to carob mixture and mix well. Grease baking pan and pour in batter. Bake in a preheated 350°F oven for 40 minutes or until a toothpick inserted near center comes out clean. Cool in pan on a rack and cut into squares.
Makes 12 to 16 brownies
4.5/3.4 grams protein per brownie

Double-Decker Brownies

This brownie is packed with wheat germ and dry milk for a super complete-protein treat. The icing adds more milk protein.

Wheat Layer
1/4 pound butter or safflower margarine, at room temperature
1/2 cup packed brown sugar
1 egg yolk
1 teaspoon vanilla extract
3/4 cup wheat germ
2/3 cup stirred whole-wheat pastry flour
1/4 teaspoon salt

Chocolate Layer
Two 1-ounce squares semisweet chocolate
5 tablespoons butter or safflower margarine, at room temperature
3/4 cup honey
2 eggs
1 egg white
1 teaspoon vanilla extract
2/3 cup wheat germ
1/3 cup stirred unbleached all-purpose flour
1/2 cup non-instant nonfat dry milk
1/4 teaspoon baking powder
1/4 teaspoon salt

Chocolate Icing, following

To make the wheat layer, with an electric mixer or in a food processor, beat butter or margarine, sugar and egg yolk together until fluffy. Sprinkle vanilla, wheat germ, flour and salt evenly over this mixture and stir until well blended. Pat evenly into an ungreased 9 X 9-inch square cake pan.

To make the chocolate layer, in a large saucepan melt chocolate and butter or margarine over low heat; stir to blend well. Beat in honey, eggs, egg white and vanilla. Combine wheat germ, flour, dry milk, baking powder and salt; add to chocolate mixture and blend well. Spread chocolate batter over wheat layer. Bake in a preheated 350°F oven for 35 to 40 minutes, or until chocolate layer is firm but moist. Cool completely in pan on a rack, spread with Chocolate Icing and chill in the refrigerator until icing is firm. Cut into squares or bars to serve.
Makes 16 squares or 32 bars
6.9 grams protein per square,
3.5 grams protein per bar

CHOCOLATE ICING In a medium saucepan, melt 1/4 cup chocolate chips or one 1-ounce square of semisweet chocolate over hot water. Stir in 3 tablespoons of honey and 1/4 teaspoon vanilla extract and remove from heat. Stir in 1/4 cup non-instant nonfat dry milk, blend thoroughly and add about 2 teaspoons of hot water, or enough to make a glaze.

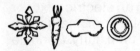

Fudgy High-Fiber Brownies

Rolled oats create a nutty texture and provide fiber in these complementary-protein brownies. This recipe contains no flour.

One 6-ounce package carob or chocolate chips
5 tablespoons butter or safflower margarine
2 eggs
1/2 cup packed brown sugar
1 teaspoon vanilla extract
3/4 cup rolled oats
1/4 cup toasted wheat germ
1/4 cup non-instant nonfat dry milk
1/2 teaspoon baking powder
1/2 teaspoon salt
1/2 cup walnuts, chopped, or mixed chopped
    walnuts and sunflower seeds

In a saucepan over low heat, melt chips and butter; cool slightly. In a large mixing bowl, beat eggs until light, then beat in sugar and vanilla. When well blended, stir in carob or chocolate mixture. In an 8 × 8-inch cake pan, mix oats, wheat germ, dry milk, baking powder and salt. Stir into wet ingredients. Stir in nuts. Grease pan and spoon in batter, spreading evenly. Bake in a preheated 350°F oven for 20 to 25 minutes, or until top is crisp and brownies are just firm. Cool in pan on a rack, then cut into squares.
Makes 12 brownies
4.2 grams protein per brownie

Bars and Squares

Bar cookies are great to bake and freeze, and to give as gifts. They store more easily than drop cookies, because they don't crumble.

Whole-Wheat Fruit Bars

3 cups stirred whole-wheat flour
3/4 cup stirred unbleached all-purpose flour
1/2 cup wheat germ
1 cup packed brown sugar
1 cup non-instant nonfat dry milk
2 teaspoons baking powder
1 teaspoon salt
2 teaspoons ground cinnamon
4 eggs, beaten
2 tablespoons grated orange rind
2 teaspoons vanilla extract
2 cups apple juice
3/4 cup safflower or corn oil
1/2 cup honey
1/2 cup dark corn syrup
2 cups raisins
One 6-ounce package dried apricots, snipped
    (about 1-1/3 cups)
1 cup salted roasted sunflower seeds

Stir together flours, wheat germ, sugar, dry milk, baking powder, salt and cinnamon. Combine eggs, orange rind, vanilla, apple juice, oil, honey and syrup. Add dry ingredients, stirring just until moistened. Stir in raisins, apricots and sunflower seeds. Spread in a greased 10 × 15-inch jelly roll pan. Bake in a preheated 350°F oven for 45 minutes. Cool and cut into bars.
Makes 40 bars
4.3 grams protein per bar

Crunchy Apricot Squares

1/4 pound butter or safflower margarine
1 cup graham cracker crumbs
1/2 cup wheat germ
1/3 cup non-instant nonfat dry milk
One 6-ounce package dried apricots, snipped
   (about 1-1/3 cups)
One 14-ounce can sweetened condensed milk
1-1/4 cups unsweetened flaked or shredded
   coconut
1/2 cup walnuts, coarsely chopped

In a 9 × 13-inch baking pan, melt butter or margarine. Mix crumbs, wheat germ, dry milk and apricots and sprinkle evenly over butter. Pour sweetened condensed milk evenly over crumbs. Top with coconut and nuts and press down gently. Bake in a preheated 350°F oven for 25 to 30 minutes, or until lightly browned and firm to the touch. Cool thoroughly before cutting into 1-inch squares. Store in the refrigerator.
Makes 32 squares
2.4 grams protein per square

Chewy Nut Squares

These make great Christmas gifts: They freeze and ship beautifully.

1/3 cup chopped unsalted soy nuts
1/2 cup chopped walnuts
1/3 cup stirred whole-wheat pastry flour
1/3 cup wheat germ
1/3 cup non-instant nonfat dry milk
1/4 teaspoon salt
1/4 teaspoon baking soda
1 egg
1 teaspoon vanilla extract
1 cup packed brown sugar

Combine nuts, flour, wheat germ, dry milk, salt and baking soda. Beat together egg, vanilla and brown sugar. Add dry ingredients, mix well and spread in a greased 8 × 8-inch baking pan. Bake in a preheated 350°F oven for 18 to 20 minutes. Cookies will be soft in the center but firm on the edges when taken from the oven. Cool in pan and cut into 1-inch squares.
Makes 32 squares
1.5 grams protein per square

Sugarless Fruit-Oat Bars

A sugarless treat with plenty of protein from milk, wheat germ, nuts, soy nuts and whole wheat. Oats and dates or apples provide fiber.

1/2 cup stirred whole-wheat flour
1/2 cup wheat germ
1/2 cup non-instant nonfat dry milk
2/3 cup rolled oats
1 teaspoon baking powder
1/2 teaspoon ground allspice
1/2 teaspoon ground nutmeg
1/2 teaspoon ground cinnamon
1/4 teaspoon salt
1/4 pound butter or safflower margarine, at room
   temperature
1 egg
1 teaspoon vanilla extract
1 teaspoon grated orange or lemon rind
1-1/3 cups chopped dates or chopped dried
   apples
2/3 cup milk
1/3 cup chopped walnuts
1/3 cup chopped unsalted soy nuts
1/3 cup unsalted sunflower seeds

Combine flour, wheat germ, dry milk, oats, baking powder, spices and salt. Beat butter or margarine, egg and vanilla until light. Mix in rind, dates or apples and milk. Add dry ingredients, beating just until well blended. Spread batter evenly into a well-greased 10 × 15-inch jelly roll pan. Sprinkle with nuts and seeds; press gently into batter. Bake in a preheated 325°F oven for about 25 minutes, or until center feels firm to the touch and sides begin to pull away from pan. Cool in pan on a rack, then cut into 2 × 3-inch bars.
Makes 25 bars
3.6 grams protein per bar

Wholesome Wheat-Nut Squares

I can't rave about these enough. They're based on a traditional Viennese recipe.

1 cup stirred whole-wheat pastry flour
1/4 cup wheat germ
3 tablespoons non-instant nonfat dry milk
1/8 teaspoon salt
1/4 pound butter or safflower margarine, at room
   temperature
1/2 cup packed brown sugar
1 egg, separated
1 teaspoon vanilla extract
2/3 cup chopped walnuts
1/3 cup unsalted soy nuts
1/2 teaspoon ground cinnamon

In an 8 × 8-inch baking pan, combine flour, wheat germ, dry milk and salt. Cream butter or margarine and 1/4 cup brown sugar. Add egg yolk and vanilla, beating well. Add flour mixture and mix until combined. Grease baking pan and, with floured fingers, pat dough into pan. Bake on the lowest rack of a preheated 350°F oven for 10 minutes. Meanwhile, beat egg white with remaining 1/4 cup brown sugar. Stir in nuts and cinnamon. With a small spatula, spread over baked dough to cover completely. Bake for 15 minutes, or until firm. Cool in pan and cut into 1-inch squares while slightly warm.

Makes 32 squares
2 grams protein per square

Fudge-Filled Bars

Milk and cheese complement the wheat germ, flours and oats in this protein-rich and absolutely delicious bar cookie.

Cookie Base and Topping
1 cup butter or safflower margarine, at room
   temperature
1-1/2 cups packed brown sugar
1 egg
1 easpoon vanilla extract
1 cup stirred unbleached all-purpose flour
1 cup stirred whole-wheat flour
1 teaspoon baking soda
1 teaspoon salt
2 cups rolled oats
2/3 cup wheat germ

Filling
One 12-ounce package carob or chocolate chips
One 15-ounce can sweetened condensed milk
2 tablespoons butter or safflower margarine
1/2 teaspoon salt
2/3 cup dry cottage cheese or bakers' (hoop)
   cheese
1 cup chopped nuts or sunflower seeds
1 teaspoon vanilla extract
2 tablespoons unbleached all-purpose flour

To make the cookie base and topping, with an electric mixer or in a food processor beat together butter or margarine and sugar until light and fluffy. Blend in egg and vanilla. Combine flours, baking soda and salt; add to wet ingredients and mix well. Stir in oats and wheat germ. Press half of mixture onto bottom of a greased 9 × 13-inch baking pan. Reserve remaining mixture for topping.

To make the filling, melt together carob or chocolate chips, sweetened condensed milk, butter or margarine and salt in a heavy saucepan over low heat until smooth. Stir in cheese, nuts, vanilla and flour. Spread evenly over cookie base; sprinkle reserved cookie base and topping mixture over chocolate layer; press down slightly. Bake in a preheated 350°F oven for 35 to 40 minutes. Cool in pan and cut into 1 × 1-1/2-inch bars.

Makes 48 bars
2 grams protein per bar

Creamy Cheese Squares

Neufchatel cheese complements the protein in wheat, wheat germ and nuts.

1 cup stirred whole-wheat pastry flour
1/3 cup rolled oats
1/4 cup wheat germ
1/4 teaspoon salt
1-1/2 teaspoons baking powder
1/2 cup chopped walnuts
6 tablespoons butter or safflower margarine, at room temperature
1/2 cup packed brown sugar
One 8-ounce package Neufchatel cheese, at room temperature
2 teaspoons grated lemon rind
1/2 teaspoon vanilla extract
3 tablespoons sugar
1 egg

In an 8 X 8-inch baking pan, combine flour, oats, wheat germ, salt, baking powder and nuts; mix well. Cream butter or margarine and sugar until fluffy. Stir in dry ingredients, mixing until mixture is crumbly. Remove 1 cup of this mixture and set aside; grease baking pan and press remaining crumbly mixture in pan. Bake in a preheated 350°F oven for 12 minutes. Meanwhile, mix cheese, lemon rind, vanilla, sugar and egg until smooth. Spread cheese mixture over layer in pan and sprinkle on reserved crumbly mixture. Bake about 25 minutes, or until center is firm. Cool; cut into 1-inch squares. Store in the refrigerator.
Makes 32 squares
2.1 grams protein per square

Always-Ready Slice-and-Bake Cookies

These nutritious cookies are perfect to keep on hand in the refrigerator or freezer. Wrap in foil to freeze, and cut and bake while still frozen. Bake up a few at a time or enjoy a whole batch.

Sunflower Seed Refrigerator Cookies

1 cup stirred whole-wheat flour or whole-wheat pastry flour
1/2 cup stirred soy flour
1 cup wheat germ
2 cups rolled oats
1/2 teaspoon salt
1 teaspoon baking soda
1/2 pound butter or safflower margarine, at room temperature
1 cup packed brown sugar
1 cup Turbinado or granulated sugar
2 eggs
1 teaspoon vanilla extract
1 cup unsalted sunflower seeds

Combine flours, wheat germ, oats, salt and soda. Cream butter or margarine and sugars. Beat in eggs and vanilla. Add dry ingredients and seeds. Roll dough into several long logs about 2 inches in diameter (if dough is too soft to roll, chill for several hours). Wrap dough logs in plastic wrap and chill for several hours or freeze. To bake, slice about 1/4 inch thick, arrange slightly apart on ungreased baking sheets and bake in a preheated 350°F oven for 10 minutes, or until crisp and dry.
Makes about 9 dozen
14.9 grams protein per dozen

Carob or Chocolate Sunflower Refrigerator Cookies

Another good treat to have on hand to help you avoid junk food.

1-1/4 cups stirred whole-wheat pastry flour
1/4 cup soy flour
1/3 cup non-instant nonfat dry milk
1/2 cup wheat germ
3 tablespoons carob powder or cocoa
1/2 teaspoon baking powder
1/4 teaspoon salt
1/2 cup unsalted sunflower seeds
6 ounces (1-1/2 sticks) butter or safflower
    margarine, at room temperature
1 cup packed brown sugar
1 egg, beaten
1 teaspoon vanilla extract

Mix together flours, dry milk, wheat germ, carob powder or cocoa, baking powder and salt. Grind sunflower seeds to a coarse powder in a blender or food processor (without a blender, either chop seeds fine with a knife, or place seeds in a plastic bag or between 2 sheets of waxed paper and roll into a powder with a rolling pin). Blend seeds, butter or margarine, sugar, egg and vanilla. Add this mixture to the dry ingredients and work them together with your hands until dough is smooth. Form dough into a roll about 2 inches in diameter. Wrap dough and chill for 4 hours or freeze. To bake, cut dough into 1/4-inch-thick slices. Place slightly apart on cookie sheets and bake in a preheated 325°F oven for 15 minutes, or until cookies are crisp. Cool on racks.
Makes about 4 dozen
19 grams protein per dozen

Sugarless Slice-and-Bake Date Cookies

These cookies have a delicious natural sweetness provided by the dates and coconut and contain no other sweetener.

2/3 cup stirred unbleached all-purpose flour
1/2 cup stirred whole-wheat pastry flour
1/2 cup wheat germ
1/2 cup non-instant nonfat dry milk
1/4 teaspoon salt
1 teaspoon baking powder
1/4 pound butter or safflower margarine, at room temperature
2 eggs
1-1/2 teaspoons vanilla extract
1 teaspoon grated orange or lemon rind
1-2/3 cups chopped dates
1 cup unsweetened shredded coconut
1/2 cup chopped walnuts
1/2 cup chopped unsalted sunflower seeds

Combine flours, wheat germ, dry milk, salt and baking powder. Beat butter or margarine, eggs and vanilla until light. Add grated rind. Gradually beat in dry mixture until blended. Mix in dates, coconut, nuts and seeds. Form dough into two 1-1/2-inch rolls and wrap in aluminum foil; freeze until firm enough to slice easily or until ready to bake. To bake, cut rolls into 3/8-inch-thick slices. Place slices on lightly greased cookie sheets and bake in a preheated 350°F oven for 12 minutes, or until golden and firm to the touch. Cool on racks.
Makes about 5 dozen
18.3 grams protein per dozen

Refrigerator Nut Slices

Good snack cookies; they keep and ship well.

1/4 pound butter or safflower margarine, at room temperature
1/2 cup Turbinado or granulated sugar
1 tablespoon molasses
1/8 teaspoon salt
5 tablespoons finely chopped nuts
1 cup stirred whole-wheat pastry flour
1/4 cup soy flour
1/4 cup wheat germ
1/2 teaspoon baking soda

Cream butter or margarine, sugar, molasses and salt until fluffy. Stir in the nuts. Stir together flours, wheat germ and baking soda. Gradually stir into creamed mixture until blended. Roll dough into a 10-inch roll about 1-1/2 inches in diameter. Wrap airtight and chill 1 hour or longer. With a sharp knife cut into 3/16-inch-thick slices. Place 1 inch apart on lightly greased cookie sheets. Bake in a preheated 350°F oven for 8 to 10 minutes, or until light brown and crisp. Remove to racks to cool.
Makes about 4 dozen
8.9 grams protein per dozen

Peanut-Oat Refrigerator Cookies

Peanut butter, rolled oats, wheat germ, whole wheat, milk and nuts add up to a cookie loaded with nutrition.

1 cup stirred whole-wheat pastry flour
1/2 cup rolled oats
1/3 cup wheat germ
1/4 cup non-instant nonfat dry milk
1/2 teaspoon salt
1/4 teaspoon baking soda
1/4 cup chopped peanuts or walnuts
4 tablespoons butter or safflower margarine, at
    room temperature
1/4 cup creamy old-fashioned peanut butter
1/3 cup packed brown sugar
1/2 cup honey
1 egg, beaten
1/2 teaspoon vanilla extract

Combine flour, oats, wheat germ, dry milk, salt, baking soda and nuts. Cream butter or margarine, peanut butter and sugar together. Add honey gradually, beating continuously. Beat in egg and vanilla. Stir in dry ingredients. Shape into a roll about 2 inches in diameter (if dough is too soft to shape, chill for about an hour in the freezer). Chill roll for 4 hours or freeze. Cut into 1/8-inch-thick slices and place slightly apart on ungreased cookie sheets and bake in a preheated 350°F oven for 8 to 10 minutes or until crisp. Remove and cool on racks.
Makes about 3 dozen
24.5 grams protein per dozen

Drop Cookies

Basic Nourishing Cookie Mix

This recipe makes 6 bags of cookie mix, each of which will make about 3-1/2 dozen cookies. The basic mix can be altered according to the following variations. It's nice to have a bag of mix available when someone in the family gets a sudden cookie craving. The cookies are easy for children to make, and the mix makes thoughtful (and nourishing) gifts (be sure you include the Cookie-Mix Cookie recipe, following).

2-1/2 cups each stirred whole-wheat flour and
    stirred unbleached all-purpose flour
3/4 cup soy flour
1-1/2 cups non-instant nonfat dry milk
1-1/2 cups wheat germ
2 cups rolled oats
4-1/2 cups (2 pounds) packed brown sugar
1/4 cup baking powder
1 tablespoon salt
1 tablespoon ground nutmeg
2 tablespoons ground cinnamon
3 cups raisins or chopped dates
1-1/3 cups unsalted sunflower seeds
1 cup chopped walnuts

In a very large mixing bowl or saucepan mix all ingredients thoroughly, making sure sugar is well distributed and there are no lumps. Divide mix into 6 plastic bags or jars.
Makes 6 bags (about 3-1/4 cups mix per bag)

CHOCOLATE CHIP OR COCONUT-CHOCO-LATE CHIP COOKIE MIX Prepare basic cookie mix, reducing nutmeg to 1 teaspoon and cinnamon to 1 tablespoon. Omit raisins and replace them with three 6-ounce packages carob or chocolate chips. For Coconut-Chocolate Chip Cookies, add 2 cups unsweetened flaked or shredded coconut (about 4-1/4 cups mix per bag).

COCONUT COOKIE MIX Prepare basic cookie mix, reducing nutmeg to 1 teaspoon and cinnamon to 1 tablespoon. Omit raisins and replace them with 2 cups unsweetened flaked or shredded coconut.

COCONUT RAISIN COOKIE MIX Prepare basic cookie mix, adding 2 cups unsweetened flaked or shredded coconut (about 4-1/4 cups mix per bag).

Cookie-Mix Cookies

2 eggs
1/2 cup safflower or corn oil
1 teaspoon vanilla extract
1 bag cookie mix, pages 141-42

In a large bowl, beat together eggs, oil and vanilla. Mix in 1 bag of cookie mix. Drop by tablespoons 1-1/2 inches apart onto lightly greased cookie sheets. Bake in a preheated 350°F oven for about 10 minutes or until cookies are lightly browned and firm to the touch. Cookies will become crisp when cooled on racks.
Makes about 3-1/2 dozen
16.8 grams protein per dozen

No-Bake Apple Drops

A chocolate-apple combination that is very appealing.

1/4 pound butter or safflower margarine
2 cups Turbinado, granulated or packed brown
   sugar
2 tablespoons carob powder or cocoa
1 cup grated apple
Pinch salt
2 cups rolled oats
3/4 cup wheat germ
1/3 cup non-instant dry milk
1/2 cup chopped nuts
1/2 cup unsalted sunflower seeds
1 teaspoon vanilla extract

In a large saucepan, melt butter or margarine. Add sugar, carob powder or cocoa, grated apple and salt. Boil 1 minute. Remove from heat and immediately add oats, wheat germ, dry milk, nuts, sunflower seeds and vanilla. Mix well. Drop by heaping teaspoonfuls onto waxed paper. Chill in the refrigerator. Store in the refrigerator or freeze.
Makes 5-1/2 dozen
15.9 grams protein per dozen

Hero Cookies

These are hearty snack cookies, good for kids who like to cook. Be sure to use High-Protein Granola for maximum nutrition.

1-1/2 cups stirred whole-wheat flour
1/2 cup non-instant nonfat dry milk
1-1/2 teaspoons baking soda
1 teaspoon salt
2 teaspoons ground cinnamon
1/2 teaspoon ground nutmeg
2 cups wheat germ
3/4 pound butter or safflower margarine, at room temperature
2-1/2 cups Turbinado, granulated or packed brown sugar
1/2 cup honey
4 eggs
2 teaspoons vanilla extract
3 cups rolled oats
3 cups Homemade High-Protein Granola, page 171
1 cup raisins
One 6-ounce package carob or chocolate chips

Combine flour, dry milk, baking soda, salt, cinnamon, nutmeg and wheat germ. Cream butter or margarine, sugar, honey, eggs and vanilla; beat until smooth. Stir in dry ingredients, oats, granola, raisins and carob or chocolate chips. Drop by teaspoonfuls 1-1/2 inches apart onto greased cookie sheets. Bake in a preheated 350°F oven for 12 to 15 minutes, or until golden and slightly crisp. Remove and cool on racks.
Makes about 8 dozen
28.7 grams protein per dozen

Peanut-Raisin Cookies

This unusual yeast-rising cookie is filled with whole-grain goodness, complementary protein and a great peanut-raisin combination.

1-1/3 cups wheat germ
1/2 cup stirred soy flour
2 tablespoons non-instant nonfat dry milk
1-2/3 cups rolled oats
1 tablespoon (1 envelope) dry yeast
1/2 teaspoon salt
1/4 teaspoon ground cinnamon
3/4 cup chopped unsalted peanuts
1/3 cup safflower or corn oil
2/3 cup honey or molasses
2 eggs
1/2 cup apple or pineapple juice
1 teaspoon vanilla extract
1/2 cup raisins

Mix wheat germ, soy flour, dry milk, oats, yeast, salt, cinnamon and peanuts. In a large bowl, beat together oil and honey or molasses; add eggs and beat again. Then add juice, vanilla and raisins; mix well. Add dry ingredients to liquid mixture and mix well. Let batter rest 20 minutes before baking. Drop by teaspoonfuls about 1-1/2 inches apart onto greased cookie sheets. Bake in a preheated 375°F oven for 10 to 15 minutes, or until golden brown and firm to the touch. Remove and cool on racks.
Makes about 5 dozen
24.8 grams protein per dozen

Orange Coconut Drops

These are nice cookies for company and special occasions. They are crispy and delicate with an orangy flavor.

1/2 pound butter or safflower margarine, at room temperature
1-1/2 cups packed brown sugar
2 eggs
1 tablespoon thawed frozen orange juice concentrate
1 tablespoon grated orange rind
1-1/2 cups stirred whole-wheat pastry flour
1/4 cup soy flour
1/4 cup non-instant nonfat dry milk
1-1/3 cups rolled oats
1-1/4 cups wheat germ
1-1/2 teaspoons baking powder
3/4 teaspoon salt
1/2 cup unsweetened shredded or flaked coconut

Cream together butter or margarine and sugar until light and fluffy. Beat in the eggs, one at a time. Mix in orange juice concentrate and grated rind. Combine the flours, dry milk, oats, wheat germ, baking powder, salt and coconut. Mix wet ingredients into dry. Drop by rounded teaspoonfuls 1-1/2 inches apart onto lightly greased cookie sheets. Bake in a preheated 375°F oven for 9 to 11 minutes, or until firm to the touch. Cool on cookie sheet for 1 minute, then cool on racks.
Makes 3-1/2 dozen
30.6 grams protein per dozen

Glazed Apple Cookies

The glaze on these cookies adds protein. The cookies themselves are filled with complementary protein ingredients as well as the fiber and nutrition of fresh apples.

2/3 cup stirred unbleached all-purpose flour
2/3 cup stirred whole-wheat flour
1/2 cup wheat germ
1/3 cup non-instant nonfat dry milk
1 teaspoon baking soda
1/2 teaspoon salt
1 teaspoon ground cloves
1 teaspoon ground cinnamon
1/2 teaspoon ground nutmeg
1/4 pound butter or safflower margarine, at room temperature
1-1/4 cups packed brown sugar
1/3 cup honey
1 egg
3 tablespoons apple juice or milk
1 cup finely chopped unpeeled apples
1/2 cup unsalted sunflower seeds or chopped unsalted soy nuts
1/2 cup chopped nuts
1 cup chopped dark or light raisins
Vanilla Glaze, following

Mix flours, wheat germ, dry milk, baking soda, salt, cloves, cinnamon and nutmeg. Cream butter or margarine and sugar together until creamy. Beat in honey gradually. Beat in egg and juice or milk, then blend in apples, dry ingredients, seeds, nuts and raisins. Drop by rounded tablespoonfuls 2 inches apart onto greased cookie sheets. Bake in a preheated 400°F oven for 11 to 14 minutes, or until lightly colored and dry to the touch. Remove to racks and while cookies are still hot, spread them evenly with vanilla glaze.

Makes about 3-1/2 dozen
27 grams protein per dozen

VANILLA GLAZE Mix together 1/4 cup non-instant nonfat dry milk and 1/4 cup sifted powdered sugar. Add just enough milk or water to make a glaze.

Applesauce Oatmeal Cookies

These are loaded with all kinds of nutritious ingredients—they make great snacks for kids.

1/2 pound butter or safflower margarine, at
   room temperature
2 cups packed brown sugar
1 egg
One 16-ounce can unsweetened applesauce
1-1/3 cups stirred whole-wheat flour
1/3 cup stirred soy flour
1/2 cup non-instant nonfat dry milk

1 teaspoon baking soda
1/2 teaspoon baking powder
1 teaspoon salt
1-1/2 teaspoons ground cinnamon
1/2 teaspoon ground cloves
1/2 teaspoon ground nutmeg
3/4 cup rolled oats
3/4 cup wheat germ
1 cup raisins
1/2 cup chopped nuts
1/2 cup unsalted sunflower seeds
3/4 cup carob or chocolate chips (optional)

Cream together butter or margarine and sugar until light and fluffy. Add egg, beating thoroughly. Stir in applesauce. Stir together flours, dry milk, baking soda, baking powder, salt, cinnamon, cloves and nutmeg. Stir in oats and wheat germ. Add dry ingredients to creamed mixture. Stir in raisins, nuts, seeds and optional chips. Cover and chill for at least 2 hours. Drop by heaping teaspoonfuls 2 inches apart onto greased cookie sheets. Bake in a preheated 400°F oven for 10 to 12 minutes, or until firm to the touch. Cool on racks.

Makes about 8 dozen
16.6 grams protein per dozen

Seed and Nut Clusters

These crunchy meringue snacks can double as cookies or candies. Pumpkin and sunflower seeds are especially high in protein, vitamins, minerals and fiber.

1 cup unsalted shelled raw pumpkin seeds
1 cup broken walnuts
1/2 cup slivered blanched almonds
1/2 cup unsalted raw sunflower seeds
3 egg whites
1 cup Turbinado or granulated sugar
3/4 cup stirred whole-wheat pastry flour
1/4 teaspoon salt

On a rimmed baking sheet, toast pumpkin seeds, walnuts, almonds and sunflower seeds in a pre-heated 325°F oven for 12 to 15 minutes; cool. Beat egg whites until soft peaks form. Very gradu-ally add 1/2 cup of the sugar, beating to form stiff peaks. Stir together remaining 1/2 cup of sugar, flour and salt. Fold into egg white mixture. Fold in toasted seeds and nuts. Drop by rounded tea-spoonfuls, slightly apart, onto greased cookie sheets. Bake in a preheated 325°F oven for 10 to 12 minutes, or until crisp. Cool 2 minutes before removing from cookie sheets, then cool on racks.
Makes 4 dozen
24.8 grams protein per dozen

Whole-Wheat Nut and Chip Cookies

Nutritious ingredients give chocolate chip cookie lovers something more than just good taste.

1/2 cup stirred whole-wheat flour
1/2 cup wheat germ
2 tablespoons non-instant nonfat dry milk
1/2 teaspoon baking soda
1/4 pound butter or safflower margarine, at room temperature
1/2 cup packed brown sugar
1 egg
1/2 teaspoon vanilla extract
One 6-ounce package chocolate or carob chips
1/2 cup unsalted sunflower seeds
1/2 cup chopped unsalted peanuts

Thoroughly stir together flour, wheat germ, dry milk and baking soda. Cream together butter or margarine and sugar. Blend in egg and vanilla and beat until smooth. Add flour mixture; blend well. Stir in chocolate or carob chips, sunflower seeds and nuts. Drop by teaspoonfuls 2 inches apart on greased cookie sheets. Bake in a pre-heated 375°F oven for 8 to 10 minutes, or until lightly browned and firm to the touch. Remove and cool on racks.
Makes about 3 dozen
24.5 grams protein per dozen

Sunflower Seed Lace Cookies

2/3 cup unsalted raw sunflower seeds
1/4 pound butter or safflower margarine, at
   room temperature
3/4 cup packed brown sugar
1/4 teaspoon salt
1/2 cup rolled oats
1/4 cup wheat germ
1/4 cup soy flour or non-instant nonfat dry milk
1/3 cup finely chopped almonds, pecans or
   walnuts
1 teaspoon vanilla extract
2 teaspoons grated orange rind and
   1/2 teaspoon grated lemon rind, or 1/2
   teaspoon ground cinnamon and 1/4 teaspoon
   ground nutmeg
1 tablespoon milk

In a shallow pan, roast the sunflower seeds in a preheated 350°F oven for 15 minutes; cool. Cream together butter or margarine and sugar until light and fluffy. Stir in salt, oats, wheat germ, soy flour or dry milk, nuts, vanilla, rinds or spices and roasted sunflower seeds. Add milk, blending well. Drop by teaspoonfuls about 2 inches apart onto ungreased cookie sheets. Bake in a preheated 350°F oven for about 8 minutes, or until lightly browned; cookies will be very thin and lacy. Cool 2 to 3 minutes, then loosen edges of cookies with a spatula and cool them about 2 minutes longer until you can remove them. If cookies harden before they can be removed from sheets, reheat in oven for a few minutes to soften. Cool on racks.
Makes 2-1/2 dozen
17.6 grams protein per dozen

Shaped Cookies

Molasses Crisps

You can make nutritious gingerbread men from this recipe.

1/4 cup honey
1/4 cup molasses
1/4 pound butter or safflower margarine, melted
1-1/3 cups stirred whole-wheat pastry flour
1/3 cup stirred soy flour
1/3 cup non-instant nonfat dry milk
1 teaspoon baking soda
1/2 teaspoon salt
1/4 teaspoon ground ginger

In a mixing bowl, combine honey, molasses and melted butter or margarine. Sift together flours, dry milk, soda, salt and ginger; mix with honey mixture. Chill dough several hours in the refrigerator. Divide dough in half. Roll out one half of dough 1/8-inch thick on a lightly floured board or floured waxed paper. Cut with a cookie cutter; repeat with second half of dough. Place on lightly oiled cookie sheets. Bake in a preheated 350°F oven for 12 minutes, or until lightly browned. Remove from pan quickly and cool on racks.
Makes about 5 dozen
8.7 grams protein per dozen

Molasses Ginger Snaps

These wonderful gingery cookies are filled with high-protein soy flour—but only the good flavor is evident.

1/2 cup stirred unbleached all-purpose flour
1/2 cup stirred whole-wheat flour
1 cup stirred soy flour
1 teaspoon baking soda
1/2 teaspoon salt
1-1/2 teaspoons ground ginger
1 teaspoon ground cinnamon
6 ounces (1-1/2 sticks) butter or safflower
    margarine at room temperature
1-1/3 cups Turbinado or granulated sugar
1 egg
1/3 cup light molasses

Stir together flours, baking soda, salt and spices. Cream together butter and 1 cup sugar. Add egg and beat until light and fluffy. Beat in molasses. Stir into dry ingredients. Cover and chill for 1 hour or more. Roll dough into 1-inch balls. Roll in remaining 1/3 cup sugar. Place 2 inches apart on greased cookie sheets. Bake in a preheated 375°F oven for 10 to 12 minutes, or until lightly browned. Remove and cool on racks.
Makes 4 dozen
11.8 grams protein per dozen

Peanut Butter Biggies

Apple and peanut butter combine to form a delightful flavor as well as adding protein and fiber to the other nutritious ingredients.

1-3/4 cups stirred whole-wheat pastry flour
1/4 cup non-instant nonfat dry milk
2/3 cup rolled oats
1/3 cup wheat germ
2 teaspoons baking soda
1/2 teaspoon ground cinnamon
1/2 teaspoon salt
1/2 pound butter or safflower margarine, at
    room temperature
1-1/2 cups packed brown sugar
1 cup chunky old-fashioned peanut butter
2 eggs
1-1/2 cups coarsely chopped apples

Combine flour, dry milk, oats, wheat germ, baking soda, cinnamon and salt. Beat butter or margarine and sugar together until light and fluffy. Add peanut butter and eggs and beat until creamy. Add dry ingredients to peanut butter mixture. Mix well. Stir in apples. Shape dough to form 1-1/2-inch balls. Place 1-1/2 inches apart on ungreased cookie sheets and flatten with the tines of a fork to make a criss-cross pattern. Bake in a preheated 350°F oven for 14 to 16 minutes, or until lightly browned and firm to the touch. Remove and cool on racks.
Makes about 3-1/2 dozen
38.9 grams protein per dozen

Wheat-Germ Peanut Butter Crisps

These are my three-year-old nephew Ryan's favorite cookie. Lucky Ryan—he's getting so much good nutrition in the form of a nice crispy cookie.

1 cup stirred whole-wheat pastry flour
3/4 cup rolled oats
1 cup wheat germ
1/3 cup non-instant nonfat dry milk
1 teaspoon baking soda
1/2 teaspoon salt
6 ounces (1-1/2 sticks) butter or safflower
   margarine, at room temperature
1/2 cup chunky old-fashioned peanut butter
1 cup packed brown sugar
1 egg
1 teaspoon vanilla extract

Combine flour, oats, wheat germ, dry milk, baking soda and salt. Cream butter or margarine, peanut butter and sugar together until light and fluffy. Beat in egg and vanilla. Combine wet and dry ingredients. Shape tablespoonfuls of dough into 3/4-inch balls. Place on ungreased cookie sheets 2 inches apart. Flatten with the bottom of a glass to a 3/8-inch thickness. Bake in a preheated 350°F oven for 8 to 10 minutes, or until crisp. Cool on racks.
Makes 4 dozen
23.6 grams protein per dozen

CANDIES

Candy is a concentrated source of carbohydrates. This is fine for marathon runners or champion swimmers, but most of us don't need the extra pure-energy food, and of course, we all know that it shouldn't replace the nutritious foods we need for a balanced diet.

The candies in this chapter are a source of both nutrients and energy. Instead of the usual raft of imitation colorings, flavorings and chemical stabilizers, they contain wholesome ingredients, without losing the satisfying taste we expect from candy. Most of these candies are so simple that children can make them by themselves. I like to give them as gifts because my friends appreciate knowing I care about their health as well as their palate.

Note: Candies marked with a snowflake symbol may be wrapped in foil and frozen for up to three months. Remember to refrigerate candies made with dry milk.

Plain and Fancy
Peanut Butter Balls

Peanut butter and dry milk are the high-protein base for these and several following candies. Kids like the way they taste, and parents like the nutritional benefits.

1 cup creamy old-fashioned peanut butter
1-1/4 cups honey
1 cup unsweetened shredded or flaked coconut
   or 1 cup chopped dates, or 1/2 cup each
   (optional)
1-1/4 cups non-instant nonfat dry milk
Sesame seeds, chopped unsalted peanuts,
   wheat germ or unsweetened shredded or
   flaked coconut (optional)

In a saucepan over very low heat, stir peanut butter and honey together until liquified. Stir in optional coconut and/or dates, then add dry milk. Roll into logs or balls and then into optional sesame seeds, peanuts, wheat germ or coconut. Chill well. Slice logs about 3/8 inch thick. Place between sheets of waxed paper, cover and store in the refrigerator.
Makes about 7-1/2 dozen
15.1 grams protein per dozen

Peanut Butter Granola Candies

3 cups Homemade High-Protein Granola,
   page 171
1 cup non-instant nonfat dry milk
1/2 cup chopped unsalted peanuts
1/2 cup chopped unsalted soy nuts
1/2 cup creamy old-fashioned peanut butter
3/4 cup honey
2 eggs
4 tablespoons butter or safflower margarine

In a large bowl, mix granola, dry milk, peanuts and soy nuts. In a saucepan over low heat, mix peanut butter and honey until liquified. Beat in eggs one at a time until mixture boils and forms a ball. Remove from heat and stir in butter. Pour over dry mixture and mix thoroughly. Pat into a greased 9 X 9-inch pan. Chill well and cut into 1-inch squares. Place between sheets of waxed paper and cover; store in the refrigerator.
Makes about 6-1/2 dozen
26.4 grams protein per dozen

GRANOLA CAROB OR CHOCOLATE LAYERS
Prepare Peanut Butter Granola Candies and pat into pan. Melt 1/2 cup carob or chocolate chips in a double boiler over boiling water and spread over candy mixture. Chill well and cut into 1-inch squares. Place between sheets of waxed paper and cover; store in the refrigerator.

Carob or Chocolate Peanut Butter Fudge

1-1/3 cups non-instant nonfat dry milk
1/2 cup carob powder, or 6 tablespoons cocoa
1 cup creamy old-fashioned peanut butter
1-1/4 cups honey
1 teaspoon vanilla extract

Combine dry milk and carob powder or cocoa in a small bowl. In a saucepan over very low heat, stir the peanut butter and honey together until liquified. Stir in vanilla and dry milk mixture. Lightly grease an 11 X 13-inch baking pan, then fit the bottom and sides with waxed paper. Pour fudge mixture into pan, cover with aluminum foil and chill. Cut into 1-inch squares. Place between sheets of waxed paper, cover and store in the refrigerator.
Makes about 11 dozen
10.5 grams protein per dozen

COCONUT-COATED PEANUT BUTTER FUDGE
Prepare Carob or Chocolate Peanut Butter Fudge. Before pouring fudge into dish, sprinkle waxed paper with 2/3 cup unsweetened shredded or flaked coconut. Pour in fudge and top with another 2/3 cup coconut.

PEANUT BUTTER NUT FUDGE Follow recipe for Carob or Chocolate Peanut Butter Fudge, reducing dry milk to 1 cup. Stir in 1 cup chopped nuts (or a mixture of half nuts and half unsalted soy nuts) before stirring in milk mixture.
14 grams protein per dozen

Sesame Balls or Squares

3/4 cup creamy old-fashioned peanut butter
1 cup honey
1/2 teaspoon vanilla extract
2 teaspoons lemon juice
1-1/2 cups unhulled sesame seeds
1-1/4 cups non-instant nonfat dry milk

In a saucepan over very low heat, stir peanut butter and honey together until liquified. Stir in vanilla, lemon juice, 1 cup sesame seeds and dry milk. Roll into 1-inch balls, then roll balls in remaining 1/2 cup sesame seeds. Or line a 9 X 13-inch baking pan with waxed paper and sprinkle with 1/4 cup sesame seeds, then carefully pour in candy mixture and sprinkle with remaining seeds. Press down so that seeds will stick to candy. Chill thoroughly and cut into 1-inch squares. Place between sheets of waxed paper, cover and store in the refrigerator.
Makes about 6 dozen
22.3 grams protein per dozen

Sesame Seed Candy

1-1/4 cups unhulled sesame seeds
3/4 cup finely chopped unsalted soy nuts
1/3 cup wheat germ
1/2 cup packed brown sugar
1/2 cup honey
1/4 teaspoon salt
3/4 teaspoon ground ginger, cinnamon or
   cardamom

Spread sesame seeds (and soy nuts, if not roasted) in a thin layer on a rimmed baking sheet. Place in a preheated 350°F oven for about 15 minutes, or until light golden, shaking pan occasionally. Thoroughly combine seeds, soy nuts and wheat germ. In a 10- to 12-inch frying pan, combine honey, brown sugar, salt and spice. Bring mixture to a boil over medium heat, stirring constantly; cook for 2 minutes. Remove pan from heat and immediately stir in seed mixture; mix thoroughly. Turn into a greased 9 × 13-inch baking pan. With a large greased spoon, press candy firmly and evenly over bottom of pan. Cool at room temperature for about 15 minutes, then lift out with a wide spatula. Use a large knife to cut candy into 1 × 2-inch rectangles. Let dry on racks until very firm, about 2 hours. With plastic wrap, wrap pieces individually or wrap several pieces together in a single layer. Store at room temperature.
Makes about 4 dozen
17.3 grams protein per dozen

ORANGE SESAME HONEY CANDY Use 2 tablespoons grated orange rind in place of ginger, cinnamon or cardamom in preceding recipe.

Fruit and Seed Bars

Crunchy, nutty and honey flavored.

1/2 cup unhulled sesame seeds
2/3 cup chopped nuts
3/4 cup chopped unsalted soy nuts
1/4 cup wheat germ
1/2 cup unsweetened shredded coconut
1/2 cup honey
1/2 cup packed brown sugar
1/4 teaspoon salt
1/2 cup finely chopped dried mixed fruit or dates

Thoroughly combine seeds, nuts, wheat germ and coconut. In a 10- to 12-inch frying pan, combine honey, brown sugar, salt and chopped dried fruit. Bring mixture to a boil over medium heat, stirring constantly; cook for 2 minutes. Remove pan from heat and immediately stir in seed and nut mixture, mixing thoroughly. Turn into a well-greased 9 × 13-inch baking pan. With a large greased spoon, press candy firmly and evenly over pan bottom. Cool at room temperature for 30 minutes, then lift out with a wide spatula. Use a large knife to cut candy into 1-1/2 × 3-inch rectangles. Let dry on racks for about 3 hours, or until no longer sticky. Wrap pieces individually in plastic wrap or wrap several pieces together in a single layer; store at room temperature.
Makes 24 bars
2.5 grams protein per bar

LEMONY FRUIT-SEED BARS Add 1 tablespoon grated lemon peel to nut mixture in preceding recipe.

Chewy Granola Candies

These "candy" nibbles are more nutritious than most commercial granolas.

3/4 cup rolled oats
1/2 cup wheat germ
3 tablespoons non-instant nonfat dry milk
1/4 cup unsweetened shredded coconut
1/4 cup chopped dried apricots
1/4 cup chopped pitted prunes or dates
1/2 cup coarsely chopped nuts
1/2 cup chopped unsalted soy nuts
1/2 cup unsalted sunflower seeds
1/4 cup unhulled sesame seeds
2 tablespoons currants or raisins
2 tablespoons safflower or corn oil
3 tablespoons packed brown sugar
3 tablespoons honey
1/2 teaspoon vanilla extract

In a large bowl, blend oats, wheat germ, dry milk, coconut, apricots, prunes or dates, nuts, seeds and currants or raisins thoroughly. In a small pan cook oil, sugar and honey, stirring, until bubbly; stir in vanilla. Pour over granola mixture and stir to coat evenly. Spread mixture in a single layer on a buttered rimmed baking sheet. Bake in a pre-heated 325°F oven for 20 minutes, stirring mixture several times. Remove from oven. With a wide spatula, lift mixture out of pan onto a piece of buttered waxed paper, shaping mixture into a rough rectangle about 1/2 inch thick. Let cool, then break into large pieces; package airtight in jars or cans.
Makes about 3-1/2 cups
86.4 grams protein

Fruityrolls

1 cup dried apricots
1/2 cup unsalted soy nuts
1-1/2 cups unsweetened shredded coconut
3 tablespoons lemon juice
1/4 cup honey
1/2 cup non-instant nonfat dry milk
Ground nuts

Grind apricots, soy nuts and coconut together in a food grinder or food processor. Add lemon juice, honey and dry milk and mix well. Shape into 1-inch balls and roll in ground nuts. Place between sheets of waxed paper, cover and store in the refrigerator.
Makes about 5 dozen
8.4 grams protein per dozen

Delicious Orange Fondant

It's hard to believe this luscious orange candy is filled with protein-rich ingredients as well as vitamin C. No one seems to object to its being good for you.

1/2 cup sweetened condensed milk
5 tablespoons thawed frozen orange juice concentrate
3/4 teaspoon vanilla extract
2 tablespoons grated orange rind (optional)
1-1/2 cups non-instant, nonfat dry milk
1-3/4 cups sifted powdered sugar

In a mixing bowl, combine condensed milk, orange juice and vanilla. Mix well. Mix in orange rind. Combine dry milk and powdered sugar and mix into orange mixture about 1/3 cup at a time. Mixture will be stiff and hard to stir toward the end. If mixture becomes too stiff to stir, turn it out on waxed paper and knead in remaining dry milk and sugar. Roll into 1-inch balls, place on a waxed paper-covered plate, cover with plastic wrap and chill. Place between sheets of waxed paper, cover and store in the refrigerator.
Makes about 6 dozen
10.6 grams protein per dozen

ORANGE FONDANT VARIATIONS Follow above recipe, mixing 1 cup finely chopped walnuts or almonds, unsweetened flaked coconut, or snipped dried apricots with dry milk and powdered sugar.

Carob Brittle

This is chocolaty and crunchy. The protein count is for the entire amount.

1-1/4 cups honey
1/4 cup carob powder
1 tablespoon water
4 tablespoons butter or safflower margarine
2 teaspoons baking powder
1 teaspoon vanilla extract
2/3 cup coarsely chopped almonds

Mix honey, carob powder, water and butter or margarine in a heavy saucepan. Bring to a boil, stirring constantly, and continue cooking until syrup reaches 280°F on a candy thermometer. When dropped into cold water, a drop of the syrup will separate into hard and brittle threads. Remove syrup from heat and quickly stir in baking powder, vanilla and nuts. Pour mixture into a lightly greased jelly roll pan and spread thinly. When cool, break into pieces. Store airtight in plastic wrap or jars.
Makes about 6 cups
37.6 grams protein

Delicious Chocolate or Carob Fondant

If kids (or adults) are going to eat candy, it may as well offer them something besides quick energy. These candies contain lots of nutrients from the dry milk as well as from the nuts.

Three 1-ounce squares semisweet chocolate, or
   1/2 cup chocolate or carob chips
3/4 cup sweetened condensed milk
1 tablespoon vanilla extract
1-1/2 cups non-instant nonfat dry milk
1-1/2 cups sifted powdered sugar

In a large saucepan, melt chocolate or carob over hot water. Stir in condensed milk and vanilla. Combine dry milk and sugar and stir about 1/3 cup at a time into chocolate or carob mixture. If mixture becomes too difficult to stir toward the end, turn it out onto waxed paper and knead in the last of the dry ingredients. Form into 2-inch balls and chill. Or form logs about 1-1/2 inches in diameter, place on a waxed paper-covered plate and cover with plastic wrap; chill, then slice logs into bite-sized pieces. Place between sheets of waxed paper, cover and store in the refrigerator.
Makes about 5-1/2 dozen
11.6 grams protein per dozen

DELICIOUS CHOCOLATE-COCONUT BALLS Follow the recipe for Delicious Chocolate or Carob Fondant, mixing 2/3 cup unsweetened flaked coconut into dry milk. Form into balls and roll balls in additional flaked coconut before chilling.

DELICIOUS CHOCOLATE OR CAROB-NUT FONDANT Follow the recipe for Chocolate or Carob Fondant, mixing 1 cup finely chopped walnuts, almonds, peanuts or a mixture of these into dry milk and sugar. Or, roll logs or balls while still warm into 1 cup chopped unsalted roasted peanuts or sunflower seeds.
18.5 grams protein per dozen

Nut Creams

1/2 cup sweetened condensed milk
1/2 cup packed brown sugar
2 tablespoons butter or safflower margarine
1 teaspoon vanilla extract
About 2/3 to 3/4 cup non-instant nonfat dry milk
About 48 walnut or almond halves

In the top of a double boiler, mix condensed milk, sugar and butter or margarine. Heat over boiling water for about 10 minutes, or until sugar is melted. Remove from heat, cool thoroughly, and stir in vanilla and enough dry milk to make the mixture thick but not stiff (candy will harden when chilled). Drop teaspoonfuls onto greased aluminum foil or greased cookie sheets. Put a walnut or almond half on top of each candy. Chill. Place between sheets of waxed paper, cover and store in the refrigerator.
Makes about 4 dozen
15.9 grams protein per dozen

High-Protein Frozen Desserts

What is America's favorite dessert? No, it's not apple pie but ice cream! Kids appear to thrive on it and supermarkets devote more freezer space to ice cream than to frozen vegetables. But despite it's popularity, this delicious American tradition, like apple pie, is nutritionally in the same category as empty-calorie junk food.

We've all heard by now about the chemical additives, fillers and colorings that are put into ice cream but are not required by law to appear on the label, for ice cream is a "standard identity food" and escapes strict labeling laws. So you are never quite sure what you're eating when you treat yourself to most commercial ice creams. Even the terms "pure" and "natural" in ice cream simply mean it contains only cream, natural flavorings and sugar. This product may be safer to eat, but it does not solve the problem of good nutrition.

Most ice creams are very high in sugar and butterfat (or some other kind of fat, depending on the purity of the product). Frozen yogurts may be somewhat better because of their low butterfat content, but there are many ways their nutritional value could be improved.

It was inevitable that I would have to find some nutritious substitutes for traditional ice cream for this book. I started to adapt ice cream recipes by adding nonfat dry milk to the ice cream mixture in place of some of the cream, thereby reducing the butterfat level. Many of the recipes developed for this book also contain eggs or egg whites for added nutrition. Some contain cottage cheese or yogurt, and some are made without any cream at all.

In addition to the extra protein, many of the frozen desserts in this chapter contain fruit or fruit juice concentrates, nuts or seeds. And for extra nutrition, wheat germ or high-protein granola may be sprinkled on as a topping. For a vegetable frozen dessert, see Pumpkin Ice Cream in the "Delicious Vegetable Desserts" section.

I hope you'll have fun with these recipes. Before you begin, I'd like to share what I've learned about making frozen desserts successfully. To achieve a smooth texture in a frozen dessert, you need to inhibit the formation of large ice crystals, especially when making still-frozen desserts (those frozen in the refrigerator rather than in an ice cream machine). The high butterfat content of regular ice cream (and the unknown chemicals in some commercial ice creams) prevents the clumping of ice crystals, but when the butterfat content is lowered, additions such as gelatin, eggs, starch and air bubbles are necessary to prevent an "icy" product. All of the following points are important when preparing the frozen desserts in this chapter:

● Be sure dry milk is absolutely fresh or your ice cream dessert will taste chalky. Always store dry milk in the refrigerator in an airtight container.

● Always be sure gelatin is completely dissolved by cooking the gelatin mixture over low heat or over boiling water until the mixture reaches the boiling point and no granules of gelatin are visible. Stir constantly but never allow the mixture to boil.

● Be sure when beating evaporated milk that the bowl, beaters and milk are *icy* cold. Chill them in the freezer.

● Be sure starch and eggs are thoroughly cooked before proceeding further with the recipe; this mixture should be as thick as pudding.

● Be sure any ice cream dessert mixture is thoroughly chilled before freezing it, with or without an ice cream maker.

● Fold any whipped milk, whipped cream or beaten egg whites carefully into the ice cream mixture to retain a maximum amount of air bubbles.

● Fold in nuts, seeds, fruits or other solid ingredients after the ice cream is partially frozen. This will insure more even distribution of the solid pieces so they will not sink to the bottom of the container.

● Beat as much air as possible into still-frozen desserts. An electric mixer with a wire whip beater is ideal for this, though a regular electric mixer may be used successfully.

● The desserts that may be frozen in an ice cream maker are the correct proportions for a 1-quart ice cream maker. You may want to double or even triple the recipes to accommodate larger ice cream makers.

● These desserts tend to be slightly harder than ordinary ice cream when taken right out of the freezer, so for maximum enjoyment, allow each serving of ice cream dessert to stand at room temperature for several minutes before serving it.

High-Protein Vanilla Ice Cream No. 1

6 tablespoons Turbinado or granulated sugar or warm honey
3/4 cup non-instant nonfat dry milk
1 tablespoon (1 envelope) unflavored gelatin
1-1/2 cups whole or low-fat milk
3/4 cup whipping cream
1 teaspoon vanilla extract
2 egg whites

Combine sugar, dry milk and gelatin; mix thoroughly (if using honey, see below). Place liquid milk in a bowl and sprinkle dry milk mixture over gradually while beating with a whisk. Or place liquid milk in a blender, cover and turn on blender, uncover and add dry mixture; do not allow mixmixture to foam. Pour this mixture into a double boiler and heat it over hot water, stirring constantly, until sugar and gelatin are dissolved, about 3 minutes. If using honey, blend honey and liquid milk in a bowl, then sprinkle dry milk over gradually while beating with a whisk. Or place honey and liquid milk in a blender, cover and turn on blender, uncover and add dry milk; do not allow mixture to foam. Place this mixture in the top of a double boiler, sprinkle gelatin over and allow it to soften for about 5 minutes. Cook over boiling water, stirring constantly, until gelatin is dissolved, about 3 minutes.

For machine-frozen ice cream, add cream and vanilla to cooked mixture and chill thoroughly, about 40 minutes. Add egg whites and beat with a whisk until well combined. Place in an ice cream freezer and freeze according to manufacturer's instructions. For still-frozen ice cream, place cooked mixture in a medium-sized mixing bowl, add cream and vanilla and freeze until firm, about 4 hours. Remove from freezer, cut into chunks, add egg whites and beat at high speed with an electric mixer until smooth and fluffy, about 5 minutes (stop beating before ice cream is completely thawed). Place in a 1-quart or 2 pint-sized containers, cover and freeze until firm, about 4 hours.

Makes about 1 quart or 4 cups
13.1 grams protein per cup

High-Protein Vanilla Ice Cream No. 2

A still-frozen ice cream.

1/3 cup Turbinado or granulated sugar or honey
2 tablespoons unbleached all-purpose flour
1/2 cup non-instant nonfat dry milk
1 cup evaporated milk
1 teaspoon vanilla extract
1/2 cup whipping cream

In a small saucepan, blend sugar, flour and 1/4 cup dry milk. Stir in 1/2 cup evaporated milk. (If using honey, blend flour and 1/4 cup dry milk well. Blend honey and 1/2 cup evaporated milk thoroughly and add to flour mixture.) Cook this mixture over medium heat, stirring constantly, until mixture boils for 1 minute and becomes as thick as pudding. If any lumps appear, beat mixture with a wire whisk. Stir in vanilla. Place in a mixing bowl and chill in the freezer for about 40 minutes.

Meanwhile, place remaining 1/2 cup evaporated milk in a bowl and sprinkle remaining 1/4 cup dry milk over gradually while beating with a whisk. Or place evaporated milk in a blender, cover and turn on blender, uncover and add dry milk, not allowing mixture to foam; pour into a bowl. Place this mixture in a mixing bowl and chill in the freezer, along with your electric mixer beaters, until ice crystals begin to form around the edge of the milk, about 35 minutes.

Beat chilled evaporated milk mixture with chilled beaters until very stiff. Beat chilled cooked mixture until it is fluffy. Whip cream until soft peaks form. Beat about one third of the whipped milk into the whipped cooked mixture, then fold in remaining whipped milk and whipped cream. Pour into a 1-quart or 2 pint-sized containers and freeze until firm, about 4 hours.

Makes about 1 quart or 4 cups
9.5 grams protein per cup

High-Protein Vanilla Ice Milk

Ice milk is not as creamy as ice cream—but it's lower in fat and higher in protein.

1/2 cup non-instant nonfat dry milk
1/3 cup Turbinado or granulated sugar or honey
2 tablespoons unbleached all-purpose flour
1/2 cup whole or low-fat milk
1 cup evaporated milk
2 tablespoons whipping cream
1 teaspoon vanilla extract

In a small saucepan, combine 1/4 cup dry milk, sugar and flour; mix well. Mix in whole or low-fat milk and 1/4 cup evaporated milk. (If using honey, mix it thoroughly with milk and evaporated milk, then add to flour mixture.) Cook over medium heat, stirring constantly, until mixture boils for 1 minute and becomes as thick as pudding. Remove from heat and stir in cream and vanilla.

Place remaining 3/4 cup evaporated milk in a bowl and sprinkle remaining 1/4 cup dry milk over gradually while beating with a whisk. Or place evaporated milk in a blender, cover and turn on blender, uncover and sprinkle in dry milk, not allowing mixture to foam.

For machine-frozen ice cream, combine cooked mixture and evaporated milk mixture and chill thoroughly in the freezer, about 40 minutes. Place in an ice cream machine and freeze according to manufacturer's instructions. For still-frozen ice cream, place cooked mixture and evaporated milk mixture in separate mixing bowls, place them in the freezer along with your electric mixer beaters, and chill until ice crystals begin to form around the edge of milk, about 35 minutes. Beat chilled evaporated milk mixture until it is very stiff. Beat chilled cooked mixture until fluffy. Mix about one third of the whipped milk mixture into whipped cooked mixture, then fold in remaining whipped milk mixture. Pour into a 1-quart container or 2 pint-sized containers and freeze until firm, about 4 hours.
Makes 1 quart or 4 cups
14 grams protein per cup

High-Protein
French Custard Ice Milk

A still-frozen ice milk. This recipe contains three eggs, the equivalent of five cups of milk, and only one tablespoon of sugar or honey per serving. So you can see that this ice milk is truly good food.

1-1/3 cups whole or low-fat milk
1 egg
2 eggs, separated
1/2 cup Turbinado or granulated sugar or warm honey
1/2 cup non-instant nonfat dry milk mixed with 1 tablespoon unbleached all-purpose flour
1 teaspoon vanilla extract
2/3 cup evaporated milk

In a mixing bowl, combine milk, egg, egg yolks and 1/4 cup sugar or honey. Sprinkle dry milk and flour over while beating with a whisk. Or place milk, egg, egg yolks and 1/4 cup sugar or honey in a blender. Cover and turn on blender, then uncover and sprinkle in dry milk and flour, not allowing mixture to foam. Place this mixture in a small saucepan and cook over low heat, stirring constantly for 6 to 8 minutes or until mixture is as thick as pudding. Remove from heat and stir in vanilla. Place in a mixing bowl and chill thoroughly in the freezer, about 40 minutes.

Meanwhile, place evaporated milk in a mixing bowl and chill in the freezer along with your electric mixer beaters until ice crystals begin to form around edge of milk, about 35 minutes. With chilled beaters, whip chilled evaporated milk until very stiff. Beat egg whites until soft peaks form, then add remaining 1/4 cup sugar or warm honey a teaspoon at a time while continuing to beat whites into stiff peaks. Fold half of the egg whites into chilled cooked mixture; fold in remaining whites and then whipped evaporated milk. Place in a 1-1/2-quart or 3 pint-sized containers, cover and freeze until firm, about 4 hours.
Makes about 1-1/4 quarts or 5 cups
12.2 grams protein per cup

Ice Cream or Ice Milk Variations

HIGH-PROTEIN CHOCOLATE OR DARK CHOCOLATE ICE CREAM OR ICE MILK Follow directions for High-Protein Vanilla Ice Cream No. 1 or 2, High-Protein Vanilla Ice Milk or High-Protein French Custard Ice Milk. Add 1 ounce (1 square) finely grated semisweet or unsweetened chocolate to the dry milk. Increase honey or sugar to 1/2 cup. Decrease vanilla to 1/2 teaspoon. If desired, fold in 1/3 to 1/2 cup chopped almonds after ice cream or ice milk is partially frozen.

HIGH-PROTEIN CAROB OR COCOA ICE CREAM OR ICE MILK Follow directions for High-Protein Vanilla Ice Cream No. 1 or 2, High-Protein Vanilla Ice Milk or High-Protein French Custard Ice Milk, adding 2 tablespoons carob powder or 4 teaspoons cocoa to dry milk powder. Use 1 teaspoon vanilla and increase sugar or honey to 1/2 cup. If desired, add 1/2 cup finely chopped walnuts or almonds after ice cream or ice milk is partially frozen.

HIGH-PROTEIN CAROB OR CHOCOLATE CHIP ICE CREAM OR ICE MILK Follow directions for High-Protein Vanilla Ice Cream No. 1 or 2, High-Protein Vanilla Ice Milk or High-Protein French Custard Ice Milk. Chop 1/2 cup carob or chocolate chips in a blender or food processor and add to ice cream or ice milk after it is partially frozen.

HIGH-PROTEIN MINT CHIP ICE CREAM OR ICE MILK Follow the directions for High-Protein Vanilla Ice Cream No. 1 or 2, High-Protein Vanilla Ice Milk or High-Protein French Custard Ice Milk, using only 3/4 teaspoon vanilla extract and adding 3/4 teaspoon mint extract. Chop 1/2 cup carob or chocolate chips in a blender or food processor and fold into ice cream or ice milk after it is partially frozen.

HIGH-PROTEIN COFFEE ICE CREAM OR ICE MILK Follow the directions for High-Protein Vanilla Ice Cream No. 1 or 2, High-Protein Vanilla Ice Milk or High-Protein French Custard Ice Milk, adding 2 tablespoons instant decaffeinated coffee powder to dry milk. Use 1/2 teaspoon vanilla.

HIGH-PROTEIN PISTACHIO ICE CREAM OR ICE MILK Follow directions for High-Protein Vanilla Ice Cream No. 1 or 2 or High-Protein Vanilla Ice Milk, replacing 1 teaspoon vanilla extract with 1/4 teaspoon vanilla and 1/4 teaspoon almond extract. Fold in 1/2 cup shelled pistachio nuts after ice cream or ice milk is partially frozen.

HONEY SESAME OR SESAME-SUNFLOWER SEED FROZEN CUSTARD Follow directions for High-Protein French Custard Ice Milk using honey. Fold in 1/2 cup unhulled sesame seeds or 1/4 cup unhulled sesame seeds and 1/4 cup unsalted sunflower seeds after ice milk is partially frozen.

HIGH-PROTEIN BLACK WALNUT ICE CREAM OR ICE MILK Follow the directions for High-Protein Vanilla Ice Cream No. 1 or 2 or High-Protein Vanilla Ice Milk. Fold in 1/2 cup chopped black walnuts after ice cream or ice milk is partially frozen.

DATE OR DATE-NUT ICE CREAM OR ICE MILK Follow the directions for High-Protein Vanilla Ice Cream No. 1 or 2 or High-Protein Vanilla Ice Milk, reducing sugar or honey to 1/4 cup. Fold in 2/3 cup finely chopped dates after ice cream or ice milk is partially frozen. If desired, add 1/3 to 1/2 cup chopped walnuts or unsalted sunflower seeds along with the dates.

High-Protein Mocha Ice Cream

3 tablespoons unbleached all-purpose flour
3/4 cup non-instant nonfat dry milk
1 tablespoon carob powder or cocoa
2 teaspoons instant decaffeinated coffee powder
6 tablespoons Turbinado or granulated sugar or honey
1-1/2 cups whole or low-fat milk
3/4 cup whipping cream
1 teaspoon vanilla extract
2 egg whites

In a saucepan, combine flour, dry milk, carob powder or cocoa and coffee powder. For still-frozen ice cream, add 6 tablespoons sugar, for machine-frozen add only 2 tablespoons. With a wire whisk, blend in milk until mixture is smooth. (If using honey, blend honey and milk together before mixing with dry ingredients, using 6 tablespoons honey for still-frozen ice cream and 2 tablespoons for machine-frozen.) Cook milk mixture over medium heat, stirring constantly, until mixture boils for 1 minute and becomes as thick as pudding. Remove from heat and cool slightly. Stir in cream and vanilla.

To still-freeze, place this mixture in a mixing bowl and freeze until it is almost solid, about 3 hours. Remove from freezer and cut into chunks. Add egg whites and beat until mixture is fluffy, about 4 to 5 minutes (mixture should not be completely thawed but you should beat in as much air as possible). Pour into a 1-quart container or 2 pint-sized containers and freeze until firm, about 4 hours. To freeze in a machine, place cooked mixture in the freezer and chill thoroughly, about 40 minutes. Beat egg whites until fluffy; add 4 tablespoons sugar or honey a teaspoonful at a time while beating to stiff peaks. Fold egg whites into the chilled mixture. Place in an ice cream machine and freeze according to manufacturer's instructions.

Makes about 1 quart or 4 cups
12.1 grams protein per cup

High-Protein Peach Ice Cream

2 or 3 peaches, peeled and sliced, or 2-1/2 cups
  frozen or canned sliced peaches
2 tablespoons lemon juice
1/8 teaspoon salt
2/3 cup non-instant nonfat dry milk
1/2 cup Turbinado or granulated sugar or warm
  honey
1-1/2 tablespoons unbleached all-purpose flour
3/4 cup whole or low-fat milk
2 eggs, separated
1/2 cup whipping cream

Puree 1-3/4 cups peaches in a blender or food processor to make 1 cup puree. Coarsely chop remaining peaches and reserve. Add lemon juice and salt to puree. With the motor running, sprinkle in dry milk, blending just enough to mix; set aside. In a saucepan, combine 1/4 cup sugar and the flour. With a wire whisk, blend in liquid milk until mixture is smooth. (If using honey, blend 1/4 cup of it with the milk before mixing in flour.) Cook milk mixture over medium heat, stirring constantly, until mixture boils for 1 minute and becomes as thick as pudding. Add a small amount of this mixture to egg yolks, then add egg yolks to mixture in pan and cook and stir over low heat 1 minute more. Blend into peach mixture and chill thoroughly in the freezer, about 40 minutes.

To freeze in a machine, blend unwhipped cream into chilled peach mixture. Beat egg whites until soft peaks form. Add remaining 1/4 cup sugar or warm honey 1 tablespoon at a time, beating until stiff peaks form. Fold egg whites into peach mixture, place in an ice cream freezer and freeze according to manufacturer's instructions. After ice cream is partially frozen, add chopped peaches and finish the freezing process. To still-freeze, whip cream. Beat egg whites as directed above, adding sugar, then fold, along with whipped cream, into chilled peach mixture. Freeze in a covered 1-quart container or 2 pint-sized containers until partially frozen. Fold in chopped peaches and freeze until firm.

Makes about 1 quart or 4 cups
8.8 grams protein per cup

High-Protein
Strawberry Ice Cream

1 tablespoon (1 envelope) unflavored gelatin
3/4 cup whole or low-fat milk
1/2 cup Turbinado or granulated sugar or honey
2 cups fresh or unsweetened frozen strawberries
1/2 cup whipping cream
3/4 cup non-instant nonfat dry milk
2 egg whites

In a saucepan, sprinkle gelatin over milk; allow gelatin to soften for about 5 minutes. For still-frozen ice cream, add 1/2 cup sugar or honey to this mixture; for machine-frozen add only 6 table-spoons. Cook this mixture over low heat, stirring constantly until gelatin is dissolved, about 3 minutes. Puree berries in a blender or food processor and measure; you should have 1 cup puree. Add cream and sprinkle in dry milk while the blender is running; blend only until combined. Blend in gelatin-milk mixture.

For still-frozen ice cream, freeze this mixture in a mixing bowl until almost solid, about 3 hours. When frozen, cut into chunks, add egg whites and beat until fluffy but not completely thawed. Pour into a 1-quart container or 2 pint-sized containers and freeze until firm, about 4 hours. For machine-frozen ice cream, do not freeze ice cream mixture but chill thoroughly in the freezer, about 40 minutes. Beat egg whites until soft peaks form, then gradually add 2 tablespoons sugar while beating egg whites into stiff peaks. Fold in chilled mixture, place in an ice cream

freezer and freeze according to manufacturer's instructions.
Makes about 1 quart or 4 cups
11.3 grams protein per cup

Easy High-Protein Berry Freeze

Use your favorite berries in this delicious low-fat treat.

2/3 cup evaporated milk
About 3 cups fresh or frozen unsweetened
    strawberries, boysenberries, raspberries or
    blackberries
2/3 cup warm honey or Turbinado or granulated
    sugar
1 cup non-instant nonfat dry milk
1 tablespoon lemon juice

Puree berries in a blender or food processor and measure them—you should have 2 cups of puree. Add honey or sugar and sprinkle in dry milk gradually while the blender or food processor is running; chill thoroughly in the freezer, about 40 minutes. Meanwhile, chill evaporated milk in a mixing bowl in the freezer, along with your electric mixer beaters, until ice crystals begin to form around the edge of the milk, about 35 minutes.

With chilled beaters, whip chilled evaporated milk until fluffy. Add lemon juice and continue beating until very stiff. Fold one third of the whipped milk into chilled berry mixture, then fold in remaining whipped milk. Freeze in a 1-quart or 2 pint-sized containers until firm, about 4 hours,

or freeze in an ice cream machine according to the manufacturer's instructions.
Makes 1 quart or 4 cups
11 grams protein per cup

TROPICAL FRUIT FREEZE Follow recipe for Easy High-Protein Berry Freeze, substituting 1 cup mashed bananas (about 2 medium) and 3/4 cup orange juice for the berries. Reduce honey or sugar to 1/3 to 1/2 cup. Use 4 tablespoons lemon juice.

Berry Cottage-Cheese Freeze

Cottage cheese and nonfat dry milk are the protein ingredients in this delicious low-fat still-frozen dessert.

1/4 cup thawed frozen apple juice concentrate
4 teaspoons unflavored gelatin
About 1-1/2 cups fresh or frozen unsweetened strawberries, boysenberries, raspberries or blackberries
6 tablespoons Turbinado or granulated sugar or warm honey
2/3 cup cottage cheese
1/4 cup whipping cream
3/4 teaspoon vanilla extract
2/3 cup water
2/3 cup non-instant nonfat dry milk
1 tablespoon lemon juice

Place apple juice concentrate in a small saucepan, sprinkle gelatin over and allow it to stand 5 minutes. Warm over low heat, stirring constantly, until gelatin is dissolved, about 3 minutes. Puree fruit and measure it—you should have 3/4 cup puree. Combine sugar or honey, cottage cheese, whipping cream and vanilla in a blender or food processor and blend until smooth (or press cottage cheese through a sieve, then mix thoroughly with sugar or honey, whipping cream and vanilla). Add gelatin-juice mixture and berry puree and blend until combined. Place in the freezer until thoroughly chilled, about 40 minutes.

Meanwhile, place water in a bowl and sprinkle dry milk over gradually while beating with a whisk. Or place water in a blender, cover and turn on blender, then uncover and sprinkle in dry milk, not allowing mixture to foam. Place in a bowl and chill in the freezer, along with your electric mixer beaters, until ice crystals begin to form around the edge of the milk, about 35 minutes.

With chilled beaters, whip chilled milk mixture until soft peaks form. Gradually add lemon juice and beat until stiff. Blend chilled berry mixture until smooth and fold whipped milk into it. Pour into a 1-quart or 2 pint-sized containers and freeze until firm, about 4 hours.
Makes about 1 quart or 4 cups
12 grams protein per cup

APPLE COTTAGE-CHEESE FREEZE Follow the above recipe, replacing berries with 2/3 cup unsweetened applesauce. Reduce vanilla to 1/2 teaspoon and sugar or honey to 4 tablespoons.

High-Protein Frozen Orange Custard

This delicious still-frozen dessert rates high on taste tests. In addition, it's high in vitamin C, iron and protein.

1/2 cup water
1 egg
2 eggs, separated
1/2 cup Turbinado or granulated sugar or warm
  honey
1/2 cup non-instant nonfat dry milk
3 tablespoons thawed frozen orange juice
  concentrate
2/3 cup evaporated milk

In a mixing bowl, place water, egg, egg yolks and 6 tablespoons sugar or honey and mix well. Sprinkle dry milk over gradually while beating with a whisk. Or place water, egg, egg yolks and sugar or honey in a blender and cover blender. Turn on blender, uncover and sprinkle in dry milk, not allowing mixture to foam. Cook this mixture in the top of a double boiler, stirring constantly, until mixture becomes thick enough to coat a spoon, about 5 minutes. Remove from heat and beat in orange juice. Place in a mixing bowl and chill in the freezer until thoroughly chilled, about 40 minutes. Meanwhile, place evaporated milk in a mixing bowl in the freezer along with your electric mixer beaters until ice crystals begin to form around the edge of the milk, about 35 minutes.

When both mixtures are chilled, beat chilled evaporated milk with chilled beaters until stiff. Beat egg whites until soft peaks form, then add remaining 2 tablespoons sugar or honey a teaspoon at a time, beating whites until stiff. Fold half of the egg whites into chilled orange mixture, then fold in remaining whites and whipped milk. Place in a 1-quart or 2 pint-sized containers and freeze until firm, about 4 hours.
Makes about 1 quart or 4 cups
11.5 grams protein per cup

HIGH-PROTEIN FROZEN LEMON OR LIME CUSTARD Follow directions for High-Protein Frozen Orange Custard, adding 1/4 cup lemon juice and 1/2 teaspoon grated lemon rind, or 1/4 cup lime juice and 1/2 teaspoon grated lime rind. Omit orange juice concentrate and orange rind.

Vanilla Frozen Yogurt

3 cups unflavored yogurt
1 cup non-instant nonfat dry milk
1 tablespoon vanilla extract
1 teaspoon grated lemon rind
One 3-ounce package cream cheese, at room
  temperature
1 cup granulated sugar or honey
1/3 cup water
1 tablespoon (1 envelope) unflavored gelatin
3 egg whites
1/8 teaspoon cream of tartar
Fruit, unsalted sunflower seeds or Homemade
  High-Protein Granola, page 171

In a blender or food processor, blend yogurt, dry milk, vanilla, lemon rind and cream cheese until smooth; place in a mixing bowl and chill thoroughly in the freezer, about 40 minutes. If using sugar, bring water to a boil. Mix sugar and gelatin and combine with boiling water in a small saucepan; bring to boiling, stirring until sugar dissolves. (If using honey, soak gelatin in cold water in a saucepan for 5 minutes, then stir in honey and bring to a boil, stirring.) Boil sugar and gelatin or honey and gelatin mixture rapidly, without stirring, for 5 to 8 minutes, or until syrup registers 236°F on a candy thermometer or until a drop of syrup forms a soft ball in cold water.

Beat egg whites with cream of tartar until soft peaks form; pour syrup in tiny drops slowly over egg whites while beating constantly with an electric mixer. Continue beating until very stiff peaks form and mixture cools, altogether about 15 minutes. Add one fourth of the meringue to chilled yogurt mixture and stir to combine well; fold in remaining meringue. Pack in 2 quart-sized or 4 pint-sized containers and freeze until firm, about 4 to 6 hours, or freeze in an ice cream machine according to the manufacturer's instructions. To serve, top with fruit, sunflower seeds or granola.

Makes about 1-3/4 quarts or 7 cups
12.4 grams protein per cup

Fruit Frozen Yogurt

Try any of the following in this recipe: peaches, plums, sweet cherries, pineapple, apples (or applesauce), bananas, nectarines, mangoes or papaya.

1 cup puree made from fresh, thawed unsweetened frozen or unsweetened canned fruit
1/2 cup non-instant nonfat dry milk
1-1/2 cups unflavored yogurt
1/4 to 2/3 cup Turbinado or granulated sugar or honey
1 tablespoon (1 envelope) unflavored gelatin
1/4 cup whole or low-fat milk
2 teaspoons lemon juice
2 egg whites
1/4 cup sugar

Blend fruit puree, dry milk, yogurt and sugar or honey. In a small saucepan, sprinkle gelatin over milk and allow it to stand for 5 minutes. Warm milk over low heat, stirring constantly, until gelatin is completely dissolved, about 3 minutes. Add lemon juice and gelatin mixture to fruit mixture; chill thoroughly in the freezer, about 40 minutes.

Beat egg whites until soft peaks form. Add 1/4 cup sugar very slowly, a tablespoon at a time, while continuing to beat egg whites into stiff peaks. Fold egg whites into chilled yogurt mixture. Pour into a 1-1/2-quart or 3 pint-sized containers and freeze until firm, about 4 hours. For a smoother yogurt, freeze in an ice cream machine according to the manufacturer's instructions.

Makes about 1-1/4 quarts or 5 cups
9.3 grams protein per cup

Banana Frozen Yogurt

A still-frozen frozen yogurt.

1 tablespoon (1 envelope) unflavored gelatin
1/4 cup whole or low-fat milk
1/3 cup Turbinado or granulated sugar or honey
1/4 teaspoon salt
1 cup mashed ripe bananas (3 medium)
2 teaspoons lemon juice
1/3 cup non-instant nonfat dry milk
1 cup unflavored yogurt
2 egg whites

In a small saucepan sprinkle gelatin over milk and allow to stand for 5 minutes. Warm over low heat, stirring constantly, until gelatin dissolves, about 3 minutes. Stir in sugar or honey and salt. Remove from heat. Blend bananas, lemon juice, dry milk and yogurt in a blender until smooth and well combined, then blend in gelatin mixture. Pour into a mixing bowl and freeze until almost solid, about 3 hours.

Cut frozen mixture into chunks and add egg whites. Beat at high speed with an electric mixer until smooth and fluffy, but not completely thawed, about 10 minutes. Pour into a 1-1/2-quart or 3 pint-sized containers and freeze until firm, about 4 hours.
Makes 1-1/4 quarts or 5 cups
7.2 grams protein per cup

Lemon-Lime Frozen Yogurt

Egg yolks and dry milk add extra nourishment to this dessert.

1/4 cup water
1 tablespoon (1 envelope) unflavored gelatin
3 egg yolks
1 cup Turbinado or granulated sugar or honey
1 cup sugar or honey
5 tablespoons lemon juice
3 tablespoons lime juice
1 tablespoon lemon rind
2 cups unflavored yogurt
1/2 cup non-instant nonfat dry milk
1/2 cup whipping cream, whipped

Place water in top of a double boiler; sprinkle gelatin over and allow it to soften for 5 minutes. Beat in egg yolks and sugar or honey until well blended. Stir lemon and lime juice into gelatin mixture. Cook over simmering water, stirring constantly, until mixture is slightly thickened and gelatin is dissolved, about 8 to 10 minutes. Remove from heat; stir in lemon rind. Cool. Place yogurt in a bowl and sprinkle dry milk over while beating with a whisk; blend into gelatin mixture. Pour into a 9 × 9-inch pan. Freeze, stirring occasionally, until partially frozen, about 2 to 3 hours.

Spoon partially frozen mixture into a chilled large mixing bowl. Beat with an electric mixer until very smooth, about 3 to 5 minutes. Fold in whipped cream. Spoon into a 1-1/2-quart or 3 pint-sized containers and freeze until firm, about

4 hours, or freeze in a machine according to the manufacturer's instructions.
Makes about 1-1/4 quarts or 5 cups
11.2 grams protein per cup

Your Own Ice Cream or Frozen Yogurt Bars

You can turn any of the above recipes into ice cream bars by pouring the ice cream mixture into 3- or 5-ounce waxed paper cups. Insert a stick and freeze.

Your Own Soft Frozen Yogurt

Cut any homemade frozen yogurt into chunks and place in a mixing bowl. Allow it to thaw for about 10 minutes, then beat at high speed until smooth and creamy but not completely thawed. Return mixture to the freezer for about 10 minutes.

Fruity Yogurt Pops

One 16-ounce can sliced peaches or apricots, drained, or one 10-ounce package frozen strawberries or raspberries, thawed
1/4 cup Turbinado or granulated sugar or warm honey
1-1/2 cups unflavored yogurt
1 teaspoon lemon juice
Few drops almond extract

Place all ingredients in a blender and blend until smooth. Pour into 3-ounce waxed paper cups or muffin tins with paper muffin liners. Insert wooden sticks. Freeze until firm.
Makes 10 to 12 pops
1.4 grams protein per pop

VITAMIN C YOGURT POPS Combine 2-1/2 cups unflavored yogurt with one 6-ounce can frozen orange juice concentrate. Stir in 7 tablespoons honey or sugar and freeze as above.
Makes 9 pops
2.5 grams protein each

BANANA-PINEAPPLE YOGURT POPS Blend 2 cups unflavored yogurt, 1/2 cup mashed banana, 1 teaspoon lemon juice, 2/3 cup crushed pineapple and 6 tablespoons honey or sugar and freeze as above.
Makes 9 pops
2 grams protein each

Peanut Yogurtcicles

3/4 cup creamy old-fashioned peanut butter
1/3 cup honey
1 cup unflavored yogurt
1 cup whole or low-fat milk
3 tablespoons carob powder

Combine peanut butter and honey and blend thoroughly. Stir in yogurt. Blend milk and carob powder and stir into peanut butter mixture. Pour into 3-ounce waxed paper cups or muffin tins lined with paper muffin liners. Insert wooden sticks and freeze until firm.
Makes 9 yogurtcicles
7.9 grams protein per yogurtcicle

Healthy Basics

Your Own Yogurt

A very easy recipe with more protein than commercial yogurt.

3/4 cup warm water
1/2 cup non-instant nonfat dry milk
3 cups whole or low-fat milk
1/4 cup unflavored yogurt

Place water in a bowl and gradually sprinkle dry milk over while beating with a whisk; blend thoroughly. Or place water in a blender, cover and turn on blender, uncover and sprinkle in dry milk, not allowing mixture to foam. In a saucepan, scald liquid milk, then cool to room temperature. Thoroughly mix in yogurt. In a glass or pottery mixing bowl, mix dry milk-water mixture and liquid milk-yogurt mixture.Cover and wrap in a towel. Place in a warm spot, 85°F to 110°F, for 4 to 8 hours, or until firm (a gas oven with a pilot light is ideal for

this: Heat oven to 200°F for 3 minutes, then turn off and place wrapped bowl inside). Do not disturb mixture until set. Chill yogurt for several hours before serving.
Makes about 3-1/2 cups
12 grams protein per cup

Homemade "Evaporated" Milk

You can make your own "evaporated" milk by adding dry milk to liquid milk. This mixture has more protein and less fat than canned evaporated milk, and may be substituted wherever evaporated milk is called for in this book.

2 cups whole or low-fat milk
2/3 cup non-instant nonfat dry milk

Place liquid milk in a bowl and gradually sprinkle dry milk over while beating with a whisk; blend thoroughly. Or place liquid milk in a blender, cover and turn on blender, uncover and sprinkle

in dry milk, not allowing this mixture to foam.
Makes about 2 cups
37.4 grams protein per cup

Your Own Ricotta Cheese

Save the whey from this recipe for use in other recipes. It contains lots of good nutrients. Use it as liquid in baking, in soups, or as the water used in making yogurt.

4 cups whole milk
2 tablespoons lemon juice

Place milk in a saucepan and heat to scalding (150°F); don't allow milk to reach the boiling point. Remove from heat. Add lemon juice to milk and stir; it will curdle. Cover and let sit overnight or 12 hours at room temperature. Place 2 thicknesses of cheesecloth in a strainer or colander and place a bowl under it. Pour cheese mixture into strainer and drain several hours until curd is dry.
Makes about 1-1/2 cups
21.3 grams protein per cup

Homemade High-Protein Granola

Unlike many granolas, this version is high in complete protein. It's great plain, in cookies and bars, or used on top of frozen desserts.

3 cups rolled oats or mixed rolled oats and
   wheat and rye flakes
1/2 cup unprocessed wheat bran
1/2 cup unhulled sesame seeds
1 cup untoasted wheat germ
1/2 cup stirred soy flour
1/2 cup non-instant nonfat dry milk
1/2 cup unsalted broken cashews, almonds or
   peanuts
1/2 cup unsalted sunflower or hulled pumpkin
   seeds, or unsweetened shredded coconut
1/2 cup finely chopped dates, dried apples or
   prunes, or finely snipped dried apricots
1/2 cup raisins or currants
1/2 cup safflower or corn oil
1/2 cup honey
3 tablespoons packed brown sugar (optional—
   for a sweeter granola)
1 teaspoon vanilla extract
1/4 teaspoon salt

Combine all dry ingredients except dried fruit in a very large mixing bowl. Combine honey and optional sugar and oil in a small bowl and distribute over dry ingredients, folding in until well coated. Pour into a large roasting pan or 2 jelly roll pans and bake in a preheated 250°F oven for about 1 hour or until light brown in color, stirring occasionally. Immediately fold in dried fruit while mixture is still warm. Cool and store in an airtight container.
Makes about 7-1/2 cups or
fifteen 1/2 cup servings
9.4 grams protein per serving

Sesame Honey Granola

Honey lightly sweetens this sesame seed version of granola.

5 cups rolled oats
1 cup stirred soy flour
1 cup non-instant, nonfat dry milk
1 cup unsweetened shredded coconut
1 cup unsalted sunflower seeds
1 cup untoasted wheat germ
1 cup chopped walnuts
1 cup unhulled sesame seeds
1 cup safflower or corn oil
1 cup honey
2 teaspoons ground cinnamon

In a large bowl, mix together oats, flour, dry milk, coconut, sunflower seeds, wheat germ, walnuts and sesame seeds. In another large bowl, stir together oil, honey and cinnamon; add oat mixture and stir until evenly moistened. Spread mixture out on 2 large 10 × 15-inch rimmed baking pans. Bake, uncovered, in a preheated 250°F oven, stirring every 15 minutes, until granola is caramel colored, about 1 to 1-1/4 hours. Let cool thoroughly, then store in an airtight container.
**Makes about 14 cups
or twenty-eight 1/2-cup servings
8.3 grams protein per serving**

Healthy Biscuit Mix

This nutritious biscuit mix takes only minutes to put together. Keep some on hand to use in many of the recipes in this book or for your own creations; this recipe may easily be doubled.

2 cups stirred whole-wheat flour
2 cups stirred unbleached all-purpose flour
2/3 cup wheat germ
1-1/4 teaspoons salt
2 tablespoons plus 1/4 teaspoon baking powder
6 tablespoons vegetable shortening or safflower
  margarine

Place flour, wheat germ, salt and baking powder in a bowl and mix together. With a pastry blender or a food processor, cut in the shortening or margarine until mixture resembles oatmeal. Store covered in the refrigerator.
**Makes about 6-1/2 cups
16 grams protein per cup**

Easy High-Protein Freezer Dough

For burger buns, hot dog buns, pizzas and sandwiches. Don't let this yeast dough scare you off. Even if you've never made bread this is a very quick and foolproof recipe. Just be sure the water is 110°F.

2 cups boiling milk
3 tablespoons honey
1 tablespoon butter or safflower margarine
3 teaspoons salt
3 tablespoons (3 envelopes) active dry yeast
1 teaspoon honey
1/2 cup warm (110°F) water
3 cups stirred unbleached all-purpose flour
1/4 cup soy flour
1/4 cup non-instant nonfat dry milk
1 cup wheat germ
About 2-1/2 cups stirred whole-wheat flour, or
    more as needed

In a large bowl, combine milk, honey, butter or margarine and salt; cool to lukewarm. In a warm cup or bowl, dissolve yeast and honey in warm water. Let yeast stand until bubbly, about 5 minutes. Combine yeast mixture with lukewarm mixture. Mix flours, dry milk and wheat germ. Add flour mixture to liquids, beating well with an electric mixer, then gradually stir in as much of the whole-wheat flour as the dough will absorb, mixing well. Knead 3 to 5 minutes on a lightly floured surface. To let dough rise in the refrigerator, divide dough into three balls and place each in a greased bowl; cover with plastic wrap. Place in refrigerator for at least 3 hours or up to 24 hours. To let dough rise at room temperature, place in a greased bowl, cover and let rise in a warm place for 1 hour.

Dough may now be baked or frozen. To bake without freezing, punch dough down and form into loaves or bun shapes. Place loaves in 3 greased 5 × 9-inch loaf pans or place buns on greased cookie sheets, cover lightly and let rise in a warm place until almost doubled in size. Bake in a preheated 375°F oven 12 to 15 minutes for buns, about 40 minutes for loaves; buns will be lightly browned and loaves will sound hollow when tapped on top, with no soft spots when loaves are removed from pans and undersides of loaves are pressed. Cool on racks.

To freeze dough, punch down and form into 3 balls, wrap in aluminum foil and freeze, or form into loaves and/or buns, freeze solid, unwrapped, then wrap in aluminum foil and place in freezer.

Makes 3 loaves or 18 to 24 buns
51.4 grams protein per loaf
8.6/6.4 grams protein per bun

Note: Dough may be kept frozen for 2 months. Be sure it is kept solidly frozen in the back of the freezer, or it will not rise after thawing.
● To bake frozen loaves or buns, place frozen buns about 2 inches apart on greased baking sheets, place loaves in greased 5 × 9-inch loaf pans. Cover lightly and let rise in a warm place until almost doubled. Bake as directed in recipe.
● To bake unshaped frozen dough, thaw first. Form into loaves or buns, place buns about 2 inches apart on greased baking sheets and loaves in greased loaf pans. Cover lightly and let rise in a warm place until almost doubled in size. Bake as directed in recipe.

Fortified Frozen Bread Dough

You can make your own pizzas and several of the dishes in this book using commercially prepared frozen bread dough. Here's how it can be nutritionally fortified.

One 1-pound loaf frozen bread dough (preferably whole-wheat), thawed
2 tablespoons soy flour
1/4 cup wheat germ

On a floured board, roll out dough into an 8 × 10-inch rectangle. Sprinkle with soy flour, then wheat germ. Fold or roll dough up to encase soy flour and wheat germ, and knead dough to incorporate these ingredients. Some flour or wheat germ may spill out, but this will be picked up in the kneading process. When dough looks blended, prepare as directed in the individual recipe.
Makes 1 loaf
47.5 grams protein per loaf

READY-WHEN-YOU-ARE HIGH-PROTEIN PIE CRUSTS

Complementary protein ingredients are used in all of the following pie crust recipes so that the crusts add complete protein to any pie. When unbleached white flour is used, wheat germ is included to enrich the protein and vitamin content. All of these crusts can be made and frozen in foil pie plates so they will be on hand when you want to put a pie or cheesecake together quickly.

There are two basic types of pie crusts: crumb and pastry. Crumb crusts may be baked before freezing; roll-out crusts should be frozen in a pie pan unbaked. Prick the pie crust before freezing it, and then you can bake it without thawing. Pastry dough may also be frozen in a ball—wrap airtight in foil and thaw before rolling out.

High-Protein Graham Cracker Crumb Crust

1 cup graham cracker crumbs
3 tablespoons non-instant nonfat dry milk
1/2 cup wheat germ
1/4 cup packed brown sugar
6 tablespoons butter or safflower margarine, melted

Combine cracker crumbs, dry milk, wheat germ and brown sugar in a mixing bowl. Pour melted butter over and mix thoroughly. Press into a 9- or 10-inch pie pan. Bake in a preheated 375°F oven for 6 to 8 minutes, or until lightly colored. Cool.
Makes one 9- or 10-inch shell
30.9 grams protein per shell

Nutty Bran Crumb Crust

Bran adds fiber and nuts add crunch to this crust. Make several at once and freeze them.

1/2 cup dry whole-wheat bread crumbs
1/4 cup unprocessed wheat bran
1/4 cup wheat germ
1/3 cup finely chopped walnuts
3 tablespoons non-instant nonfat dry milk
4 tablespoons packed brown sugar
4 tablespoons butter or safflower margarine, melted

Combine all ingredients except butter or margarine in a bowl; mix well. Sprinkle butter or margarine over dry ingredients and mix them thoroughly. Press into a 9- or 10-inch pie pan or a spring form pan. Bake in a preheated 350°F oven for 8 to 10 minutes or until lightly colored.
Makes one 9- or 10-inch shell
30.3 grams protein per shell

Granola Crumb Crust

4 tablespoons butter or safflower margarine
3 tablespoons honey or packed brown sugar
3/4 cup rolled oats
1/3 cup unsweetened flaked coconut
1/2 cup wheat germ
1/4 teaspoon salt
1/4 cup finely chopped nuts or unsalted sun sunflower seeds, or a mixture of both
2 tablespoons non-instant nonfat dry milk

In a large saucepan, stir butter and honey or sugar together over medium heat until butter is melted. Add remaining ingredients and stir over medium heat for 3 minutes. Let cool slightly, then press mixture into a lightly greased 9-inch pie pan or 12 individual foil muffin cups. Bake in a preheated 350°F oven for 8 to 10 minutes, or until lightly colored. Cool thoroughly.
Makes one 9-inch shell or 12 tart shells
34 grams protein per 9-inch shell
2.8 grams protein per shell

Flaky Wheat Germ Pastry

For two single crusts, a double crust, or six to eight tart shells.

1 cup stirred unbleached all-purpose flour
2/3 cup stirred whole-wheat pastry flour
1/4 cup wheat germ
1/4 cup non-instant nonfat dry milk
1 teaspoon salt
6 ounces (1-1/2 sticks) butter or safflower
   margarine
1 egg
1 egg yolk
About 4 tablespoons ice water

Mix together flours, wheat germ, dry milk and salt. With a pastry blender or a food processor, cut butter or margarine into dry ingredients until mixture resembles oatmeal. Beat egg and egg yolk with 2 tablespoons ice water and sprinkle this mixture over dry ingredients, blending with a fork or in a food processor. Continue to mix while sprinkling about 2 tablespoons ice water over, until dough can be formed into a ball. Divide into 2 balls. Dough may be used immediately or wrapped in plastic wrap and chilled until ready for use. If chilled dough is too hard to roll, bring to room temperature before rolling out.

To make a single baked pie crust, roll 1 ball of dough out on a board lightly floured with whole-wheat flour or between 2 pieces of waxed paper. Roll dough into a circle 1 inch larger than pie pan. If using waxed paper, peel off 1 piece, invert dough over pan and push it down into pan; avoid stretching dough. Peel off second piece of waxed paper and prick bottom and sides of dough with a fork. Make a decorative edge on crust. Bake in a preheated 375°F oven for about 10 minutes or until lightly browned. To make a double-crust pie, trim bottom crust even with rim of pan. Pour in filling. Roll out second crust and arrange over filling. Make a decorative edge. Cut several slits in top crust to allow steam to escape while baking. Bake as directed in pie recipe.

**Makes 2 single or 1 double 9- or
10-inch crust   or 6 to 8 tart shells
24.2 grams protein per crust,
8.1/6 grams protein per tart shell**

No-Roll Whole-Wheat Pastry

3 cups stirred whole-wheat pastry flour
1/4 cup non-instant nonfat dry milk
3/4 teaspoon salt
1/2 cup safflower or corn oil
1 egg, slightly beaten
1 tablespoon lemon juice or vinegar
5 tablespoons ice water

In a mixing bowl, combine flour, milk and salt. Beat oil, egg, lemon juice and water together in another bowl. Stir ingredients together with a fork until moistened. Roll into 2 balls and wrap in plastic. Chill at least 25 minutes. Flatten 1 ball of dough into a disk with your hand, place in a 9- or 10-inch pie pan and pat into shape. Or follow the directions for rolling out crust in the Flaky Wheat Germ Pastry recipe, page 176. For a pre-baked single shell, prick with a fork and bake in a pre-heated 450°F oven for 8 to 12 minutes or until lightly browned.
Makes two 9- or 10-inch shells
28.5 grams protein per shell

Praline Crust

This is an absolutely delicious crust—especially for pumpkin, sweet potato, pumpkin chiffon or zucchini pies.

1/2 recipe Flaky Wheat Germ Pastry, page 176, or No-Roll Whole-Wheat Pastry, preceding
1/4 cup finely chopped pecans
2 tablespoons wheat germ
1 tablespoon non-instant nonfat dry milk
6 tablespoons packed brown sugar
3 tablespoons butter or safflower margarine, at room temperature

Prepare and roll out pastry 1 inch larger than a 9- or 10-inch pie pan. Line pan with pastry and make a decorative edge. Combine the remaining ingredients in a bowl, blending thoroughly. Press this mixture gently into bottom of shell with the back of a large spoon. Prick sides of shell with a fork. Bake in a preheated 450°F oven for 10 minutes, or until lightly colored; cool. Pour in filling and bake once more if pie recipe requires it.
Makes one 9- or 10-inch shell
55.3 grams protein per shell

TOPPINGS, FROSTINGS AND GLAZES

Instead of adding empty calories to desserts, you can increase the protein count of cakes, puddings and other sweets with these delicious toppings, frostings and glazes.

Whipped Ricotta Topping

Two tablespoons of this topping add three grams of protein to anything you eat it with—a big improvement over whipped cream, which is pure fat. You may want to double this recipe, as it goes fast.

1/2 cup ricotta cheese
1/4 teaspoon vanilla extract
1/4 cup sifted powdered sugar

Using an electric mixer, a blender or a food processor, beat all ingredients together until fluffy.
Makes about 1/2 cup or 4 servings
3 grams protein per serving

Note: Freeze topping in 3-ounce paper cups covered with aluminum foil (label bottom of cup).

HONEY RICOTTA TOPPING Follow preceding recipe, replacing powdered sugar with 2 to 5 tablespoons honey. Add 1/2 teaspoon grated lemon peel, if desired. If topping is too runny, beat in a little non-instant nonfat dry milk.

Ricotta Frosting

A slightly less-sweet version of Whipped Ricotta Topping, this frosting is unbelievably delicious. And you won't feel guilty about eating it or serving it to your children.

2 cups ricotta cheese
1 teaspoon vanilla extract
3/4 cup or more sifted powdered sugar

With an electric mixer, or in a blender or a food processor, blend all ingredients until smooth. For a sweeter frosting, add more sugar.
Enough for an 8- or 9-inch layer cake
or one 9 × 13-inch cake
48 grams protein

Brandy Dessert Sauce

This is really a non-alcoholic sauce, since the alcohol in the brandy evaporates when it is cooked. Because it contains milk and eggs, it adds a lot of complete protein to steamed puddings and other desserts.

4 egg yolks
1/2 cup packed brown sugar
2 to 4 tablespoons brandy, or 1-1/2 teaspoons brandy flavoring and 1/2 teaspoon vanilla extract
1/2 cup non-instant nonfat dry milk
1 teaspoon lemon juice
1/3 cup ice water
2 egg whites

In the top of a double boiler, beat egg yolks with a whisk until thick and pale. Add sugar a little at a time and continue beating until very creamy. If using brandy, blend in and cook, stirring, over hot but not boiling water until thickened. Remove from heat, place in a mixing bowl and chill thoroughly in the freezer, about 40 minutes, along with a small mixing bowl and your electric mixer beaters. If using brandy flavoring and vanilla, add them to egg yolk mixture after it is cooked and chilled.

In the chilled bowl, combine dry milk, lemon juice and ice water and beat with chilled beaters until mixture reaches the consistency of whipped cream. Beat egg whites until soft peaks form. Fold whipped milk mixture and then egg whites into chilled cooked egg yolk mixture.
Makes about 1-1/3 cups
34 grams protein

VANILLA DESSERT SAUCE Follow the above recipe, substituting 1-1/4 teaspoons vanilla extract for brandy.

Creamy Cheese Frosting

One 8-ounce package Neufchatel cheese, at room temperature
1/4 cup honey
1 teaspoon vanilla extract
1 cup non-instant nonfat dry milk
1 cup sifted powdered sugar
Milk, if necessary

With an electric mixer or in a food processor, cream cheese, honey and vanilla together until well blended. Stir in dry milk, then sugar. If frosting is too stiff, add a little liquid milk to reach desired consistency. If frosting is too runny, add more dry milk.
Enough for an 8- or 9-inch layer cake
or one 9 × 13-inch cake
57.6 grams protein

Good-for-You Frosting

5 tablespoons butter or safflower margarine,
  at room temperature
1 cup non-instant nonfat dry milk
1-1/3 cups sifted powdered sugar
1 teaspoon vanilla extract
Milk

Cream butter or margarine until fluffy. Blend in dry milk and then sugar until mixture is uniform. Mix in vanilla and add milk drop by drop until desired consistency is reached. Make frosting soft enough to spread easily, as it will firm up after it is spread on the cake.
Enough for an 8- or 9-inch layer cake
or 9 × 13-inch cake
32 grams protein

GOOD-FOR-YOU LEMON FROSTING Follow the directions for Good-for-You Frosting. Substitute 2 teaspoons grated lemon rind for vanilla. Use about 1/4 cup lemon juice in place of milk.

GOOD-FOR-YOU ORANGE FROSTING Follow the directions for Good-for-You Frosting, substituting 1 tablespoon grated orange rind for vanilla. Use 2 tablespoons thawed frozen orange juice concentrate and as much water as needed in place of milk. Add water to thin, if necessary.

Vanilla Ricotta Frosting and Filling

2-1/2 cups ricotta cheese
1/3 cup honey
2/3 cup sifted powdered sugar
1-1/4 teaspoons vanilla extract
Non-instant nonfat dry milk, if necessary

With an electric mixer, or in a blender or food processor, blend all ingredients together until smooth. If mixture is too runny, mix in a little dry milk.
Enough for an 8- or 9-inch layer cake
60 grams protein

Maple Syrup Frosting

4 tablespoons butter or safflower margarine, at
  room temperature
1/3 cup maple syrup
1/2 cup or more non-instant nonfat dry milk

Cream butter or margarine with syrup until thoroughly mixed. Blend in dry milk until creamy. Add as much dry milk as necessary to reach desired consistency.
Enough for a 9 × 9-inch cake
16 grams protein

Good-for-You
Fudgy Frosting

5 tablespoons butter or safflower margarine
1/3 cup honey
Two 1-ounce squares unsweetened chocolate
1 cup non-instant nonfat dry milk
1 cup sifted powdered sugar
1 teaspoon vanilla extract
About 2 tablespoons vanilla extract
About 2 tablespoons cream or milk

Melt butter or margarine, honey and chocolate in the top of a double boiler over simmering water until chocolate is melted. Remove from heat. Stir in dry milk and sugar until mixture is well combined. Add vanilla. Mix in cream or milk drop by drop until desired consistency is reached. Make frosting soft enough to spread easily, as it will firm up after it is spread on the cake.
**Enough for an 8- or 9-inch layer cake
or one 9 × 13-inch cake
33 grams protein**

Good-for-You
Honey-Carob Frosting

4 tablespoons butter or safflower margarine, at room temperature
1/3 cup honey
3/4 cup non-instant nonfat dry milk
1/4 cup carob powder
1 teaspoon vanilla extract
Pinch each cinnamon and nutmeg
Milk

Cream butter or margarine and honey together until smooth. Blend in dry milk, carob powder, vanilla and spices. Add milk drop by drop until desired consistency is reached. Make the frosting soft enough to spread easily, as it will firm up after it is spread on the cake.
**Enough for an 8- or 9-inch layer cake
or one 9 × 13-inch cake
25 grams protein**

Coconut-Pecan Frosting and Filling

1 cup evaporated milk
1/2 cup honey
3 egg yolks, slightly beaten
1/4 pound butter or safflower margarine
1 teaspoon vanilla extract
1 cup unsweetened flaked coconut
1 cup chopped pecans

Combine all ingredients except coconut and pecans in a heavy saucepan. Cook, stirring often, for 12 to 14 minutes or until very thick. Remove from heat and add coconut and pecans. Cool.
Enough for an 8- or 9-inch layer cake
38.8 grams protein

Milk and Honey Glaze

This glaze and the Quick Milk Glaze and Fabulous Apple Juice Glaze, following, are great for bundt cakes or cakes baked in a tube pan, and for regular cakes, too. They have fewer calories than most icings or glazes because they contain no butter. Frozen glazes should be warmed before using.

1/2 cup non-instant nonfat dry milk
5 tablespoons honey
1 teaspoon vanilla extract
Water, if necessary

Blend all ingredients together; add water to thin, if necessary. Glaze will be slightly runny, but will harden after it is applied to cake.
Enough for an 8- or 9-inch layer cake
or a 10-inch bundt or tube cake
16 grams protein

CAROB OR CHOCOLATE MILK-AND-HONEY GLAZE Mix 1 tablespoon cocoa or carob powder into dry milk in above recipe.

LEMON OR ORANGE MILK-AND-HONEY GLAZE Substitute 2 tablespoons lemon juice or thawed frozen orange juice concentrate for vanilla in Milk and Honey Glaze. Reduce honey to 4 tablespoons.

Quick Milk Glaze

1/4 cup non-instant nonfat dry milk
1/3 cup sifted powdered sugar
1/2 teaspoon vanilla extract or 1/4 teaspoon
  almond extract
Milk

Combine dry milk and sugar. Add vanilla or almond extract and add milk a little at a time until the desired consistency is reached. Glaze will be slightly runny but will harden after it is applied to cake.
**Enough for an 8- or 9-inch layer cake
or a 10-inch bundt or tube cake
8 grams protein**

CAROB OR CHOCOLATE QUICK MILK GLAZE
Blend 1 tablespoon carob or cocoa into dry milk before adding liquid.

LEMON OR ORANGE QUICK MILK GLAZE Use 1 teaspoon grated lemon rind in place of vanilla or almond extract; use orange juice or lemon juice in place of milk.

Fabulous Apple Juice Glaze

1/4 cup thawed frozen apple juice concentrate
1/4 cup non-instant nonfat dry milk
2 tablespoons sifted powdered sugar (optional)

Blend all ingredients together. Glaze will be slightly runny but will harden after it is applied to the cake.
**Enough for an 8- or 9-inch layer cake
or a 10-inch bundt or tube cake
8 grams protein**

INGREDIENT GLOSSARY

BRAN
Unprocessed wheat bran (also called millers' bran) adds extra fiber to the diet. Sprinkle on salads and add to muffins, cereals, casseroles, etc. Found in health food stores and many supermarkets.

BUTTER OR MARGARINE
Sweet (unsalted) butter or unsaturated margarine are the best shortenings to use in baking. The first ingredient on the margarine label should be *liquid* vegetable oil, preferably safflower or corn oil. Avoid margarines with the preservatives BHA and BHT. Found in supermarkets and health food stores.

CAROB POWDER
A chocolate-like substance ground from carob pods; often used to replace cocoa. Many people who are allergic to chocolate substitute carob. It does not contain a stimulant, nor does it inhibit the absorption of calcium as chocolate does. Found in most health food stores and in the health food section of many supermarkets.

CHEESES
Most yellow cheeses are colored, but manufacturers are not required to put this information on the label. Try to obtain uncolored Cheddars at health food stores. Natural cheeses are nutritionally superior to processed products, which contain fillers. Cheese is very easily digested and is an excellent source of protein, except for cream cheese, which is largely butterfat. Found in supermarkets, specialty cheese shops and health food stores.

DRIED FRUITS
Dried fruits found in most supermarkets have been treated with sulfur to retain their color and soft texture. Health food stores sell unsulphured dried fruits and though they are not as colorful, they're better for you.

DRY MILK
All of the recipes in this book have been tested with non-instant nonfat dry milk. It is probably nutritionally superior to instant dry milk because it has been dried at a lower temperature. Non-instant dry milk also contains more food value per measure because it is more compact. Instant dry milk may replace non-instant in all recipes except those for frostings and candies, where a smooth texture is essential. Substitute instant dry milk for non-instant by adding 1 tablespoon additional dry milk for every 1/4 cup; thus 1-1/4 cup instant dry milk will replace 1 cup of non-instant. Always store all dry milk refrigerated in closed containers, or it will develop off-flavors that will spoil your product. Baked goods and candies made with dry milk should also be stored in the refrigerator. Found in health food stores and some supermarkets.

FRUIT PEELS
Many citrus fruits have been colored as well as sprayed for disease. Try to obtain organic citrus fruit when using peels as flavoring. Grate the whole peel, then freeze what you don't need

wrapped in aluminum foil. Found in health food stores.

GRANOLA
Use the high-protein recipe on page 171. Most commercial granolas are not protein-balanced. They contain mostly carbohydrates and few vitamins and minerals, though they are a "natural" product. If you do buy granola, try to get one with wheat germ and some soy; found in health food stores and some supermarkets.

HIGH-PROTEIN POWDER
All protein powders do not have the same protein-calorie ratio. The best product I have found so far contains 24 grams of protein per 100-calorie serving. A good product will contain no sweeteners (sugars), artificial flavorings or preservatives. Read the label. Found in health food stores and in the health food section of some supermarkets.

NUTS AND SEEDS
A good source of complete protein when complemented with soy products, dry milk or wheat germ. It's best to buy unsalted, unroasted nuts in bulk and store them *refrigerated*. Unhulled (brown) sesame seeds contain the germ plus more fiber and are superior nutritionally to the hulled (white) variety. Many health food stores and some supermarkets carry them in bulk.

OILS
Cooking and salad oils are usually solvent-extracted and preserved with antioxidants (BHA and BHT). Buy only unsaturated pressed natural oils. Refrigerate them after opening to avoid rancidity. Cotton plants are usually heavily sprayed for insects and these sprays are absorbed into the seeds, so avoid cottonseed oil. Safflower oil is the least saturated; corn and soy bean oil are also acceptable. Found in supermarkets and health food stores.

PEANUT BUTTER
Grind your own or buy the natural unhydrogenated type ("old-fashioned") without any dextrins or freshness preservers, mono- or diglycerides. Peanuts should be the only ingredient on the label. Found in supermarkets and health food stores.

PREPARED MEATS
Most prepared meats, sausages, lunch meats, ham, corned beef, sausages, hot dogs and bacon are processed with sodium nitrate and nitrite to give them a red color and to preserve their "freshness." Avoid these as they have been known to produce a number of undesirable effects on the body. You can buy nitrate-free sausages, bacon and other prepared meats. They must be kept frozen. May be mail-ordered from Harmony Farms, La Crescenta, California, and Health Valley Meats, Norwalk, California.

RICE
Brown rice is the best choice for high nutritional value. The hull, or bran, contains fiber, vitamins and minerals. Converted or enriched is the next best choice but the fiber content is much lower. Found in supermarkets and health food stores.

ROLLED OATS
A good source of fiber. Buy "old-fashioned" or "regular" oatmeal. Instant oatmeal is cooked and then dried out; this destroys much of its nutritional value. Found in supermarkets and health food stores.

SOY FLOUR

A complete-protein product made from ground soy beans. Nonfat or low-fat soy flour is higher in protein. Good for complementing the incomplete amino acids in any wheat flour or in nuts and seeds. When adding it to baked goods, use in moderation, as it will not rise and will "weigh down" the baked product. Found in health food stores and in the health food section of some supermarkets.

SUGARS AND HONEY

Turbinado, brown sugar and honey contain slightly more nutrients than granulated sugar. Turbinado sugar contains some molasses and may be found in health food stores. "Raw" sugar, often marketed in supermarkets, is similar in appearance to Turbinado but may not contain molasses.

UNBLEACHED ALL-PURPOSE FLOUR

Contains less protein, vitamins, and fiber than the whole-wheat flours but may be "enriched" by adding wheat germ to the recipe (3 to 4 tablespoons per cup). Obtain unbleached, non-bromated or phosphated flour. White flour is used to produce a lighter, finer, more desirable texture in some baked goods. Stir before measuring. Found in supermarkets.

WHEAT GERM

The "heart" of the wheat. Contains most of the vitamins and minerals in wheat. Its protein is complete. The untoasted variety is more nourishing than the toasted variety, though toasted wheat germ may be preferred in some recipes. *Always refrigerate.* Be sure the wheat germ you buy is fresh and not rancid if it is not vacuum packed. Found in supermarkets and health food stores.

WHOLE-GRAIN PUFFED CEREALS

Be sure to get natural whole-grain cereals such as brown rice, red wheat, corn, millet or oats. Found in health food stores and some supermarkets.

WHOLE-WHEAT BREAD CRUMBS

Use stale whole-grain bread or dry it out in the oven. Crush in a food processor, blender or in a bag with a rolling pin. Store refrigerated.

WHOLE-WHEAT FLOUR

Highest in protein, fiber and vitamins of all the commonly used flours. Produces a heavier product than white flour. Be sure to stir before using. Whole-wheat flours should be stored in the refrigerator to prevent the deterioration of vitamins and the development of rancidity due to oxidation of the wheat germ oil. Found in health food stores and most supermarkets; be sure to look for "stone ground."

WHOLE-WHEAT PASTRY FLOUR

Made from a softer wheat than regular whole-wheat flour. Contains wheat germ and bran. Good for cakes, cookies and pastries as it produces a lighter product than regular whole-wheat flour. Stir before measuring. Found in most health food stores and some supermarkets; try to get stone ground.

YOGURT

It's easy to make your own yogurt that is higher in protein than commercial varieties (see page 170). Don't buy the overly sweetened, artificially colored and flavored fruit yogurts. Instead, mix frozen orange juice concentrate, applesauce, crushed frozen or fresh berries or canned juice-pack fruit into your yogurt and add a little sweetener if you wish.

INDEX

BIOGRAPHICAL NOTES

Linda Burum has taught home economics in California high schools for ten years. This book grew out of her efforts to teach the value of good nutrition to her students. Her knowledge of food has been widened by her extensive travels in Europe and the Far East. She is a teacher of foods and nutrition, gourmet cooking and international foods at Culver City High School and lives in Santa Monica with her husband, Stephen.